GREECE & ROME STUDIES
VOLUME II

GREECE & ROME STUDIES

GREEK TRAGEDY

Edited by
IAN McAUSLAN
and
PETER WALCOT

Published by
OXFORD UNIVERSITY PRESS

on behalf of
THE CLASSICAL ASSOCIATION
1993

Oxford University Press, Walton Street, Oxford OX2 6DP

Oxford New York Toronto
Delhi Bombay Calcutta Madras Karachi
Kuala Lumpur Singapore Hong Kong Tokyo
Nairobi Dar es Salaam Cape Town
Melbourne Auckland Madrid
and associated companies in
Berlin Ibadan

Oxford is a trade mark of Oxford University Press

Published in the United States
by Oxford University Press Inc., New York

British Library Cataloguing in Publication Data
Data available

Library of Congress Cataloging in Publication Data
Greek tragedy / edited by Ian McAuslan and Peter Walcot.
(Greece & Rome studies)
Includes indexes
1. Greek drama (Tragedy)—History and criticism. I. McAuslan,
Ian. II. Walcot, Peter. III. Series.
PA3133.G683 1993
882'.0109—dc20   92-26819
ISBN 0-19-920300-8
ISBN 0-19-920301-6 (Pbk)

Typeset by Latimer Trend & Company Ltd, Plymouth
Printed in Great Britain by
Biddles Ltd,
Guildford and King's Lynn

PREFACE

FOR this second volume of Studies, we have selected seventeen articles published in the journal *Greece & Rome* during the past two decades. The 1970s had begun with the issue of T. B. L. Webster's *Greek Tragedy* in the series New Surveys in the Classics (1971); few volumes of the journal since then have failed to include at least one article on Tragedy; and during the 1980s we have also published separate studies in the New Surveys series on the three major tragedians: *Euripides*, by C. Collard (1981), *Sophocles*, by R. G. A. Buxton (1984), and *Aeschylus*, by S. Ireland (1986).

The present volume begins in what we hope is an appropriately agonistic vein with Simon Goldhill's 'Reading Performance Criticism'— itself a reply to an earlier piece in the journal; thereafter, we have grouped the articles by playwright. The nature of a journal is such that articles from a given period are unlikely to provide full cover of a given topic. We hope, however, that this selection is wide-ranging enough to be found useful.

Richard Buxton ended his 1984 New Survey with the hope that the reappraisal of the playwright which he had detected in recent scholarship 'might be more often tested in the place where Sophocles belongs: the theatre' (*Sophocles*, 34). We are pleased to note as we move into the 1990s that Greek Tragedy very much holds its place on the live stage, and that it continues to inspire poets, composers, actors, and audiences. Within the past year alone we have witnessed Seamus Heaney's *The Cure at Troy*, John Buller's *BAKXAI*, Fiona Shaw's Electra, Janet Suzman's Phaedra, and the Royal Shakespeare Company's cycle *The Thebans*, in a new translation by Timberlake Wertenbaker, which has played to capacity audiences.

May 1992

IAN MCAUSLAN
PETER WALCOT

CONTENTS

READING PERFORMANCE CRITICISM

By SIMON GOLDHILL

Baseball is like *zem*, except that a ball is used
(Harry Matthews, *The Sinking of the
Odarek Stadium*)

Contexts

Fred Astaire once remarked of performing in London that he knew when
the end of a play's run was approaching when he saw the first black tie in
the audience. Perhaps this is an American's ironic representation of the
snobbishness of pre-War London (though he was the American who sang
the top-hat, white tie and tails into a part of his personal image). Perhaps it
is merely an accurate (or nostalgic) picture of the dress code of the
audiences of the period. The very appeal to such a dress code, however—
in whatever way we choose to read the anecdote—inevitably relies on a
whole network of cultural ideas and norms to make its point. It implies
tacitly what is easily recoverable from other sources about the theatre of
the period: the expected class of the audience; the sense of 'an evening's
entertainment'—attending the fashionable play of the season, with all the
implications of the theatre as a place not merely for seeing but also for
being seen; the range of subjects and characters portrayed on the London
stage of the period; the role of London as a European capital of a world
empire (with a particular self-awareness of itself as a capital); the expected
types of narrative, events, and language, that for many modern readers
could be evoked with the phrase 'a Fred Astaire story'. If we want to
understand the impact of the plays of Ibsen or Brecht or Osborne or
Beckett, it cannot be merely through 'dramatic techniques', but must also
take into account the social performance that is theatre. Ibsen's commitment to a realist aesthetic is no doubt instrumental to the impact of his
plays, but it is because his (socially committed) dramas challenged the
proprieties of the social event of theatre that his first reviewers were so
hostile. Brecht develops an aesthetic of alienation (the famous *Verfrem-
dungsaffekt*) but it cannot be discussed separately from his views of the
bourgeois audience and the need to use the social event of theatre to help
change society. Osborne and Beckett, with their different challenges to the
characterizations, narrative, and language of earlier theatre, set out to
disrupt what it means to go to the theatre. We may need a subtle and
lengthy investigation to discover how any form of literature may affect

social realities, but there can be little doubt that going to the theatre is itself a social performance, what anthropologists have called 'social drama'. The audience member who tries, say, to stop Othello strangling Desdemona has misunderstood the nature of this social drama, as much as throughout the history of the stage playwrights have attempted to redefine the theatrical event for audiences.

I am aware that by starting with an anecdote that depends on an elaborate and outmoded dress code, I have run the risk of alienating a proportion of the readership of this piece. (There are, I take it, few areas of European and American culture where the terms 'black tie' and 'white tie' can function as social signals in quite the way Fred Astaire utilizes them.) There is a point to this effect, however. It is first to recall that there is a constantly developing history of the theatre that can turn us all into outsiders—even to a performance of fifty years ago. Performance criticism, if it wishes to understand performance as an event, and drama *in and as* performance, cannot hope to rest solely with aesthetic criteria, or with an analysis of narrowly defined dramatic techniques. Rather, performance criticism must utilize a full range of analytic tools to investigate the intricate system of norms, expectations, ideologies, and transgressions that make performance a social drama. In *Reading Greek Tragedy*, and an article entitled 'The Great Dionysia and Civic Ideology' (*JHS* 107 (1987)), I have tried to develop something of this background for Greek drama of the fifth century to show how such a social context necessarily and crucially affects the understanding of the plays. I have tried there also to demonstrate how Oliver Taplin—whom I, like Wiles, take as representative because he is (rightly) 'the most respected of contemporary British writers on staging'—repeatedly represses this social and political context in order to develop his aesthetic and emotional view of Greek drama (with a consequent misrepresentation of the dramas in performance). To understand fifth-century Athenian *theatron*, we need to be anthropological historians as well as dramatic critics, and the inevitable dangers of appropriating ancient drama to modern models must be investigated, not ignored. The assumption that 'going to the theatre', 'watching a play', 'the emotional experience of an audience', are universal, cross-cultural norms takes the (humanist) sword to the complex specificities of performance as a particular type of event in a particular cultural and historical context. It might be more useful to claim that no fifth-century Athenian ever went to the theatre, at least in any way easily assimilable to the differing modern experiences of theatre.

My first point, then, is that theatrical performance can only be understood adequately if an attempt is made to see the performance within its cultural context—which may be radically different from society to society and era to era, but which will never be less than a constitutive factor in understanding drama in action. The risks of (mis)appropriation—signalled in my epigraph to this paper—constantly require a cautious critical suspicion of difference: it simply will not do to treat Greek theatre from a perspective (over)determined by two thousand years and more of historical development without at least opening the question of how such a development distorts our view.

Discovering a Grammar

Wiles is right, however, that the core of Taplin's enterprise is to discover the 'grammar of dramatic technique', the 'clarification of scenic devices' which 'must now be obligatory for any serious editor or translator of a Greek text'. So let us turn to this question of the 'grammar of dramatic technique'. I shall begin with a ground-clearing point. Now it is interesting that when Wiles quotes at length from *Reading Greek Tragedy* (hereafter *RGT*) and expresses surprise that I seem to ignore the illumination to be gained from certain studies of staging, he begins his quotation in the middle of a sentence. Interesting, because the first, unquoted part of the sentence outlines a general commitment to a study of fundamental aspects of performance (*RGT*, p. 282; Wiles, 138): 'In general terms, certain sorts of restrictions may be felt to follow from the nature of the theatre of Dionysus, the organizaton of its space, the number and masking of its actors etc.—throughout this book' (and here Wiles begins) 'I have tried to view tragic drama in the specificity of its fifth-century production and there have been recent interesting studies in the spatial dynamics of Greek theatre.' The footnote to this passage refers explicitly and with praise to several studies, including that of Oliver Taplin, one of the two works Wiles oddly suggests it is surprising not to see illuminating my argument here.

I start here with Wiles' rhetorical strategy of partial quotation not to score debating points about sloppy reading, but rather to point to a crucial way in which the whole emphasis of the argument on staging has been changed to create a polarization of 'Taplin' *v.* 'Goldhill'. Part of the context which I have just argued to be basic to understanding performance, consists precisely in such elements as the spatial dynamics of the acting area, ideas of masking, the *choros*, the social implications of dancing—the (historically specific) possibilities of representation which inform theatrical performance. *RGT*, even in its choice of title, is not an attempt simply to deny the importance of performance, and its stance cannot be set in rigid opposition to a critical position which espouses performance as a criterion and interest. Rather, throughout the work, there is a concern to articulate the problematic and varying relationship between theatre as social performance and the scripts for performance. The chapter from which Wiles quotes, is called 'Performance and Performability', and it is concerned with the conditions and possibilities of performance, the problems of representation—that is, *how* performance is to be discussed. It begins, indeed, with a consideration of the *choros* in terms of dramatic convention. In no way do I wish to be thought to be fighting a rearguard action in 'the battle to demonstrate plays are written for theatres': of course the vast majority of them are. What I want to discuss is what is at stake in such an assertion: to say that 'plays are written for theatres' seems a possible *starting point* for discussion, but as a *conclusion* it merely begs a series of questions.

Let me turn now to more specific questions of the 'grammar of dramatic technique'. I have three brief points that I want to make here. The first is merely to note that a grammar of theatrical device cannot be determined or conceived without a semantics. So, to take a most conventional piece of stagecraft from pre-War London, the opening stage direction where 'a domestic servant enters stage left and crosses stage right through the drawing room . . .', cannot function as a technique apart from the way it defines a set of expectations and has a range of implications within the play and for the audience watching the play. (One qualification: the more such implications are made *explicit* for an audience the less likely it is such action will remain a 'theatrical code' rather than seeming a cliché or a parody or an anachronism: it is hardest to understand the 'theatrical codes'—or to take them for granted—in periods of most extreme change.) The normal is always also normative; it proclaims a norm. So too with more detailed examples of 'stagecraft', as can be seen from a case where performance criticism has proved particularly illuminating for many readers, namely, Oliver Taplin's discusson of doors in the *Oresteia*. Taplin writes in a fascinating way about Clytemnestra's control and loss of control of the entrance to the house in the *Agamemnon* and the *Choephoroi* (*The Stagecraft of Aeschylus* (hereafter *STOA*), pp. 306–8, 340–6). Yet, if this action at the door is to be understood, indeed if it can even be *perceived* as a '*significant action*', we also need to know what is implicit in it, e.g. something of the significance of the *oikos* in Athenian culture, the idea of the boundary which the door instantiates, and also the role of the female with regard to that boundary. We may also not wish to leave out the literary tradition of, say, the *Odyssey* with its concern for thresholds and the proper performance of gender roles. The control of dramatic space may be a way of representing power in the dramatic characters' relationship, but what sort of understanding is it that ignores the determining factors of gender and social role in the representation of power? Since we cannot assume either that gender and social roles are self-evident from culture to culture, and era to era, or that Clytemnestra could appear at the door without being implicated in such values—as if the theatrical audience could possess a pure unmediated unsocialized gaze—we must therefore recognize that we have to analyse what is implicit in Clytemnestra's very appearance if we want to understand what is seen. Taplin writes (*STOA*, p. 4): 'My observations, however preliminary, are meant to point the way to a deeper appreciation of the play as a work of art. Any clarification of theatrical or dramatic technique—or even the pertinent formulation of a question—may help, given a critical framework, towards constructive interpretation.' I would wish to qualify this admirable awareness of what's at stake in a discussion of dramatic technique—an awareness all too often lacking in other stagecraft critics—only by reasserting that critical frameworks, like constructive interpretations, are open to (continuing) question and indeed to the continuing input of the sort of methodological enquiry Taplin is here practising. I would, in other words, reframe Taplin's cautious expression of the relation between discussion of staging and constructive interpretation as: 'discussion of staging of necessity informs and is informed by constructive interpretation.' The critical enterprise which sets out to discover merely 'dramatic technique' inevitably shows itself merely unaware of the degree to which considerations of technique and considerations of the widest aspects of interpretation are mutually implicative. Stagecraft analyses '*significant* action' and the perception and determination of significance is always already interpretative. When Wiles writes (144) 'Goldhill's mistake is to assume that Taplin's critical rhetoric is necessarily and inextricably bound up with the activity of investigating performance', I do not see how either 'Goldhill' or 'Taplin' can agree. The 'critical frame' can never be absolutely 'dispensable' (ib.), or dismissed as a 'second order of enquiry' (140). Or: We are all always already in the frame.

My second and third points about the grammar of dramatic technique are both concerned with the problematic circularity involved in the development of stagecraft criticism. For the ancient world, we have very little information about staging that is not derived from the dramatic scripts themselves. There is, for example, very little contemporary writing to match the vast archives for later European drama, that offer such an array of perspectives on theatre (as well as different problems of interpretative strategy). Contemporary, detailed descriptions of performances; writers' theoretical and practical comments; stage directions; prints and photographs; personal letters; public handbills; reviews; details of financial and artistic transactions; and many other sources for later theatrical criticism are all lacking for the fifth century. Fifth-century painted pottery may help picture costumes, but in the absence of any other representations (and, of course, the costumes themselves), it is hard to judge with any certainty to what degree imagination and convention play a part in these records of performance. We know more about the size and shape of the theatre itself, but what can be deduced from these facts remains largely a question of argument and interpretation. (It is, however, an area of criticism that has advanced greatly in recent years.) So when Wiles writes with such confidence (138) 'we know the conventions of costume, space, casting etc. observed in all fifth-century performance', it seems necessary first to reiterate just how little we do know about all these areas of performance and just how dependent we are on what is a very small selection of 'all fifth-century performance'.

The result of this paucity of information from outside the scripts is that it is overwhelmingly the scripts themselves that are used to discover the conventions ... with which to read the scripts. (This is a hermeneutic circle that inevitably arises in many (all?) branches of critical enquiry, particularly those concerned with genre and conventionality—and it is the attempt to escape this circularity that has motivated much modern critical theory.) It will not do, however, to attempt to escape the implications of this circularity by claiming that 'We can reconstruct the staging require-ments of one play because we know the conventions ... in all fifth-century performance' (138), since this is simply to ignore how the knowledge of conventions is produced—particularly for modern readers and performers of ancient plays—from observing these individual plays. Now we may wish to claim that the 'Athenian audience were competent readers of the (performance) text by virtue of sharing the same body of (performance) codes as the dramatist and actors' (140), but this (ancient) competence cannot be used to veil the modern reader's position as an outsider. And the process of determining and understanding 'competence'—norms, conven-tions, tacit knowledge—*from the outside* has become a crucial problematic of modern anthropology (linguistics, philosophy . . .), not least because of the observer's difficulty of perceiving how he is positioned inside a determining conceptual framework. I agree that there are conditions of possibility for representation that it is the task of a critic working on dramatic texts to investigate. A critic must be especially wily, however, constantly to remain aware of his complicity, his performance in the insider/outsider act of interpretation.

This theoretical discussion will no doubt appear in sharper focus with an example, and the way in which Wiles attempts to circumvent the circularity that I have been discussing will serve nicely to emphasize its inevitable problems. In his treatment of the 'palace-miracle scene' in the *Bacchae*, Wiles explains that his aim is precisely 'to lay bare the grammar of Euripides' technique, to explore the codes shared by the Athenian writer, actors, scenic designers, and audience' (144). The only way to proceed, he claims, is 'to seek out formal resemblances' (ib.) from other plays, and so he turns reasonably enough to the collapsing palace roof in *Heracles*. He immediately encounters a difficulty, however: 'Whether this was a device used elsewhere we do not know; it must suffice to say that the Athenian audience were not encountering a collapsing palace for the first time' (ib.). Now the difficulty is first that the search for 'formal resemblances' produces a single example—does one case constitute a code?—and second—and far more importantly—that it does not seem to make a difference to Wiles whether this is the sum total of parallels, or whether the *Heracles* episode is one of numerous similar (lost) scenes. Yet would it not be relevant if Euripides were the only playwright to attempt such a scene and these were the only two occasions on which it was attempted? Would there not be at least a case to be answered for a significant relationship between the two scenes (beyond the 'formal resemblance')? Would it, for example, make no difference to the recognition scene of Euripides' *Electra* if a certain sequence of three recognition tokens were used in fifteen previous plays rather than just one, the *Choephoroi*? Can the difference between common convention and significant echo be simply effaced in this way? Such problems are especially marked though all too rarely discussed, in reading a fragmentary corpus in search of a shared body of convention.

How, then, does Wiles go on to deal with the 'formal resemblance' between the scenes in the *Heracles* and the *Bacchae*? 'In order to reconstruct the meanings which the "palace-miracle" scene in the *Bacchae* held for the first Athenian audience we would need to know what happened in the *Herakles*' (ib.). I agree that what happened in the *Heracles* will crucially affect an understanding of the *Bacchae*. Yet in practice all Wiles can offer for the *Heracles* is the selfsame choices and possibilities that confront the critic in the 'palace-miracle' scene and that the *Heracles* was intended to clarify. 'If the *skene* collapsed in the *Herakles* . . .', 'If the audience of the *Herakles* merely imagined a falling palace . . .' (ib.) etc. It is probably worth underlining Wiles' uncertainty here about convention in contrast to his earlier confidence. Like all of us, Wiles *does not know* whether Athenian theatrical convention includes the possibility of a falling *skene*; the symbolic or metonymic representation of a falling *skene*; the requirement of an audience to imagine, with or without noise or other effects, a collapsing building—either the *skene* or a structure conceptualized as 'just off stage'. Nor does he know whether convention included all or only some of these possibilities. Nor does he indicate any way for us to find out—from the texts or any other source. Now Wiles is right that what happened in the *Heracles* is a determining factor in understanding the *Bacchae* for the Athenians and for us. I do not doubt that the proper understanding of conventions and codes should inform the appreciation of a scene. Yet as Wiles shows, the 'formal resemblances' between *Bacchae* and *Heracles* cannot be resolved into a convention, nor even can they be used to outline the range of possibility with any certainty.

Wiles concludes 'We have to reconstruct the dramatic codes before we investigate meanings' (ib.). I have already argued that meanings are always already implicated in dramatic codes (and it will not have escaped attention that both *Heracles* and *Bacchae* in which this problem of representation occurs, are concerned thematically with illusion, madness, seeing wrongly etc.). Now we find that the attempt at reconstruction, however admirable its aim, cannot escape its own circularity of procedure. Wiles can only restate some possibilities, some probabilities—differences as well as resemblances. Even if there was a well-defined convention in fifth-century theatre to cover these two scenes, there is no possibility of its being reconstructed with any certainty or rigour from the extant material. Perhaps Wiles's example is an extreme case, but it is one which shows in starkest form the logical problems facing stagecraft analysis of ancient theatre.

I hope it is clear from the above analysis that I am not denying that conventions exist in theatrical representation, or that they are a proper and necessary subject for critical enquiry. What I am questioning is the particular ways in which that enquiry may proceed with rigour from a modern perspective. 'Academic rigour' is not only 'clarifying and justify- ing the choices made' (Wiles, 150), but also looking at how choices get made. So, for my third and final point on such grammars, I wish to turn to less starkly problematic examples, and to make an observation with which I expect both Taplin and Wiles would agree. It is that conventions in theatre are constructed with more or less rigour but always as *a range of possibilities*. To take a simple example, it is conventional in Greek tragedy, as Taplin has argued, for characters to be announced on entrance; but the manner, form, and significance of announcement are importantly dif- ferent. What is more, particularly with writers as boldly experimental as Aeschylus, Sophocles, and Euripides, not only is the range of possibilities of a convention explored and extended, but also conventions are sub- verted, manipulated, and even parodied. Knowing the conventions of drama, its grammar, is necessary but not sufficient for an adequate reading of the great plays of fifth-century tragedy (which I have called elsewhere a 'genre of transgression'). If we knew, say, that in *Heracles* there was an off- stage noise to represent the collapse of an off-stage building and that this was conventional for Athenian theatre, it could not tell us *what* happened in the *Bacchae*, only that what happened in the *Bacchae* needs to be understood against the convention established in the *Heracles*. 'Conven- tion', 'dramatic codes' cannot remove the play of difference from the different plays of the tradition.

Performance as Text

Wiles writes (146): 'A performance, I repeat, is a "text".' And (ib.): 'The inverted commas point to an unease. Why this fetishism of "the text"?' (This second remark refers, however, in the first instance at least, to a sentence and fetish of mine.) A 'fetish for the text' (which I willingly acknowledge) may arouse in classicists the expectation of a particular type of philological project which *RGT* will not fulfil. The term 'text' is used because of the connotations with which it has been invested by numerous critics from many disciplines, whose work in my opinion is among the most stimulating and sophisticated currently available. Roland Barthes, Paul de Man, Geoffrey Hartman, Jacques Derrida, Shoshana Felman, Barbara Johnson, Julia Kristeva, Michel Foucault, Stephen Heath *et al.* (as the references in my work make evident) have deepened my understanding of the notions of 'text' and 'textuality' (the qualities that make up a text). Using the word 'text' signals a complex, shared code. One can only understand the function that the term 'text' performs (in my text), if one reconstructs the conventions by which a critic acts on the contemporary critical stage. The word 'text' is also a performative (to borrow from the technical vocabulary of speech-act theory). Within such a critical context, it is at best disingenuous of Wiles to suppose that my use of the word 'text' can be used to enforce an opposition between the written word and performance, between reading and staged action. Of course 'performance is a text': I repeat: 'The actor's interrelations on stage are subject to the constructive interpretation of the audience ... From each point, the author's text is subject to reading (in its widest sense). Dramatic experience at all levels from directing to watching involves a series of readings, of interpretations' (*RGT*, pp. 283–4). Reading in its widest sense—the constructive interpretation of different signs and of narrative; in general, the construction of meaning—is, I argued and still believe, fundamental to theatre in action. It is somewhat disappointing to find that what I hoped was a careful attempt to break down the naïve oppositions between 'action' and 'interpretation', 'reading' and 'performance' has been reconstructed precisely as 'the old question of stage versus study' (141).

The combination of Taplin's insistence that stagecraft is the articulation of significant action and Wiles's insistence that performance is a text leads me to make one final point that is often forgotten in discussion of stagecraft. The visual—that element which Taplin rightly stresses for the *theatron*—does not lead necessarily to clarity and does not obviate interpretation. Now some visual images depend on the repression of a viewer's interpretative strategies to make their point. Part of Barthes's argument in the famous theoretical essay in his *Mythologies* is that for pictures to communicate as myth, 'seeing must equal believing'. The repression of interpretative strategies does not mean that the images are without significance. Far from it. Rather, the significance of the image is regarded as 'natural', 'self-evident', 'clear'. The significance of many visual images on stage depends on precisely such a process, such a code (which, I have already argued, it is crucial for an outsider to try to understand). In this sense, certain stage actions are clear to an audience (even if it requires an historical enquiry for the modern critic to see what is clear to the ancient spectator). Yet, the meaning of much of what is 'significant action' on stage cannot be taken for granted even by a contemporary audience, since it consists of strikingly novel visual images and a visual narrative (which can change even the most hackneyed of images). Thus, both specific actions—like Agamemnon stepping on the tapestries in the *Oresteia*, to take an obvious and notorious example—and repeated actions—like the appearance in the *Oresteia* of first Clytemnestra and then Orestes over the dead bodies of a man and a woman—seem designed to produce questions or complexities of understanding for an audience. It is not quite that 'visual images have limited meaning until words guide the spectator how to "read" them' (Wiles, 149): contemporary art historical studies show again and again that it is not a problem of too limited a meaning that makes pictures hard to 'read'. Rather, it is first that visual images themselves, as signs, are always subject to constructive interpretation (and, of course, different members of an audience can and do produce quite different interpretations of what a particular visual image in a performance signifies). Second, the relation between word and image sets up a further involved interplay, which can be seen in all its complexity even in the relation between a picture and its title. (Again, modern art history has much of use for stagecraft analysis here.) So, I will end in agreement with Wiles (141): 'the visual image does not restrict meaning, it opens up meaning.' Or: performance does not determine sense, the activity of reading does. Or: there can be no theory of performance without a theory of representation.

BIBLIOGRAPHICAL NOTE

This article was written in response to David Wiles's piece 'Reading Greek Performance' (*G & R* 34 (1987), 136 ff.). For this volume it seems worth while adding a brief bibliographical note to help those interested in these questions to follow up some of the key issues.

The most sensible starting-point for 'performance criticism' remains Oliver Taplin's *The Stagecraft of Aeschylus* (Oxford, 1977), which has spawned many volumes, few as extensive or scholarly as his own. It does require a knowledge of Greek. His own *Greek Tragedy in Action* is a commonly used introduction, although the intellectual frame of this book lacks the scope or sophistication of the Aeschylus volume. Narrower conventions are explored with a certain intellectual narrowness by D. Bain, *Actors and Audience* (Oxford, 1977); *Masters, Servants and Orders in Greek Tragedy* (Manchester, 1981); more useful than either of these is D. Mastronarde's *Contact and Discontinuity* (Berkeley, 1979), which at least attempts to explore the interrelations of stage conventions and theatrical meaning. M. Halleran's *Stagecraft in Euripides* (London and Sydney, 1985) is extremely slight; D. Seale's *Vision and Stagecraft in Sophocles* (London, 1982) takes a crucial theme, the connection of sight and theatrical work, but offers a rather pedestrian treatment. J. M. Walton's *The Greek Sense of Theatre* (London, 1984) covers the whole range of Greek theatre for the drama student. Most recently, David Wiles has produced *The Masks of Menander* (London, 1991), which focuses stage-craft discussion on New Comedy. Many articles have continued to consider the technical aspects of theatre—the development of the *ekkuklema*, the crane, etc. These are likely to be of interest primarily to specialists. There is also still published a bit of trivial posturing of the 'What I would do if I were the director' sort—e.g., G. Ley, 'Scenic Notes on Euripides' *Helen*', *Eranos* 89 (1991), 25–34.

More recently, much of the most interesting work has been on 'performance' in a wider sense, looking at the Great Dionysia as a social performance. *Nothing to do with Dionysos?*, edited by J. Winkler and F. Zeitlin (Princeton, 1990), is an important collection of essays on this topic, that takes the work of Vernant and Vidal-Naquet in a new and profitable direction. Work is also being done widely at present on the relation between performance and audience that looks very promising indeed, not least because it sees theatre rightly as one of a series of fifth-century democratic institutions. I have made some preliminary remarks along these lines on Aristophanes in *The Poet's Voice* (Cambridge, 1991) and on Pindar, for which see also Leslie Kurke's fine monograph *The Traffic in Praise* (Cornell, 1991). Nicole Loraux's *Les Enfants d'Athéna* is about to be translated, as is the work of Christian Meier. J. Ober, *Mass and Elite in Democratic Athens* (Princeton, 1989) also has suggestive comments.

Much early stagecraft criticism took a lead from Shakespearian criticism, and there is still a lot to be learnt from Elizabethan and Jacobean studies: particularly S. Orgel, *The Illusion of Power* (Berkeley, 1975); L. Tennenhouse, *Power on Display* (London and New York, 1986); P. Berry, *Of Chastity and Power* (London, 1989); A. Sinfield, *Literature in Protestant England* (London, 1983). These studies show how detailed understanding of performance raises a wide series of questions, all too often unapproached by classical critics. There is, then, much to be done . . .

PRESENTATION OF CHARACTER IN AESCHYLUS[1]

By P. E. EASTERLING

Everyone who reads Aeschylus sympathetically does so, I should guess, with at least an implicit understanding of the point I shall be attempting to make in this paper; my reason for elaborating it at such length is that it is barely acknowledged in some of the recent scholarly literature, and the new orthodoxy on characterization is in danger of becoming no more helpful than the old.

It will be as well to start with the old doctrine, noting in passing that it is still remarkably alive and vigorous in some quarters. According to this view there is no fundamental difference between Aeschylus and modern dramatists in their treatment of character; its exponents see his plays as building up unique human portraits in which every detail of language adds subtle touches to an elaborate and consistently drawn personality, which is assumed to be a major focus of the dramatist's interest. Thus in *Septem* when the Theban women of the Chorus are thrown into panic, and Eteocles in his anger makes a most virulent attack on women in general, Méautis (and more recently Dawson) sees this as a trait of character, to be explained by reference to Eteocles' unfortunate family back-ground. 'It is motherhood that Eteocles hates: he has only known it, in his family, stained by incest', says Méautis.[2] In the *Persae* when Atossa hears the news of Salamis she exclaims, 'O hateful *daemon*, how you deceived the minds of the Persians! My son found his vengeance on famous Athens a bitter one, and it did not satisfy him that Marathon had destroyed Persians before' (472–5). Two hundred or so lines earlier Atossa has even had to ask the Chorus who these Athenians are (230 ff.); now she appears to know all about them. Broadhead, unable to make these passages cohere into a character portrait, concludes that 'in this part of the play the characterisation is unconvincing'; he goes on to speak of Atossa at the end of the scene becoming 'once more her normal self'.[3] The assumption, of course, is that it is a function of the play to reveal Atossa's personality, and that her words must all be put together to build a complete picture.

This kind of approach has been called into question during the last half-century, but only in the last ten or perhaps twenty years has it become the generally accepted view that 'in character for its own [sake Aeschylus] took no interest whatsoever' (I quote Professor Hugh Lloyd-Jones).[4] The ground was prepared partly by the work on Sophocles of Tycho von Wilamowitz and his followers, who showed how Sophocles appears to

sacrifice consistency of plot and character in favour of dramatic effectiveness. More recently, and more directly in connection with Aeschylus,
John Jones has argued that nineteenth-century and modern criticism has
attached too much importance to the tragic hero, and hence to character
study, and too little to the action, wishing upon Aristotle and the
tragedians notions alien to Greek thinking and to the habits of the Greek
theatre.[5] Jones must be right in emphasizing that it is the doing and
suffering of the characters—the *praxis*—that interests Aeschylus, not the
kind of personalities they are, and that the words they utter matter because
they articulate the dramatic situation, rather than because they convey the
characters' inner consciousness. And there must be some truth, at least, in
his further claim, that Aeschylus was more concerned with the study of a
whole household's fortunes than with any individual hero, an individual
whose entire existence, in any case, was defined in terms of his role in the
οἶκος. I shall return to this second point later; but it is Jones's first and
more general claim that has been most influential in helping[6] to shape the
orthodoxy.

There is nothing wrong in general terms with the current view that
Aeschylus presents most of his figures with a minimum of characterization; indeed, it usefully reminds us how much his preoccupations differed
from those of say, Ibsen, who described his creative process thus: 'Before I
write down one word, I have to have the character in mind through and
through. I must penetrate to the last wrinkle of his soul. I always proceed
from the individual; the stage setting, the dramatic ensemble, all that
comes naturally and does not cause me any worry, as soon as I am certain
of the individual in every aspect of his humanity. But I have to have his
exterior in mind also, down to the last button, how he stands and walks,
how he conducts himself, what his voice sounds like. Then I do not let him
go until his fate is fulfilled.'[7] It is hard to imagine Aeschylus working like
this, and we need to be on our guard against approaching him with the
wrong expectations. Similarly we have to be constantly reminding ourselves that the absence of naturalism in Aeschylus is only disconcerting to
us because we happen to be used to the different rules of the modern
realistic theatre, and that these are (of course) just as much conventions as
any of the formal elements in Aeschylus which on a superficial reading
strike us as wooden and artificial. So far so good, but it is when critics
come to analyse particular passages that we find them giving this approach
some most peculiar twists in their anxiety to avoid anything that smacks of
the psychological.

First there is what might be called the opportunist view, undiluted
Tychoismus as propounded by Dr. R. D. Dawe in his stimulating article on
inconsistency of plot and character in Aeschylus.[8] The implication of this
is that once you have shown how dramatic considerations take the place of

psychological ones you have answered all your questions: there is no need for a reason, other than dramatic effectiveness, why a particular action should be taken. I think there is an objection in principle to this approach. It is that 'dramatic effectiveness' is not a particularly useful criterion if no meaning is attached to the dramatic effects beyond the immediate excitement they offer the audience. Dawe's description of the technique of *Agamemnon* will illustrate my point. He speaks of 'the desire to make the utmost out of each successive scene, and to pile different kinds of dramatic thrill one upon the other in such a way that the audience is constantly being presented with a variety of spectacle and situation' (p. 51). This is rather like interpreting the *O.T.* as a masterly thriller; such interpretations are correct, as far as they go, but the trouble is that they do not go far enough. It is true that Dawe's analysis of *Septem* is much subtler and more interesting, but in the end we are still left with the question 'What are these dramatic effects for?' Clearly the study of technique alone without reference to meaning gives us only a very limited insight into what a dramatist is doing. There must be more to Aeschylus than this.

A different approach, which also has eminent exponents, notably Professors Gundert and Lloyd-Jones, is what one might call the supernaturalist view. This is really only relevant to cases where characters behave oddly; but in practice these are the only cases that cause us any difficulty: where the behaviour portrayed is very obviously 'natural' we find we have no questions to ask. The essence of the supernaturalist view is that you replace the psychological explanation of a character's strange or abnormal behaviour with an explanation in terms of Ate, the *daemon*, or the god leading a man into ruin, which in some cases you associate with a family curse. Now the trouble with this is that (like the first view) it is partly true: of course a divine explanation of human behaviour came as naturally to Aeschylus as to Homer or Herodotus. But what we must remember is that such an explanation is a *diagnosis of something actually observed in human behaviour*, and not a piece of mumbo-jumbo independent of observed phenomena. When the Greeks talked about a man being the victim of an *alastor* (or for that matter when the Hebrews said a man was full of devils) they had a real phenomenon in human life in front of them, a man behaving in a peculiar way. They diagnosed it in supernatural terms, whereas we might call it 'unconscious impulse' or 'paranoia'. At all events we should not use language that implied supernatural causation, though we should be seeing the same phenomenon. I conclude that when a character behaves oddly in an Aeschylean play it is not enough to say 'he is in the grip of Ate'. We must also ask ourselves what kind of *human intelligibility* the oddity has—unless we are content to believe that there are aspects of behaviour in Greek plays that we should expect to be quite inexplicable by our own human criteria. To say 'he behaves in this extraordinary way because a *daemon* is at work in him' and assume that one has explained the oddity seems to me like saying 'I have broken my leg *because* I have fractured my femur', pretending that two ways of saying the same thing stand in a causal relation to one another. It has often been pointed out that in Aeschylus, as in Homer, the two levels of causation, the supernatural and the human, are co-existent and simultaneous, two ways of describing the same event. I see no reason to depart from this principle here.

These applications of the 'no psychology' orthodoxy fail, I think, to lay enough stress on the simple but vital consideration that Aeschylus wishes us to believe in his characters in a deep and serious way. He may not have been interested in the exploration of personality for its own sake, but he was profoundly interested in his characters, whom he saw as *paradeigmata* of the human condition. The significance of what they do and suffer is enormous; and we shall only be able to take the full measure of it if we fully believe in them, as fully as we believe in Hamlet or Hedda Gabler. I suspect most people would say that they do indeed find themselves engaged with this sort of intensity, once they have got used to the stilted-seeming form and language and have stopped looking for naturalistic effects. Leaving aside for the moment the special case of Clytemnestra, consider Agamemnon and Orestes. Even they command our ready suspension of disbelief, though there is deep disagreement among critics about the tone of Agamemnon's speeches, and Orestes' consciousness is not given much attention, particularly in *Eumenides*. How does Aeschylus achieve it? First because he starts off with the advantage, shared by all dramatists, that the audience is willing to accept a good deal and to supply a good deal. There is what C. Garton has called 'our overwhelming natural expectation that most figures should show some continuous identity and some approximation to a human nature'[9]—a natural expectation because it arises from the physical presence on stage of a single figure impersonating a given character throughout a play; there is also the 'historical' reality of most of Aeschylus' characters, so that, just as in a modern play about Queen Victoria, he does not need to spend a long time establishing their credibility; and there is the status-definition that makes us expect kings, queens, messengers, elders to behave in certain ways, and spares the dramatist the labour of building them up from scratch.

But more than all this, which is only the common stock-in-trade of all dramatists, there is the depth of the great dramatist's (or novelist's) insight into human experience. We surely cannot be in any doubt that Aeschylus belongs to this class: the people and events—the doing and suffering—he portrays convince us with the same kind of compelling authenticity as we find in Shakespeare or George Eliot. So in thankfully dispensing with the concept 'the character of Agamemnon' we must not go on to dispense with an awareness of Aeschylus' profound and subtle insight into human motivation. It is this that gives him the power to command our response, so that believing in what Agamemnon does and suffers, we are able to sense its significance. There is nothing new in this claim, of course: the point was made perfectly clearly by H. D. F. Kitto in a discussion of characterization: 'They are all real persons, or the drama would have no effect.'[10] It is only because of the turn that most recent scholarship has taken that the issue requires to be discussed in detail.

It is time I illustrated these general claims; and it hardly seems possible to avoid Agamemnon and the carpet scene, a notorious and vigorously disputed issue which has been the focus of much of the controversy about character in Aeschylus. Let us look at the action from the moment when Agamemnon arrives at Argos (783 ff.) Here the anti-psychologists have performed a very useful service in clearing away the largely fanciful character portrait accorded to him by the critical tradition. Clearly we ought not, if we have been following Aeschylus' promptings, to be asking ourselves 'What kind of a person is Agamemnon?', but thinking 'Here at last is the king, the significance of whose actions we have been brooding over since the play opened. The head of the household is returning: what will he say and do?' And when he proceeds to speak, in language that all the time recalls the deeply disturbing themes elaborated in the first part of the play, the impact of his words is tremendous, greatly increasing our fear of what is going to happen to him. Whether his tone is haughty and overbearing or simply dignified is open to debate, given the extreme formality of the style, but in any case it doesn't greatly matter: what counts is the actual content of his speech. (That Agamemnon does not address Clytemnestra is not to be used as evidence for the presentation of his character one way or the other. First, we do not even know whether Clytemnestra is on stage at this point: the manuscript evidence is unhelpful, and it is quite possible that she is not meant to emerge from the palace until the end of Agamemnon's speech. And secondly, our knowledge of the rest of Aeschylean tragedy ought to warn us against demanding the kind of naturalism that just did not interest Aeschylus, supposing he had ever heard of it. Kitto has pointed out how little formal acknowledgement his characters make of other people on stage; when Aegisthus arrives he greets no one and barely receives a greeting, but the fact has no significance.[11])

Agamemnon begins with a greeting to the gods, which used to be thought a proof of his impiety because he calls the gods partners with him, μεταίτιοι, in his punishment of Priam and return to Greece. But Fraenkel has conclusively shown that this is perfectly acceptable Greek phraseology and carries no overtone of arrogance.[12] Even so, the whole of this section must have a most disturbing effect on the reader (or member of the audience) who notes its many echoes of the earlier part of the play and in particular of the Herald's words. The Herald has very plainly revealed that the Greeks committed dangerous excesses in their sack of Troy, and his news has brought to a climax the Chorus's feelings of disquiet about the expedition. All along they have recognized that the cause of Agamemnon and Menelaus is a just one (and the recurrent legal language has reinforced this emphasis) but they have also had very serious reservations about the whole enterprise: it was undertaken for the sake of a promiscuous woman, it has been wasteful of Greek lives, and morally it is desperately dangerous ('may I not be a sacker of cities!', 472). The Chorus have summed up all this in their words of greeting to the king (783–7 and 799–806), which help to underline both the importance of Agamemnon and the extreme complexity of his position; now he restates the same themes, and the important point for us is that he, like the Herald, unequivocally lumps together the good and the bad sides of his situation. He reminds us of the worries that the Chorus have so memorably been expressing, but he does so without giving any sign that he finds anything to be worried about himself.

'By the smoke the conquered city is easily recognized even yet. The gusts of destruction are alive, but the embers are dying with the city and sending forth rich breaths of wealth (σποδὸς προπέμπει πίονας πλούτου πνοάς). For this the gods must be paid with ever-mindful gratitude, since we have exacted payment for a presumptuous robbery, and for a woman's sake the city was laid in the dust by the fierce beast of Argos, the brood of the horse, the shield-bearing host, which launched itself with a leap at the setting of the Pleiades; and springing over the wall the ravening lion licked his fill of the blood of princes' (818–28, the translation is Fraenkel's). We notice the conflicting themes restated: the legal justification (Paris' act of robbery, recalling the Herald's words at 534) *and* the fact that it was all for the sake of a woman.[13] We see, too, that the Trojan horse is compared to a lion that 'licks his fill of the blood of princes'. Coming so soon after the αἶνος of the lion cub, this must give us pause. The lion cub was an example of something that looked good but turned out disastrous: an illustration of the way in which Paris' bringing of Helen to Troy, which was joyfully celebrated by the Trojans, turned out utterly to destroy them. We surely cannot help being chilled by the appearance here of the ravening lion, and fearing that its significance may be more ambivalent than Agamemnon implies, especially since these themes are set in the context of the total destruction of the city. When the Herald reported the fall of Troy, he also described the storm that wrecked most of the Greek ships, and we were led to interpret this storm as punishment on the Greeks for their excesses as victors; when Agamemnon talks as he does our fears of what must happen to him cannot help but be intensified.

The second section of Agamemnon's speech is an answer to the Chorus's warning to beware false friends. It is twenty-one lines long (830–50), which suggests that Aeschylus meant it to be important. Agamemnon confidently assures the Chorus that he completely understands other people's jealousy and faithlessness (perhaps his claim that Odysseus was his only faithful comrade points up the irony) and that he knows exactly how to deal with it. But *we* fear he is walking straight into a trap, and we can only shudder at his blindness.

What can we conclude from this speech? First that the prevailing modern view is right to dismiss as distracting the question 'What sort of a person is Agamemnon?' Secondly, and this is where the prevailing view is less helpful, that in dismissing this kind of psychological interpretation we ought not to be depriving ourselves of full belief in Agamemnon as a real person. He is not just a symbol or a vehicle for the development of a theme, but the king coming back home at last, and arousing our emotional response of fear and pity. Perhaps the dominant emotion generated by this speech is a kind of horrified fear: horror that a man in this plainly dangerous position can be so sure of himself and so blind, and fear that something of the most terrible kind is going to happen to him. We can feel these emotions, I suggest, because we find his words humanly intelligible: it is easy enough to imagine a highly successful person in his moment of triumph being simplistic in this sort of way.

The speech of Clytemnestra increases our fear still further. With outrageous hypocrisy she boasts about her faithful devotion (devotion that led her even to the point of attempted suicide); describes the rumours of Agamemnon's wounds and death in words that sound more like wishes than like statements; offers specious excuses for the absence of Orestes; finally, in what H. Gundert[14] aptly calls a 'cascade' of similes welcoming back her protector, she begs him not to let the foot that conquered Ilium touch the ground: instead he must walk on a 'way strewn with purple' (910). Until we reach the purple all is plain sailing. There has never been a serious critical controversy about Clytemnestra because she is so elaborately realized by Aeschylus. For the anti-psychologists she is the exception that proves the rule, a woman with a 'heart of manly counsel' and therefore a highly unusual person who has to be drawn in detail by Aeschylus in order that her action will be intelligible. Of course this is true, but a dramatist who could create Clytemnestra must not be patronized when we come to discuss his character-drawing in general; the orthodoxy, we may feel, begins to look a little inadequate if it does not bring out the power of Aeschylus' insight except in a compellingly obvious case like that of Clytemnestra.

Now we come to the contentious passage (914–57) in which Agamemnon first resists Clytemnestra's invitation, then after a rapid exchange of stichomythia accepts it and walks into the house on the purple tapestries. This requires a rather detailed discussion. Let us begin by considering what it is that Clytemnestra asks Agamemnon to do. Scholars disagree over the meaning of the walking on the purple, though presumably it was easily understood by the Greek audience. Was it—at one extreme—an act of quite unequivocal sacrilege, like using communion plate at a drinking party? Or is there no more to the act itself, as Dawe suggests, than 'walking on a rather expensive piece of material'? 'Let us not pretend', he adds, 'that only the most sensuous oriental monarchs would do such a thing: our own Royal Family does it every day.'[15]

Against the first view there is the point, well made by Jones among others, that if the purple tapestries were intrinsically sacred objects, things reserved for the use of the gods, the scene would be pretty crude: Clytemnestra would be inviting Agamemnon to do something which was quite obviously an outrage by anybody's standards. It may be helpful at this point to stop to consider precisely what these pieces of material were. Aeschylus calls them εἵματα, πετάσματα, ὑφαί, ποικίλα, and Denniston and Page have shown that we should be wrong to think of them as specifically *carpets*: they are 'fabrics which are, or resemble *clothing*'[16] (so when we speak of the 'carpet scene' we are using an imprecise shorthand). We probably ought to think of them as something like tapestries; the text describes them as woven, dyed, and patterned, and the implication of all that is said about them is that they are extremely precious. The evidence for their use is not clear-cut; all it seems safe to assume is that they were associated with Eastern civilizations, and that they were the kind of thing one might dedicate to the gods. But I do not think we are forced to see them as intrinsically sacred objects, like say, altar cloths, woven for no other purpose than dedication to the gods.[17]

However, I find it equally hard to accept the view that there is *no* religious offence in what Clytemnestra is proposing to Agamemnon. For a start, the analogy with 'our own Royal Family' is wildly misleading. The text makes it plain that the effect of walking on the tapestries is to spoil them: it is not a matter of rolling out the red carpet for Agamemnon and tidily rolling it up again for the next important visitor. The point of strewing someone's path with tapestries is of course to glorify him, to symbolize his greatness, as Clytemnestra makes clear when she says 'Let not the foot that conquered Ilium touch the ground'; it is easy enough to think of Eastern parallels. The reason why the Greeks thought it danger- ous to accept such honour has been well expressed by D. W. Lucas: 'To use expensive material for a carpet is highly wasteful and amounts to an assertion of complete confidence in the continuance of prosperity. But a human being who claims to know what the future holds for him has forgotten his place in the scheme of things. To put it on the most primitive level, he is claiming to be more than a man and so is a fit object for divine resentment.'[18] By *Greek* standards it is *hubris* both to damage the house's substance and to glorify oneself in the process, but the point is that *some people* might do it, particularly non-Greeks, orientals used to the most extravagant displays of reverence for conquerors and monarchs. Clytemnestra has just greeted Agamemnon with a string of similes so unhellenically unrestrained that Dindorf was moved to bracket the lot; the closest parallel to her language is an Egyptian song to Sesostris III praising him as saviour and guardian.[19] Now she proposes another extravagant gesture of reverential welcome, the strewing of purple tapestries, and Agamemnon's objection shows that he recognizes walking on them as the kind of thing some people—barbarians—might do, but which (speaking as a god-fearing Greek) he rejects for himself as dangerous, liable to incur $\phi\theta\acute{o}\nu o\varsigma$. The important point Clytemnestra is implicitly making is that the conquest of Troy is so special that Agamemnon deserves special treatment, and the distinction between Greek and barbarian can be blurred.

Thus the impact of the scene is rather complicated: we are made (with Agamemnon) to feel the religious danger, but we are also put in a position to envisage the thing happening, as part of a specially extravagant triumphal homecoming. The question that needs to be in our minds as we watch the scene is how far the distinction between Greek and barbarian *can* be blurred. Agamemnon's indignant objection expresses the normal Greek reaction: 'Do not pamper me like a woman, and do not adore me as if I were an oriental, with open-mouthed acclaim, nor by strewing my path with vestures bring down envy upon it. It is the gods whom we should honour with such things' (918 ff.). The rest of his speech elaborates the idea of the danger to a mortal in behaving as Clytemnestra invites him to do, which would have little dramatic point if the issue of walking over the purple was of secondary importance and merely used by Aeschylus as a convenient means of portraying a clash of wills.

Agamemnon has stated his position quite clearly, but after a dozen lines of dialogue he yields. This short passage has been the subject of heated controversy, intensified during the 1950s by the appearance in print of the opposing views of Fraenkel and Denniston–Page. Neither view was in fact wholly new, but the eminence and eloquence of their respective proponents made the contrast all the more striking: Fraenkel arguing for an Agamemnon who must be seen as a great gentleman, worn out after his arduous expedition and unwilling to show discourtesy to a lady; Denniston–Page claiming (more traditionally) that it is Agamemnon's secret wish to walk on the purple, because he is 'at the mercy of his own vanity and arrogance, instantly ready to do this scandalous act the moment his personal fears of divine retribution and human censure are, by whatever sophistry, allayed'.[20]

Let us look at the text[21] before we consider some of the more recent views on this scene. The simple point on which all the recent critics are agreed is that the scene cannot be explained in these psychological terms: the 'character of Agamemnon' must be eliminated. Suppose we follow their general approach, without, however, dropping the criterion of human intelligibility. Can we detect any relation between this scene and the way people behave in real life?

First, Clytemnestra attacks Agamemnon's religious scruples by asking him 'Would you in a time of fear have vowed to the gods to do this?' She is confusing the issue by asking him if he would have walked on tapestries *as a religious act*; she deliberately fails to distinguish between two completely different kinds of spoiling of property: the kind you do as a thank-offering to the gods for their protection or good will, as a token of your humility and gratitude,[22] and spoiling your property by walking on it, as a gesture of your own more-than-human greatness. Agamemnon ought to have pointed out this distinction, but he is confused, and instead he makes a different and much less important point. 'Yes,' he says, 'I would if an expert', εἰδώς γ' εὖ—he means a seer—'had told me to do it.' The winning of Agamemnon's assent, even if it does not commit him on this particular occasion, is important, and Clytemnestra follows up her advantage with another misleading question: 'What would Priam have done if he had achieved this victory?' This again is a false analogy; the whole point is that Agamemnon is *not* Priam, an oriental monarch who might well be expected to indulge in the kind of behaviour Greeks were very scrupulous to avoid. But Clytemnestra makes the analogy in terms of achievements: 'If Priam had won a victory like yours.' 'Oh yes,' says Agamemnon, 'Priam would have done it.' He ought to have added 'but I am not Priam', but he fails to draw this vital distinction. Clytemnestra has now won two admissions from Agamemnon: first, that he can imagine himself doing it in certain circumstances, and secondly that he can imagine someone else doing it in these. Neither admission commits him, but they prepare the ground, and when Clytemnestra concludes, 'Well then, don't fear the reproach of men', and Agamemnon does *not* say 'It's the gods that I'm worried about', we know he is going to lose. She has confused him into treating the issue as the danger of public opinion, an anxiety easily enough allayed. She points out that the person who incurs no human jealousy is not ἐπίζηλος, and as Fraenkel has noted, 'the ἐπίζηλος τύχα . . . is one of the blessings that a great lord and king particularly desires':[23] any successful Greek would like to be 'the envy of all'. Agamemnon can give only a feeble answer: 'It is not for a woman to desire conflict', which probably refers to conflict with the people, in which he is accusing Clytemnestra of trying to involve him. But Clytemnestra neatly takes it in personal terms, as referring to their present battle of words, and turns her attack on him into

a straight appeal from the woman to the man. She flatters: 'Successful
people are the ones who can afford to be conquered'; and when Agamemnon has only a question to ask ('Do you want this victory so much?') she
makes an outright appeal to his masculine superiority: '$\pi\iota\theta o\hat{v}$. You'll be the
winner in yielding to me.'

Should we be surprised after this onslaught if Agamemnon gives in?
Yes, if we suppose that people are always rationally in control of
themselves and always act as they know is best for them. But Aeschylus is
interested in real people and the compulsions that make them do self-
destructive things. As Gundert says, reminding us of Cassandra's words
later in the play (1227 ff.), Agamemnon is blind to the sophistries of
Clytemnestra,[24] as Lloyd-Jones comments, 'Agamemnon knows that what
his wife proposes is wrong, and yet she persuades him to act against his
better judgment.'[25] Yet both these critics feel they must explain Agamemnon's behaviour in terms of the curse at work on him, that otherwise it is
inexplicable. I see no reason for adducing the curse as an explanation,
though we may indeed describe what is happening in terms of supernatural as well as human causation. All I am claiming is that surely the scene
makes sense on the human level: a man succumbing to temptation and
saying as he does so, 'I know this is wrong . . .'—*video meliora proboque,
deteriora sequor*. It is humanly intelligible provided we can assume that
walking on purple is something Agamemnon, or any successful Greek,
might be expected to find attractive in itself, so long as he could be sure it
was not dangerous. This is the essential point, as I see it, for our
understanding of the scene; walking on purple is just not a feature of
modern life, but if it can be thought of as something highly flattering to
one's self-esteem, tangible proof that one has 'made it to the top', then we
can understand the sequence of Agamemnon's confusion and collapse, his
succumbing against his better judgement, under pressure from a woman
assuring him that it is all perfectly safe, daring him, almost, to accept her
challenge. Do we pity him as a tragic character, rather than regard him as
merely contemptible? Yes, because we see him, like Pentheus, as a victim,
and also because we understand the situation of knowing the better course
but, for whatever reason, being unable to make oneself take it.

A final point of interpretation: Agamemnon's removal of his shoes when
he decides to walk on the purple. This is a gesture of respect for the
precious material, and more important, a sign of god-fearing $\alpha\iota\delta\omega\varsigma$.
Agamemnon is trying to minimize the $\phi\theta\delta\nu o\varsigma$ he fears he will incur for
behaving in this presumptuous way. It contributes a visual detail which
illustrates his knowledge that he is doing the wrong thing, and of course in
human terms it is perfectly comprehensible: it represents the futile
attempts we make to deceive and comfort ourselves when we know we
have taken the wrong decision.

The claim that I have been making for the human intelligibility of the carpet scene is not at all the same thing as attributing motives to Agamemnon in terms of his character. Of course, each of us in reading will intuitively supply a colouring of motive, just as every actor will supply nuances in his acting, but in order to enter fully into this scene we have no need of the idea 'Agamemnon is a proud man' or 'Agamemnon is exhausted by all those years of warfare' or even 'he thinks she loves him, and he yields'.[26] Similarly, we have no need of a precise definition of Clytemnestra's motives in order to believe in her behaviour in this scene. I lay so much stress on believing in the characters and their actions because although great dramatists are often ambiguous they are not puzzling. To be puzzling is to run the risk of distracting or boring the audience; and every great dramatist knows that they must be gripped. So human behaviour is portrayed—through whatever artificial conventions or whatever fantasy—as something we can understand and identify with. And inconsistency, though exploited for dramatic purposes in all kinds of ingenious ways, is not allowed to break the illusion. This is why to go looking for a completely different alternative to psychology strikes me as dangerous: it neglects the way drama actually works.

Let me illustrate this point from some of the recent publications on this scene. Dawe, having most lucidly demonstrated the weaknesses of the old-style psychological approach, has nothing to offer in its place except 'dramatic necessity', which considered by itself has very little meaning. 'Agamemnon', he says, 'surrenders . . . only because it was dramatically necessary that he should do so.'[27] The only dramatic function he attributes to this scene is the defeat of Agamemnon by Clytemnestra in a clash of minds. The reasoning seems to be as follows: It will make good drama to have Clytemnestra beat Agamemnon in a battle of words before she kills him; the purple is as good a subject for a quarrel as any; let there be a quarrel over it, but don't attach any special importance to the words of the quarrel: their only function is to express Agamemnon's defeat. This leaves me wondering what sort of criteria can be used for distinguishing between the *Oresteia* and say, *Z Cars*, for Dawe has left an important question unanswered. If the quarrel is intrinsically so unimportant and humanly barely motivated, how does it come to have such a powerful and profound impact on the audience?

I have already touched on the supernaturalist view in mentioning the comments of Gundert and Lloyd-Jones. They conclude that the supernatural level of causation must be brought in as an explanation of Agamemnon's behaviour. Lloyd-Jones puts it like this: 'Would it be possible for her to persuade him, if he were not under a curse, so that in the phraseology common to Aeschylus and Homer, Zeus sends Ate to take

away his wits?'[28] The implication of this view is that we can only make
sense of Agamemnon's behaviour if we use the terminology of curses and
Ate: human explanations are not enough. I have already argued for a
simultaneous understanding of supernatural and human causation, and, as
Professor N. G. L. Hammond has noted,[29] there is also an argument from
the play's structure which points to the same conclusion. The idea of the
curse as such, the curse uttered over the race of Atreus by Thyestes, is not
brought into prominence until the last scene of the play. Even the idea of
Agamemnon's inherited guilt is not given explicit treatment until Cassandra speaks: it is she who first takes us back to the crimes of the earlier
generation, even though the Second Stasimon may already have aroused
some disturbing thoughts along the same lines in our minds. Thus we are
asked in the carpet scene to react to Agamemnon largely against the
background of his own deeds—at Aulis and Troy—and we ought to be
able to interpret his action, at any rate on the most obvious level, without
recourse to a theme that is only later in the play brought into full focus.
This is not to say that we do not feel the presence of greater-than-human
powers in the carpet scene; I shall come back to these in a moment.

What I have called the supernaturalist view has close affinities with the
symbolist, which in its purest forms sees little or no psychological
motivation of Agamemnon's yielding; instead it lays all the stress on the
fact of that yielding, expressed in his walking on the purple, as a symbol of
the working of fate or of some other aspect of the meaning of the play.
Jones, for example, claims that commentators have obscured the situation
by 'psychologising the meeting of husband and wife into a process of
temptation',[30] and Anne Lebeck maintains that 'the power of the carpet
scene is diminished by attempts to interpret the behavior of the characters
psychologically rather than symbolically'.[31] Such remarks suggest that
critics have felt a conflict between the two types of interpretation, but if
my arguments have any force this conflict disappears. I have been
emphasizing the dramatist's concern for human intelligibility not because
I wish to claim that it is an end in itself, but because I see it as a *sine qua
non*, an essential ingredient in the composition of the drama. There is no
need, therefore, to limit ourselves to this criterion when we come to
discuss the scene's function in the trilogy as a whole, which is the final
question to which we must address ourselves.

What is the carpet scene for? It cannot be thought of as having any
practical effect on the action: however Agamemnon walks into the house,
Clytemnestra can still attack him in the bath. Nor should it be given
significance as the clinching act of *hubris* without which Agamemnon's
death would not be inevitable. As Jones has pointed out, 'Agamemnon
isn't killed because he walked on the tapestries', and in any case, 'he
doesn't deserve to die for walking on the tapestries'.[32]

The scene, then, must be considered to have a symbolic function, if it has a function at all beyond that of generating excitement and tension, and to the question 'symbolic of what?' a number of related answers can be given. According to Jones, the traditional interest in Agamemnon's character has distracted attention from the real significance of the scene, which is not to be found in its study of an individual, but in its enactment of the wounding of the house. Agamemnon's homecoming is also a harming of his house, manifested in the treading on the purple, and it presages the ultimate wounding, his death, which is like cutting off the house's head. I think we must agree with Jones in recognizing the enormous importance of the house as a real identity in the trilogy, but I hesitate to see the harming of the house as the dominant theme of this scene. Even more important, I believe, is its illumination of both Agamemnon's and Clytemnestra's situation. It shows how Agamemnon's deeds and their consequences are organically linked: it looks back to Aulis and forward to his death, and it also introduces Clytemnestra's first overt step on the road to *her* decisive act, the murder of Agamemnon. It is hard to escape the belief that the poet was profoundly interested in a basic human predicament which is ultimately an experience of the individual: the tragic situation of being forced to act, often under the pressure of circumstances or impulses beyond one's control, and then having to take the consequences, in other words the familiar tension between freedom and necessity. George Eliot expressed it in terms that seem to me highly relevant to Aeschylus: 'Our deeds are like children that are born to us; they live and act apart from our will: nay, children may be strangled, but deeds never; they have an indestructible life both in and out of our consciousness.'[33]

The carpet scene brings upon the stage an Agamemnon whose blindness recalls the Chorus's description of his behaviour at Aulis: 'When the wind of his purpose had veered about and blew impious, impure, unholy, from that moment he reversed his mind and turned to utter recklessness. For men are emboldened by base-counselling wretched infatuation, the beginning of woe' (219–23). And we recall Aulis, too, in the detail about the religious expert giving advice, which Agamemnon brings into the stichomythia (934). These echoes remind us of the load of guilt that Agamemnon still carries, and of the inescapability of his having to pay for it. The scene also looks forward. Through its stress on φθόνος it makes vivid the idea of punishment coming to Agamemnon; even more, by showing his blindness it convinces us that he is walking into a trap of which he has no suspicion. And the treatment of Clytemnestra is such as to leave us in no doubt as to who is the setter of the trap and who will be the doer of the deed. The inescapability of *her* punishment is foreshadowed in her triumphant speech ἔστιν θάλασσα, her claim that the house is inexhaustibly rich and 'does not know how to be poor' (958–62), which surely has as much concentrated *hubris* in it as anything in the play.

The power of the scene is greatly intensified by the way it brings into the action itself themes that have so far been confined to the language of the play. Critics have often noted how the image of 'trampling on hallowed things', memorably elaborated in the First Stasimon as an illustration of the process of wrongdoing, is enacted in this scene when Agamemnon literally tramples on the precious purple. In the First Stasimon the agency that causes the wrongdoing is 'wretched Peitho, the child of Ate' (385–6). In the carpet scene it is Clytemnestra's persuasion that forces Agamemnon to yield. And the theme of wealth and its dangerous links with sin and punishment is here given new relevance: Agamemnon's walking on the purple is an impious use of wealth, and so is Clytemnestra's boast that the house does not know how to be poor. All these themes are of course developed further after this scene: for example, Cassandra reveals that the first crime in the chain was the 'trampling on a brother's bed' (1193); and one of the trilogy's great resolutions comes in the scene where Athena's good Peitho at last wins round the Furies.[34] As Anne Lebeck has rightly remarked, 'by the use of kindred imagery Aeschylus gives meaning and coherence to events; it is thus that he establishes the causal connection between them.'[35] Nor should we overlook the visual impact of the stage property, the purple tapestry, which, as R. F. Goheen[36] has shown, is likely to have been envisaged as blood-coloured, and thus an appropriate path for Agamemnon to tread on the way to his death. This, too, has links with the language and action of other parts of the trilogy, most obviously with the king's blood-stained robe.

And where does the *daemon* of the house, or the curse, fit into this picture, if it is not to be allowed to usurp the place of human motivation? As I have already suggested, everything that happens in the trilogy is seen both on the human and on the supernatural level. We are made aware in the behaviour of these human beings of the presence of something enormously powerful; Jones puts it very perceptively when he speaks of 'the way it unites accusers and accused in a search for some means of appeasement', and of 'its power of lending opposed individuals a deeper harmony in wrongdoing; when Agamemnon is walking along the tapestries and Clytemnestra is saying there are plenty more where those come from, the greatness of the scene touches us through our haunting awareness of conspiracy'.[37] The compulsions under which men act were given an external, supernatural character by Aeschylus and his contemporaries, who interpreted human experience as part of a larger continuum, the total working of the universe. Modern writers tend to look inwards, rather than outwards to the cosmic patterns, but the human raw material remains the same. The curse is not a remote and peculiar phenomenon, untranslatable into universal experience: we are *all* under a curse in the sense that we are caught in the web of necessity. As human beings we are forced to make choices and commit ourselves, and then to take the consequences for actions over which we are not fully in control, and our sufferings are often out of all proportion to our deserts.[38]

NOTES

1. This paper was read in April 1972 at the Bristol meeting of the Classical Association.

2. G. Méautis, *Eschyle et la trilogie* (Paris, 1936), p. 109. Cf. C. M. Dawson, *The Seven against Thebes by Aeschylus*, a translation with commentary (Englewood Cliffs, 1970), p. 48.

3. *The Persae of Aeschylus*, edited by H. D. Broadhead (Cambridge, 1960), p. xxvii.

4. *L'Antiquité Classique* 33 (1964), 374.

5. *On Aristotle and Greek Tragedy* (London, 1962), Sections I and II.

6. I do not mean to imply that Jones was the sole originator of the current approach to characterization; for a representative selection of other references, see A. F. Garvie, *Aeschylus' Supplices: Play and Trilogy* (Cambridge, 1969), p. 132 n. 2.

7. Quoted by R. Fjelde, *Henrik Ibsen: Four Major Plays* (New York, 1965), p. xiv.

8. *PCPhS* n.s. 9 (1963), 21–62.

9. *JHS* 77 (1957), 250.

10. *Greek Tragedy*[3] (London, 1961), p. 104.

11. Op. cit., p. 109.

12. *Aeschylus, Agamemnon*, edited by Eduard Fraenkel (Oxford, 1950), on 811.

13. Dawe draws attention to the importance of this detail (art. cit., 48). I take it that γυναικὸς οὕνεκα is meant neutrally enough by Agamemnon (cf. the Chorus's Ἑλένης ἕνεκ' at 800), but for the audience it is heavily loaded.

14. Θεωρία, *Festschrift W.-H. Schuchhardt* (Baden-Baden, 1960), p. 70.

15. Art. cit., 48 n. 2.

16. *Aeschylus, Agamemnon*, edited by J. D. Denniston and Denys Page (Oxford, 1957), on 909.

17. At 946 Fraenkel and Denniston–Page take θεῶν with ἀλουργέσιν rather than with φθόνος in the following line; if this is correct it is proof that these tapestries, at any rate, were thought of as belonging specifically to the gods. But the arguments for the traditional construction (θεῶν | μή τις πρόσωθεν ὄμματος βάλοι φθόνος) seem to me more valid; I see no awkwardness in Agamemnon's very strong stress on the gods here, but a natural emphasis on the real source of his fear (cf. the same preoccupation at 951–2).

18. *The Greek Tragic Poets*[2] (London, 1959), p. 95.

19. Fraenkel (on 899–902) gives references.

20. On 931 ff.

21. My discussion owes much to several of the recent critics, and above all to the editions of Fraenkel and Denniston–Page themselves.

22. Clytemnestra proposes to make this kind of sacrifice of property herself at 1574 ff.

23. On 939 f.

24. Art. cit., 77.

25. *Agamemnon by Aeschylus*, a translation with commentary (Englewood Cliffs, 1970), p. 67. Cf. *CQ* 12 (1962), 195–7.

26. J. T. Sheppard, *CAH* v (1927), p. 124.

27. Art. cit., 50.

28. *Agamemnon by Aeschylus*, p. 67.

29. *JHS* 85 (1965), 42–3.

30. Op. cit., 85.

31. *The Oresteia, a Study in Language and Structure* (Washington, 1971), p. 76. True, she admits that 'it would be wrong to assert that Agamemnon is only a symbol', and that 'he acquiesces because he cannot do otherwise, and, at the same time, because he wishes to', but she quotes with approval B. Daube's remark 'Dass Agamemnon nachgibt ... wird nicht

psychologisch begründet. Der Dichter benützt vielmehr magische Motive als Symbol für das schicksalhafte Geschehen' (*Zu den Rechtsproblem in Aischylos' Agamemnon* (Zürich and Leipzig, 1939), p. 127 n. 11).

32. Op. cit., 90.

33. *Romola*, ch. 16.

34. *Eumenides* 794 ff., and especially 970–2.

35. Op. cit., 77.

36. *AJP* 76 (1955), 115–26, who writes of the carpet as 'a thing darkly pooling blood and death while overtly sheening pomp and pride' (116).

37. Op. cit., 91.

38. This article prompted an influential critique by John Gould in *PCPhS* n.s. 24 (1978), 43–67: 'Dramatic Character and "Human Intelligibility" in Greek Tragedy'. I have made a fresh approach to the subject myself in 'Constructing Character in Greek Tragedy' in Christopher Pelling (ed.), *Characterization and Individuality in Greek Tragedy* (Oxford, 1990), pp. 83–99. (See also Simon Goldhill's essay 'Character and Action, Representation and Reading: Greek Tragedy and its Critics' in the same volume, pp. 100–27.)

THE IMAGERY OF *THE PERSIANS*

By MICHAEL ANDERSON

'If, almost a hundred years ago,' writes the critic Martin Esslin, 'Walter Pater could sum up the then prevailing trend in his famous epigram, "All art constantly aspires towards the condition of music", the dominant tendency of our own age might be described as an aspiration of all the arts to attain the condition of *images*.' Certainly it is true that the study of imagery has been a fashionable method of literary criticism for some time and, employed with the proper blend of caution and imagination, has proved itself of service in the interpretation of a number of poets, most notably perhaps Shakespeare.[1] It has long been recognized that Aeschylus is a poet who often works through 'key' or 'dominant' images; indeed, I suspect that classical scholarship may take some modest pride in having been the first in this field of study, even if it has yet to reach the dizzy heights (and sometimes the excesses) achieved by the Shakespearians.[2]

The Persians seems to me a play in which an examination of recurrent strands of imagery can throw a great deal of light on the structure of the play as a whole. In terms of our conventional notions of what a tragic plot ought to offer, *The Persians* seems static and undramatic. '*The Persians* is one of those ancient Greek plays which seem nearer oratorio than drama', complained one reviewer after a recent production. 'I always feel that I have been locked out of the auditorium like a late-comer at the opera and I resent being penned in the foyer, hearing about the murders, massacres, sacrifices and rapes only at second-hand from messengers who stagger at intervals through the pass-door.' His words reflect the sentiments, if not the sober language, of most classical scholars, from Schütz (1782), who wrote of *The Persians*, 'multo plus autem narratur in hoc dramate, quam agitur', to G. F. Else (1965), who pronounced it 'not yet quite a drama'. And Broadhead, who has much that is valuable to say about the play, is surely mistaken in his argument that *The Persians* is cast in the mould of 'the normal type of tragedy' with Xerxes as a 'tragic hero' whose presence on the stage is delayed only by the intransigence of Aeschylus' historical material.[3]

This is not to say, of course, that the major qualities of the tragedy have not been appreciated. More than one scholar has shown how religious rather than patriotic fervour (although the two were never far apart for Aeschylus) inspires the work and gives it unity and coherence. My aim is rather to suggest, by tracing some of the recurrent imagery in the play, that Aeschylus' religious thought is linked, often to the point of complete identity, with the imaginative force of his poetry.

Contemporary literary criticism has often used the term 'imagery' very broadly to refer to a variety of associative patterns in a poem, many of which must have been produced unconsciously by the poet (when indeed they exist at all). In the following pages the term is used more narrowly, but is not applied simply to metaphors and similes. Passages of pure description or narration may take on the function of imagery within the larger structure of the play; it will be suggested that the power of the sea, and the recurring names of the Persian leaders, are images presented in this way. It is worth remembering, too, that in the theatre the spectacle presented to the audience may provide the key to an image which a study of the words alone will not supply. In short, an image is any mental picture evoked in the reader or spectator, differing from what we conventionally term a symbol in so far as it works upon the imagination in a more subtle and indirect way.

A recurrent image whose importance in *The Persians* has long been recognized is the metaphor of the yoke. When we first meet it, in the vow of those who live by sacred Tmolus to 'cast the yoke of slavery upon Hellas', ζυγὸν ἀμφιβαλεῖν δούλιον Ἑλλάδι (50), it carries no special emphasis (although we should note, perhaps, that apart from the ominous οἰχομένων Ἑλλάδ' ἐς αἶαν of 1 f., the line contains the first clear reference to the purpose of the Persian expedition); but the metaphor soon recurs, and in a more unusual sense: the royal army has crossed the Hellespont by 'casting a yoke upon the neck of the sea', ζυγὸν ἀμφιβαλὼν αὐχένι πόντου (72; cf. 130). With a characteristically vivid touch Aeschylus expands the metaphor by calling the narrow strait over which Xerxes built his bridge of boats the sea's 'neck'—an appropriate word, of course, and one used by other writers in the same sense, but nevertheless the poet's first hint that the sea is not inanimate, and may feel and suffer outrage. The image of the yoke is central to Atossa's disturbing dream: she saw her son yoke a Greek and Persian maiden together, placing the harness upon their necks. The one obeyed the rein, but the other struggled and shattered the yoke; Xerxes fell, and while his father stood by pitying him, he rent the robes about his body (181 ff.). The presage of disaster is clear, and the progress of the play turns the symbolism of the dream into reality. The extent to which Queen and Messenger are aware of Xerxes' responsibility for his own fate is a matter for dispute among scholars, as is the degree of wilful folly that is mixed with Xerxes' ignorance; but, whether or not the *daimon* who tipped the scales against the weight of fortune (345 f.), the θεῶν φθόνος that worked in league with Greek trickery to deceive Xerxes (362), or the hateful *daimon* who cheated the Persians of their expectations (472 f.)[4] are seen from the beginning to be agents of a wider force of retribution rather than inscrutably malignant powers, it is undoubtedly left to the ghost of Darius to point to the chain of cause and effect which unequivocally establishes

Xerxes' responsibility for the disaster. And here the metaphor of the yoke asserts itself again. With the help of some *daimon* (724), suggests Atossa, her son had contrived to yoke, μηχαναῖς ἔζευξεν, the strait of Helle (722). A mighty *daimon*, responds Darius, who robbed him of good sense (725); in reckless ignorance he thought to hold the sacred Hellespont, Βόσπορον ῥόον θεοῦ (746), a slave in shackles:

> θνητὸς ὢν δὲ θεῶν ἁπάντων ᾤετ', οὐκ εὐβουλίᾳ,
> καὶ Ποσειδῶνος κρατήσειν. (749–50)

It is noteworthy that Xerxes' transgression of the inviolable boundaries set between Greek and Persian is clearly one of the fundamental conceptions of the tragedy; yet it is hardly mentioned in explicit terms by the dramatist. The yoke of slavery, the yoke over the sea, the maiden who struggled against the harness, the insult to mighty Poseidon, all combine to form a cumulative poetic pattern whose significance works not upon the reason, but upon the imagination.

This pattern of significance is linked to a rich emotional pattern, well illustrated by another often-noticed feature of the play—the three occasions upon which we hear the resounding names of the Persian leaders, the kings led to war by the King of kings. The Chorus sings of them in the opening anapaests, Amistres and Artaphrenes, Megabates and Astaspes, βασιλῆς βασιλέως ὕποχοι μεγάλου (24). The proud list continues for almost twenty lines (21–39); soon it is to become a roll-call of the dead. Now Artembares, the Messenger tells his Queen, is tossed against the rugged shore of Silenia; in magnificent pictorial language images of wasted splendour, chaos, and destruction pour forth in the account of the warlords who met their end at Salamis (302 ff.). Finally, Xerxes is called to account by the elders of his reign, and for two strophes and antistrophes the names of the slaughtered leaders become a catalogue of mournful reproach (955 ff.). Here as elsewhere in his work Aeschylus was clearly attracted by the evocative power of foreign names and places, but the recurrence of these passages also serves to reinforce the developing emotional tone of the play, from a proud confidence in Persia's might (yet tinged with anxiety: for what mortal man can evade the deceit of god when Ate ensnares him (93 ff.)?), through appalled horror at the sudden devastation of Persian manhood, to the final, woeful understanding of the full extent of the disaster which Xerxes has wrought upon his nation.

Associated with these passages is the insistent theme of the emptiness and desolation of the land whose men have left it for ever. In the first line of the tragedy the Chorus reveals itself as the Council of the Persians 'who have gone away', οἰχομένων, and the verb recurs, with emphasis on the complete nature of the departure: πᾶσα γὰρ ἰσχὺς Ἀσιατογενὴς οἴχωκε (12 f.). It is the flower of Persian manhood that has gone away, so that the whole land of Asia grieves with longing (59 ff.; cf. 546). The Chorus compares the massive army as it follows Xerxes over the bridge yoking two continents to a swarm of bees that has left the hive with the leader of the host (126 ff.), a compact, vivid simile that stresses the extent of the nation's loss and suggests (to a Greek perhaps more than to a modern reader) the blind, excited, self-destructive impulse that lies behind it. The well-stocked hive abandoned by the swarm has its counterpart in the city desolate of men, κένανδρον μέγ᾽ ἄστυ Σουσίδος (119), here only a fearful possibility conceived by the Chorus in its μελαγχίτων φρήν (115 f.); but it turns to reality as surely as Atossa's dream:

νῦν δὴ πρόπασα μὲν στένει
γαῖ᾽ Ἀσὶς ἐκκενουμένα. (548–9)

Now all Susa κενανδρίαν στένει (730).[5]

It is hardly necessary to trace in detail the imagery of weeping, mourning, and lamentation that is so closely linked to the foregoing. It, too, is foreshadowed in the early premonitions of the Chorus. We hear of women who may cry and beat their breasts and tear their garments (120 ff.), and of marriage-beds that are filled with tears (133 ff.). All too soon the Chorus learns that it must weep for a lost army (256 ff.; 280 ff.). Which of our leaders must we lament, τίνα πενθήσομεν; (296), asks the Queen; and after the Messenger's account of the disaster the first consequence of Zeus' devastation to which the Chorus refers is the wailing and lamentation of the newly widowed Persian women (537 ff.). From this point the emptiness of the land and the grief of those who remain become one, and in the final scene the wild lamentation of a nation bewailing its lost manhood is vividly enacted on the stage: γαῖ᾽ αἰάζει τὰν ἐγγαίαν ἥβαν (922 f.).

This imagery of desolation is a natural consequence of the theme of *The Persians*; more surprising, perhaps, is the stress which Aeschylus places upon the notion of wealth. It is true that ostentation and luxury were characteristic of the Persian nation, and not inappropriate that the epithet πολύχρυσος should be found four times in the Parodos (3, 9, 45, 53; cf. 79 f., 159). Nevertheless it is strange that the first preoccupation of Atossa, alarmed by dreams and omens, should be

μὴ μέγας πλοῦτος κονίσας οὖδας ἀντρέψῃ ποδὶ
ὄλβον, ὃν Δαρεῖος ἦρεν οὐκ ἄνευ θεῶν τινός, (163–4)

words whose exact import has long vexed scholars, but which clearly suggest a close connection in the mind of the speaker between πλοῦτος, wealth, and the ὄλβος, well-being, established by King Darius.[6] It is a connection re-emphasized by the Messenger, who addresses his native land as πολὺς πλούτου λιμήν (250); Persia's πολὺς ὄλβος, he announces, has been destroyed at a single blow (251 f.). The theme is temporarily forgotten in the account of the Persian disaster, but with the appearance of

Darius, βροτῶν πάντων ὑπερσχὼν ὄλβον εὐτυχεῖ πότμῳ (709), its significance becomes more apparent. Darius fears lest the νόσος φρενῶν which tempted his son to affront Poseidon may endanger the great wealth he had toiled to secure, πολὺς πλούτου πόνος οὑμός (751 f.). It was Xerxes' evil counsellors, replies Atossa, who taunted him that, while his father won μέγαν πλοῦτον for his children, he did nothing to increase πατρῷον ὄλβον (754 ff.). Let men remember Greece and Athens, warns Darius in his closing speech, and not pour away their great prosperity, seeking to increase fortune beyond its allotted span:

> μέμνησθ᾽ Ἀθηνῶν Ἑλλάδος τε, μηδέ τις
> ὑπερφρονήσας τὸν παρόντα δαίμονα
> ἄλλων ἐρασθεὶς ὄλβον ἐκχέῃ μέγαν. (824–6)

Xerxes has overstepped the limits set by Zeus and squandered the well-being of his nation; and Zeus is a stern corrector τῶν ὑπερκόμπων ἄγαν φρονημάτων (827 f.). At this point two recurrent themes, the flower of Persia's manhood led on to slaughter by impetuous[7] Xerxes, and the wealth and well-being of a nation recklessly destroyed, merge in a composite image of ruined magnificence and blind ambition laid low.

Here it is well to remember the *The Persians* is a play written for performance. Atossa, arrayed in royal finery, descending from her chariot to confide in the elders of the realm her fears for the wealth of the kingdom, offers a striking picture of the very wealth that is at stake; and the appearance of Xerxes at the end, still in the robes he tore with his own hands at Salamis, is a no less telling metaphor for the well-being that has been wantonly poured away, 'the harvest which ὕβρις reaped ... made visible in the person of Xerxes'.[8]

The Persian armament was a force equipped to fight by land and sea, and both army and navy suffer decisive reversals; but it is the sea-battle at Salamis which is central to the *dramatic* structure of events, and it is to Xerxes' folly in bridging the Hellespont that Darius returns with such emphasis. The many references to the power of the sea combine to form one of the most dominant of the recurring images in *The Persians*. We have already seen how the image of the yoke links the attempt to enslave the Greeks with the injury offered to the ocean (50, 72); soon the Chorus is boasting of Persian prowess in standing firm against a mighty flood of men, μεγάλῳ ῥεύματι φωτῶν (88), and holding back the unconquered ocean's flow, ἄμαχον κῦμα θαλάσσας (90). The Persians have learnt to look upon the sea, trusting in slender cables and λαοπόροις ... μαχαναῖς (105 ff.). When next we hear of the sea, it is in the grimmer context of the first news of Persian defeat: the beaches of Salamis are filled with the corpses of the dead (272 f.), and the Chorus pictures the victims bobbing lifelessly in the sea, their mantles spreading on the surface (275 ff.).[9] In the Messenger's account of the leaders who have lost their lives (302 ff.), it may be noted how insistently Aeschylus paints the scene in terms of kings and admirals hurled from their ships, once-splendid heroes tossed against the shores of Greece, the whole panoply of Persia's might reduced to flotsam by the sea's elemental power. The description of the sea-battle (353 ff.) reaches its climax in the unforgettable image of the sea hidden by the wreckage and corpses strewn upon it, while the Greeks hack at the Persians with broken oars and spars, 'as if they were tunnies or some haul of fish' (418 ff.). It is indeed a 'sea of evil' (κακῶν πέλαγος (433); κλύδων κακῶν (599 f.)) that has overwhelmed the Persians.

It would be interesting to trace some of the more detailed verbal patterns which enrich this theme, for instance the many references to ships and naval commanders which reach their haunting climax in νᾶες ἄναες ἄναες (680), a poignant contrast of substance and shadow that appropriately precedes the opening words of Darius, the king returned from the shades to advise the living elders of his former realm.

There is a central theme which draws together all the strands of imagery we have considered, and that is the contrast of order and disorder, of divine foresight and human blindness. When the Messenger describes the disaster at Salamis, he begins with the Persian expectation of victory. If it were just a matter of numbers, the barbarian fleet would have won with ease (337 ff.). It was an ἀλάστωρ ἢ κακὸς δαίμων ποθέν (354) that destroyed the Persians. Xerxes gave his orders with a confident heart and his men prepared for their tasks in good order, οὐκ ἀκόσμως (374). But the Persian semblance of order was illusory, for Xerxes was outwitted by Greek treachery and the envy of the gods (362), and when at daybreak the Greeks attacked, ἐς μάχην ὁρμῶντες εὐψύχῳ θράσει (394), their battle-cry and trumpet-call were enough to inspire terror among the barbarians. The confident hymn of a land united in the cause of freedom—

> ὦ παῖδες Ἑλλήνων ἴτε,
> ἐλευθεροῦτε πατρίδ᾽, ἐλευθεροῦτε δὲ
> παῖδας, γυναῖκας, θεῶν τε πατρῴων ἕδη,
> θήκας τε προγόνων· νῦν ὑπὲρ πάντων ἀγών- (402–5)

was answered only by the confused babel of sound from Persian tongues. This is a narrative passage recalling recent history which would clearly revive powerful emotions in an Athenian audience, but within the tragedy's artistic structure it plays an important role, harking back both to the Chorus's premonition of the δολόμητιν ἀπάταν θεοῦ (107), the Ate that lures mortal man into her nets in friendly fashion, and to Atossa's anxious questions about the Athenians, who are the slaves and subjects of no man (242). Its story of confident dispositions which lead on to chaos and disaster is repeated at Psyttalea, where Xerxes, κακῶς τὸ μέλλον ἱστορῶν

(454), calls down further havoc upon his men, and again in the crossing of the sacred river Strymon, unseasonably frozen and melting when the sun-god scatters his rays abroad (495 ff.). For the Persians, beguiled by the gods, the very elements are harshly destructive; the Greeks, their oars skimming across the sea with regular stroke as λευκόπωλος ἡμέρα (386) first lights up the land, their war-cry taken up by Echo from the neighbouring crags, are as clearly in league with the gods as the Persians are their dupes. It is Darius who sees the divine purpose behind these events when he recalls the Persian destruction of the altars and shrines of the gods, an act of senseless impiety. The offenders have become the victims, κακῶς δράσαντες οὐκ ἐλάσσονα πάσχουσι (813 f.). Plataea will stand as a blood-stained monument to ὕβρις that flowers forth in ἄτη and reaps a harvest of tears (818 ff.).

The final image to be considered is one that strengthens the theme of self-inflicted disorder in a most vivid fashion and demonstrates a capacity for blending verbal and visual imagery which is one of the marks of Aeschylean drama. We have already encountered Atossa's dream, which ends with Xerxes, unseated, tearing the robes about his limbs while the pitying Darius stands by (197 ff.). This foreshadows the defeated King's real action after Psyttalea. Viewing the disastrous course of the battle from his throne on high, he 'tore his robes and wailed aloud', dismissing his troops ἀκόσμῳ ξὺν φυγῇ (470).[10] The theme is temporarily forgotten until Darius, towards the end of his last speech, reminds Atossa of her son's dishonour and instructs her to fetch κόσμον ὅστις εὐπρεπής (833); Atossa, deeply concerned, departs to do his bidding.

Darius has described how ὕβρις flowers forth; soon the audience is to see for itself a stark exhibition of the 'harvest of weeping', πάγκλαυτον θέρος (822). Before the entry of Xerxes the Chorus sings of the successful prosperity of Persia under the peaceful reign of ἰσόθεος Δαρεῖος (856 f.) and counts the lands which he held under his sway (864 ff.). This is more than a moment of lyrical nostalgia, for (perhaps while the Epode, 898 ff., is being recited) Xerxes enters the theatre in his covered chariot, σκηναῖς τροχηλάτοις (1000 f.), and the audience will remember the magnificent entry of the Queen with her chariot and her pomp. But Xerxes is γυμνός προπομπῶν (1036), and—surely a superb theatrical stroke—at the moment when Xerxes descends from his chariot it is seen that Atossa has not yet reached him, and he faces the elders of his realm with his very clothes in shreds about him (1017). Xerxes does not present the spectacle of a warrior bearing the honourable signs of a worsting in battle: he stands in richly woven garments, ποικίλων ἐσθημάτων (836), destroyed by his own hands. The King who has made havoc of his royalty is an embodiment, plain for all to see, of the Ate that has lured the flower of Persian manhood to its destruction.[11]

But the last portion of the harvest of ὕβρις has yet to be gathered in, and I cannot resist the suggestion that although Darius' last speech concludes with a resounding χαίρετε (840) the actor playing Darius did not in fact disappear from view but remained as a silent, brooding presence throughout the final scene.

> πίπτει δ' ἐμὸς παῖς, καὶ πατὴρ παρίσταται
> Δαρεῖος οἰκτείρων σφε· τὸν δ' ὅπως ὁρᾷ
> Ξέρξης, πέπλους ῥήγνυσιν ἀμφὶ σώματι.   (197–9)

If Darius remains, the symbolism of Atossa's dream is turned to visible reality on the stage.[12]

For the first five strophes and antistrophes of the Kommos the Chorus questions its defeated King, raising its cries of grief as the news strikes home: οἰοῖ βόα καὶ πάντ' ἐκπεύθου (955). But from 1038 to the end it is the crushed and humbled Xerxes who asserts himself and leads the lamentation, calling to the Persians to cry with him (1040), to beat their breasts (1054), to tear the grey hair from their chins (1056), to rend their robes swelling in folds (1060), to pluck the hair of their heads (1062). The stately Persians who entered the theatre chanting of their empire rich in gold go howling through the city to their homes (1068 ff.), their beards plucked out, their fine robes reduced to rags, sharing in the ἀτιμίαν ... ἀμφὶ σώματι ἐσθημάτων (847 f.) of the man who led his nation into ruin. In the person of Xerxes, Ate has come back from Salamis over the unholy bridge to continue its devastation in the very heart of Asia, so that finally the imagery of weeping and lamentation in the desolate city becomes one with the imagery of slaughter and destruction at Salamis, at Psyttalea, and in the crossing of the Strymon.[13]

NOTES

1. See for instance Caroline Spurgeon, *Shakespeare's Imagery and What it Tells Us* (Cambridge, 1935); W. H. Clemen, *The Development of Shakespeare's Imagery* (London, 1951); and the work of G. Wilson Knight, in particular Chapter I of *The Wheel of Fire* (Oxford, 1930). Martin Esslin is quoted from his introduction to Günter Grass, *Four Plays* (London, 1967).

2. In 1887 Verrall's edition of the *Seven Against Thebes* drew attention to the recurring metaphor of the storm-tossed ship (commentary on 747, 751–6, 780–3, 1069); Headlam's 'Metaphor, with a Note on Transference of Epithets', *CR* 16 (1902), 434–42, is packed with brilliant observations; J. T. Sheppard, *Greek Tragedy* (Cambridge, 1911) has a good appreciation of *The Persians*. The subject was treated to a full-length if sometimes mechanical study in Jean Dumortier, *Les Images dans la poésie d'Éschyle* (Paris, 1935). Among more recent work, I am indebted to J. A. Haldane, 'Musical Themes and Imagery in Aeschylus', *JHS* 85 (1965), 33–41.

3. Schütz, 'Excursus I ad *Persas*' in his complete edition of the plays; Else, *The Origin and Early Form of Greek Tragedy* (Cambridge, Mass., 1965), p. 87; H. D. Broadhead, *The Persae of Aeschylus* (Cambridge, 1960), pp. xvi f. The impatient critic is Alan Brien, writing in the *Sunday Telegraph* (25 Apr. 1965) on Karolos Koun's production of the tragedy.

4. φρενῶν, interpreted as 'wits' by Broadhead, who takes it to refer to 'the *initial* madness of conceiving the expedition'. For a contrasting view of the extent to which Atossa and the Messenger are fully aware of the divine purpose at this point in the play, cf. Fraenkel on *Ag.* 757–62 (whom Broadhead follows), with Rose on *Pers.* 362 and E. R. Dodds, *The Greeks and the Irrational* (Berkeley and Cambridge, 1951), p. 39. On the question of whether Xerxes' *hybris* or the envy of the gods is the prime mover of the action, Bruno Snell remarks: 'Der Zirkelschluss ist unlösbar. Hybris, Torheit, Schicksal stehen am Anfang des Unheils. Eins begründet das andere' (*Aisch. u. das Handeln im Drama, Philologus*, Supplementband xx, Heft 1 (Leipzig, 1928), p. 71).

5. If Broadhead's conjecture κενώσας Σουσίδ᾽ for κονίσας οὖδας (163; see Supplementary Notes ad loc.) is accepted, then Atossa's anxious words reflect this theme.

6. By contrast, the Athenians, Atossa learns from the Chorus, have a fount of silver stored beneath their land (238).

7. θούριος (73, 718, 754).

8. Broadhead, p. xxiii. Textual evidence for the spectacular nature of Atossa's first entry is offered only by her words ἄνευ τ᾽ ὀχημάτων χλιδῆς τε τῆς πάροιθεν (607 f.) when she next enters—proof, if any were needed, that Aeschylus does not always reinforce significant use of spectacle with explicit verbal reference. (For the opposite view, cf. Fraenkel on Agamemnon's entry, *Ag.* ii. 370.)

9. Broadhead ad loc. argues that the reading πλαγκτοῖς ἐν διπλάκεσσιν is unsound; but the words offer such a startling and yet appropriate image of the ruined Persian splendour that I am reluctant to reject them.

10. The notion of the spoiling of fine garments is foreshadowed by the Chorus's reference to the mourning of the womenfolk (125), and perhaps by πλαγκτοῖς ἐν διπλάκεσσιν (277; cf. n. 9 above).

11. *Agamemnon* is an infinitely more complex play than *The Persians*, but an interesting comparison of the dramatic roles of Xerxes and Agamemnon might be made. Both are kings returning from a campaign in which they have earned the anger of the gods for sacking cities and overturning altars—the one already crushed by defeat and the other triumphant in his ignorance of what the gods have in store for him—and in both plays the wanton abuse of costly fabrics is a theatrical image reflecting the greater impiety that lies at the heart of the dramatic action. If Lloyd-Jones is right in arguing that Agamemnon commits his crimes after Zeus has sent an Ate to take away his wits, the parallel between the two becomes more remarkable (cf. H. Lloyd-Jones, 'The Guilt of Agamemnon', *CQ* 12 (1962), 187–99).

12. It has often been observed that Atossa and her son, the two main characters of the tragedy, never meet; and although such a comment betrays a misunderstanding of Aeschylean dramaturgy, the presence of Darius during this scene would make it necessary for the same actor to take the roles of Atossa and her son and confirm what is so often the case, that Aeschylus is using the resources of his theatre to the full, but not in the way that we, with our modern notions of the dramatic, should expect.

13. A reproving footnote by Oliver Taplin (*The Stagecraft of Aeschylus* (Oxford, 1977), p. 116) almost persuades me to dismiss this article as a youthful indiscretion; but although studies of recurrent images or word-patterns (see e.g. Anne Lebeck, *The Oresteia: A Study in Language and Structure* (Cambridge, Mass., 1971)) have now yielded pride of place to rather more complex (and at their best more sensitive) readings of Aeschylus (see e.g. Simon Goldhill, *Reading Greek Tragedy* (Cambridge, 1986)), I suspect that the subject which interested me here, namely the relationship between images conjured up verbally and significant spectacle on stage, is one that still has a few secrets to yield to imaginative scholarship, in the works of other ancient dramatists no less than in Aeschylean tragedy.

DRAMATIC STRUCTURE IN THE *PERSAE* AND *PROMETHEUS* OF AESCHYLUS

By s. IRELAND

In contrast to earlier works of scholarship directed towards resolving the problems of authenticity and date of composition through considerations of metre, language, and style, there has been a tendency for more recent studies of the *Prometheus Bound*[1] to concentrate upon those aspects of thematic development which some have seen repeated in the *Supplices*, now dated to 464–463 B.C., and the *Oresteia* of 458. So, for instance, C. J. Herington[2] has demonstrated on more than one occasion the apparent divergence that exists between the cosmic system portrayed by Aeschylus in the *Persae* and *Septem* and that found in the later plays, including the *Prometheus*. In the former group he says: 'the Divine is united against man: let a human being swerve by a hair's-breadth from the rules, and the powers of earth and heaven will join together to castigate him', while in the later plays 'the human and divine cosmos is divided into the enemy camps of male and female, and of the opposites that go with them respectively: light/dark, heaven/earth, new/old; the universal fabric is torn in two.'[3] Certainly the ideas he puts forward here are acceptable in the case of the *Oresteia*, but for their extension to the *Supplices* and *Prometheus* they depend largely upon reconstructions of the lost plays that made up their respective trilogies—a hazardous course, though perhaps not altogether unjustified in the light of the available evidence. More important, however, is the danger of concentrating too much upon such aspects which, unlike many criteria used in the past, do produce apparently conclusive results: and I here wish to suggest that on other levels—that of overall dramatic structure, for instance—the *Prometheus* may well be regarded as containing features very similar to those of the poet's earliest play, the *Persae*.[4]

Though like the trilogy the *Prometheus* requires for its performance the presence of a third actor,[5] its dramatic action exploits the possibilities which result from this hardly at all. Indeed, apart from the opening scene it remains to all intents and purposes a two-actor play. This, however, is not to suggest composition when Aeschylus was still unsure of a device we are told he adopted from Sophocles, or that tragic dialogue even as late as the end of the fifth century was able to break free from that predominant concept of verbal exchange which marks the norm: two characters formally engaged in debate; but it is significant that nowhere in the *Prometheus* has the playwright chosen for dramatic reasons to introduce onto the stage at any one time three major speaking parts such as those of the trial scene in the *Eumenides*. The reason for this is not a lack of skill but a deliberate intention to concentrate attention upon a figure who, because of his constant presence and immobility, is the natural centre of interest. For this reason the development of the plot is truly episodic, a series of encounters between the Titan and those who visit and interact with him, each in some respect a victim of Zeus' power, each exhibiting a distinct reaction to the chained figure; and it is through these that the drama proceeds towards its climax.

The first such character brought into contact with Prometheus is Hephaestos, one of the 'new' gods, a victor in the recent struggle in heaven, but at the same time an unwilling partner in the events portrayed and himself threatened by the overwhelming might of Zeus, here represented by the harsh and brutal Kratos:

ἐλεύθερος γὰρ οὔτις ἐστὶ πλὴν Διός.

(50; cf. 52 f., 67 f., 77)

Throughout the scene Prometheus himself utters not a word, and what details are given come from the altercation that arises between those whose task it is to load their victim with the unbreakable bonds. At each stage of the chaining Hephaestos' feelings of kinship and sympathy, countered as they are by the hatred and distrust of Kratos, continually lead the attention of the audience back to the figure of the Titan and his suffering. Prometheus remains the centre of attention both directly, as in Kratos' opening remarks (4 ff.), answered by Hephaestos (14 ff.), and indirectly through the opposition of reaction his downfall produces (37 ff.). In this the relentless and merciless enthusiasm displayed by Kratos in pursuing his task, his brusque and harsh orders, his threats against Hephaestos, serve but to underline the unswerving ruthlessness of Zeus' rule. It is here, in the treatment meted out to Hephaestos at the outset of the action, that the justice of Prometheus' punishment and the yardstick by which it is to be gauged become only too clear.

In contrast to the brutality of Kratos is the gentle approach of the Chorus and the innocent sincerity of their interest in the Titan's misfortunes. The inquisitiveness they display both in the *parodos* and in the dialogue which follows is matched by Prometheus' own concern with himself. So for instance his wish at 152 ff. that he be buried in Tartaros, so that his captivity may not prove a source of pleasure to others, is matched throughout the play by his obsession with sight,[6] in each case the sight of his own torment. Similarly, the narrative of the help he gave to Zeus in combating the threat from the Titans (197–241) is a natural means of concentrating the attention of both Chorus and audience upon him, and again it is a device emphasized by the language employed, the frequent use of the personal pronoun and adjective, ἐγώ, ἐμός.[7] This is not to suggest that such usage becomes incongruous or an embarrassment to the action. Under the circumstances of the dramatic situation it is inevitable. Rather what the playwright has done is to reinforce through the language he uses the concentration of attention he places upon the source of interest.

Following the descent of the Oceanids from their winged chariot the entrance of Oceanus introduces a representative of the old order, one who has escaped the recent struggle unscathed and as a result still harbours illusions of influence. Again the Titan is the centre of attention,[8] and much of Oceanus' part consists of an attempt to urge him to a better course (309 f., 315 f.). Significantly too the failure of Oceanus throughout the scene to give any indication that he is at all aware of his daughters' presence results not from the exigencies of stage mechanics so often suggested in the past, but rather from the poet's own desire not to shift interest even momentarily away from the figure of the Titan. It is not through stubbornness or pride, however, that Prometheus refuses his visitor's offers of intercession and help, but his recognition of Oceanus' essential lack of power. In the gulf that separates the old god's hopes and the realities of the present régime, as shown in the fate of Atlas and Typhon, the total collapse of the former order of things becomes patently obvious.

With the departure of Oceanus the first ode, for the most part a list of the peoples now mourning the fall of their benefactor, leads into Prometheus' description of the help he gave to man. Again, and understandably, many of the details he gives return to himself as the provider of skills and knowledge among the creatures Zeus wished to annihilate. Once more it is a process underlined by the vocabulary and phraseology used, a concentration upon features that can only have been designed to direct attention to the source:

> χαλκόν, σίδηρον, ἄργυρον, χρυσόν τε, τίς
> φήσειεν ἂν πάροιθεν ἐξευρεῖν ἐμοῦ;

(502 f.; cf. 444, 457 f., 467 ff., 476 ff., 481 ff., 484 ff.)

The reaction of the Chorus is, as before, to retain the interest of the audience upon the person of Prometheus (540 ff., 545 ff., 552 ff.), and as they fall silent the entry of Io, representative of a race saved from annihilation but still hounded by the gods of Olympus, marks a climax in the emotional content of the play. In the ensuing scene the concentration of details upon her past and the future that awaits her means an inevitable decline in the emphasis hitherto directed towards the Titan. The reason is clear enough, for it is in conjunction with the girl as a fellow victim of Zeus that the true nature of Prometheus' strength is brought out: his eventual release at the hands of Io's descendant Heracles, and the knowledge of a future that threatens Zeus as much as he now threatens others. Yet though it is Io who is the subject of the narrative which follows, the source of most of the information given continues to be Prometheus, and it is upon him as narrator that attention naturally continues to be directed. Nor is the scene without pointed reference to the Titan. He is mentioned in Io's opening words (561; cf. 588, 593), and in the dialogue that follows her monody instances of direct reference to him continue to be produced.

Thus far three separate and distinct forces have been introduced in addition to that of the Chorus, an ascending scale of suffering at the hands of Zeus, each confirming that seen consistently in the person of Prometheus: Hephaestos, like Prometheus a victor in the recent struggle, yet all the time threatened by Zeus' minion Kratos; Oceanus, a member of the old order, again like Prometheus, but (though he has survived) his power has gone—a figure for whom action carries with it the danger of provoking a fierce retribution; finally Io, a direct victim of divine power, for whom, as for Prometheus, a refusal to comply means relentless punishment. As a result, with the entry of Hermes to deliver his ultimatum (944 ff.), even the Chorus of Oceanids is prepared to share in the suffering seen throughout the play and to sink into the earth with the Titan. The effect of all this upon the dramatic structure is impressive. At the centre of attention for both the characters on the stage and the audience is Prometheus. From him as from the hub of a wheel radiate the spokes: those who approach this desolate crag at the end of the world, each connected to the hub but not to one another, each maintaining by virtue of this limited contact a force of directed interest that reinforces the already extreme dramatic position of the Titan as the constant focus for events.

In turning to the *Persae* a number of differences become apparent: the use, for instance, of only two actors throughout. In essence, however, the action continues to be dominated by a single figure; before it was the constant presence of Prometheus, now it is the absence of the Persian host, and in particular, from the point of view of the characters introduced, the absence of Xerxes, in whom is embodied the might of Persia. From the very outset of the play, the opening anapaests of the Chorus, come murmurings that all may not be well, fears caused by a lack of news and amplified in the *stasimon* that follows.[9] In this, as elsewhere in the play, the Persian host is prominent, naturally so since it is they who are directly concerned with the action of the campaign and it is they who are its immediate victims; but it is significant that the name of Xerxes occurs at both the beginning and end of this section (5 and 144), framing what lies between. With the entrance of the Queen Mother the misgivings felt by the Chorus are given substance by her dream. As a dramatic force in the play the personal interest she exhibits throughout not only contrasts with the wider political interest of the Chorus but also overshadows it. For this reason her transformation of the dangers vaguely seen by the Chorus as a threat to the whole army into the symbolism of danger to her son alone (176 ff., 189 ff., 226 ff.) constitutes what can only be viewed as a major contributing factor in concentrating overall attention upon the figure of Xerxes.

In the epirrhematic outburst that marks the entry of the Messenger, the news of disaster, which provides the reality of what has so far existed only as a source of fear and disquiet, naturally focuses attention on the fate of the host; it is they after all who have suffered death and physical defeat and it is with them rather than with Xerxes that the Messenger identifies himself; he is one of their number. With the intervention of Atossa at 290 and the return to trimeter dialogue, however, emphasis shifts back to the figure of Xerxes as the Messenger senses the significance of Atossa's question at 296 ff.:

> τίς οὐ τέθνηκε, τίνα δὲ καὶ πενθήσομεν
> τῶν ἀρχελείων, ὅστ᾽ ἐπὶ σκηπτουχίᾳ
> ταχθεὶς ἄνανδρον τάξιν ἠρήμου θανών;

In the narrative that follows it is Xerxes who is made to bear responsibility for the destruction of the Persian leaders whose names are now unfolded. When the numerically superior navy of Persia is mentioned it is Xerxes' (341); when the ἀλάστωρ approaches with information that proves so disastrous, it is to Xerxes that he comes; and it is Xerxes who gives the order that wears out the Persian rowers with wasted effort throughout the night (361 ff.). Similarly, it is Xerxes who dispatches the cream of his forces to their deaths on Psyttaleia (450 ff.), and, with the host destroyed, it is with Xerxes that the retreat begins (465 ff.). Throughout, the name of Xerxes is never far away, and in the ensuing choral ode the theme of responsibility, a prominent feature of the description of Salamis, finds natural expression:

> Ξέρξης μὲν ἄγαγεν, ποποῖ,
> Ξέρξης δ᾽ ἀπώλεσεν, τοτοῖ,
> Ξέρξης
> δὲ πάντ᾽ ἐπέσπε δυσφρόνως
> βαρίδεσσι ποντίαις.

(550 ff.)

In the next scene, though it is the Chorus that raises the old King from his tomb and thus has a ready-made claim upon his attention, it is Atossa who is without doubt the most relevant character to engage him in dialogue, and the extreme nature of the Elders' reverence provides the means for producing the transition. Once again the result is a shift of emphasis to the figure of Xerxes, and throughout the dialogue his responsibility for the campaign and its outcome is made plain.[10] Similarly it is Xerxes who dominates Darius' final words to Atossa (832 ff.), just as he had dominated her own at 529 ff.

With the significance of Xerxes' folly made clear by Darius, the appearance of Xerxes himself, alone despite his mother's words at 849 ff. —necessarily so if his introduction is to have the desired effect—sums up in his person everything that has gone before. The *commos* in which he engages with the Chorus adds little substance to what has already been heard. Xerxes is rather the material representation of the host destroyed.

Just as the *Prometheus* ended with the disappearance, whether in fact or merely in the imagination of the audience, of the one who had dominated attention throughout, so the *Persae* ends with the appearance of one whose absence has been a prime source of interest. Where the latter play differs can be seen chiefly in the direction of dramatic contact. Whereas before, in the *Prometheus*, the evolution of the plot depended on the separate reactions of the Titan to those who visit him, this time, in the *Persae*, developments have to be produced by the interaction of characters other than the young king, who, despite his absence throughout the most formative sections of the play, nevertheless remains the chief focus of attention for those involved in the fate of Persia. Though it is Xerxes, the symbol of the army he led to destruction, who stands at the hub, developments are produced by those on the rim, and it is as a result of their contact with each other that the audience's attention flows back to the centre. At the same time there is the natural and necessary inclusion of the Persian host, occupying as it does the greater part of the narrative. Such emphatic treatment is of course inevitable given the circumstances of the plot, but in the context of Aeschylean drama the theme itself requires any hybristic cause of the disaster to reside not in the amorphous generality of the army as a whole but rather in a single individual. The playwright has reduced to a personal and thereby more understandable level a power which in the end over-stretches itself. For this reason it is on Xerxes that responsibility and attention rests, just as in the *Prometheus* it is the figure of the Titan that forms the central point of interest in the action. In this sense the dramatic structure of the two plays contains features that have much in common: in both there is a concentration of attention upon a single figure; both are essentially linear in their development of tension, and both end with an emphatic visual statement of the climax reached: on the one hand Prometheus' disappearance, symbol of a final attempt at physical coercion, on the other the appearance of Xerxes as the visible symbol of all that his folly has achieved.

NOTES

1. Since the first publication of this paper the question of *Prometheus*' relationship to the other plays of Aeschylus has been reopened by Mark Griffith, *The Authenticity of Prometheus Bound* (Cambridge, 1977), who argues forcibly against ascription to the playwright; see further, M. Gagarin, *Aeschylean Drama* (Berkeley, 1976); O. Taplin, *The Stagecraft of Aeschylus* (Oxford, 1977); D. J. Conacher, *Aeschylus' Prometheus Bound: A Literary Commentary* (Toronto, 1980); S. Ireland, *Aeschylus*, Greece & Rome New Surveys in the Classics 18 (1986).

2. *Arion* 4 (1965), 387–403; cf. *JHS* 87 (1967), 74–85; *The Author of the Prometheus Bound* (Texas, 1970), pp. 76–87; *Aeschylus* (New Haven, 1986), pp. 157–77.

3. *JHS* 87 (1967), 80 f.

4. See further E. Flintoff, 'The Date of the *Prometheus Bound*', *Mnemosyne* 39 (1986), 82–91.

5. It is hardly necessary to repeat here the arguments against the postulation of a lay figure to represent the Titan: see P. D. Arnott, *Greek Scenic Conventions* (Oxford, 1962), pp. 96 ff.; G. Méautis, *L'Authenticité et la Date du Prométhée Enchaîné d'Eschyle* (Geneva, 1960), p. 9; Taplin, op. cit., pp. 243–5.

6. Like that of maltreatment (αἰκία, ἀεικής, αἰκίζεσθαι, αἴκισμα) the theme of seeing (ἰδεῖν, δέρκεσθαι, ὁρᾶν, λεύσσειν, θεωρεῖν) forms of one of the most powerful in the play.

7. 204, 209, 214, 216, 219, 221, 234.

8. 285, 288, 292, 295.

9. The action of the play is analysed in detail by A. N. Michelini, *Tradition and Dramatic Form in the Persians of Aeschylus* (Leiden, 1982); cf. D. J. Conacher, 'Aeschylus' Persae, A Literary Commentary', in *Serta Turyniana: Studies in Greek Literature and Palaeography in Honor of Alexander Turyn*, ed. J. L. Heller (Urbana, 1974), pp. 143–68; S. M. Adams, 'Salamis Symphony: The Persae of Aeschylus', in *Studies in Honour of Gilbert Norwood*, ed. M. White (Toronto, 1952), pp. 46–54 = *Oxford Readings in Greek Tragedy*, ed. E. Segal (Oxford, 1983), pp. 34–41; Ireland, op. cit.

10. 718, 739 f., 744 ff., 750 f., 753 ff., 759, 782 f.

THE THEODICY OF AESCHYLUS: JUSTICE AND TYRANNY IN THE *ORESTEIA*

By DAVID COHEN

Along with the *Oedipus Tyrannus*, the *Oresteia* is perhaps the most discussed literary work of classical Greece. In recent years a substantial part of this interpretative effort has been devoted to various ongoing controversies, such as Agamemnon's guilt, or more generally, the interplay of necessity and freedom in the trilogy, but despite these numerous *Streitfragen* what is particularly striking about the criticism of the *Oresteia* is its relative unanimity on certain fundamental questions. This will no doubt sound strange to the classical scholar, all too finely attuned to the various important particulars over which he and his colleagues differ in their reading of the plays, but it none the less seems to me to be undeniable that in their assessment of the general movement of the trilogy, most interpretations are, with some variation and shading, cut from the same cloth. By this I mean that in regard to the fundamental questions of the justice of Zeus, and the resolution of the conflicts developed in the first two plays by means of the famous trial which concludes the trilogy, most critics agree as to Aeschylus' dramatic intention. In what follows, I will argue that this unanimity arises out of certain shared preconceptions concerning Aeschylus which, in my view, are not supported by the text. I will first discuss the main traditional views concerning Aeschylus' presentation of what is commonly called the Justice of Zeus, and then try to demonstrate that, in reality, Aeschylus portrays a cosmic and political order which is neither moral nor just, but rather tyrannical, in the sense that its ultimate foundations are force and fear.[1]

The widely accepted interpretation of the justice of Zeus in the *Oresteia* stems, it seems, from a more general, traditional view of Aeschylus as a deeply religious Athenian patriot. As R. P. Winnington-Ingram puts it, 'The drama, as the religion, of Aeschylus—and the two are hardly separable the one from the other—is centred in a Zeus who is conceived as the upholder of a just moral order. Aeschylus has been called the prophet of Zeus.'[2] Although such a statement might seem rather odd to an unlearned reader of *Prometheus Bound*,[3] it is none the less the dominant view of Aeschylus, and its cornerstone is the *Oresteia*. At this point it may be useful to distinguish, roughly speaking, two major variations of this traditional theory.[4] The first tends to view the question of justice as essentially unproblematic. As Hugh Lloyd-Jones claims,

From Hesiod Aeschylus takes over a doctrine of Zeus and Dike....

The supreme god of the universe is Zeus . . . he preserves justice among men. If they challenge Zeus' ordinances, he will punish them. . . .

Aeschylus strongly maintains that Zeus does not punish the innocent . . . [H]e destroys a family only when its members have been guilty of some grave crime.[5]

Aeschylus strongly maintains that Zeus does not punish the innocent: here is the central issue. If Zeus' rule is just, then the execution of his justice cannot be the agency of the punishment of the innocent. Therefore, those who suffer in the trilogy by the design of Zeus must be guilty of crime: 'Closely linked with this sense of balance in the universe and in human affairs is the necessity for reciprocity. . . . This rule of reciprocity is demonstrated by the action of the trilogy, as Agamemnon, Clytemnestra (and Aegisthus), and Orestes all kill and in return are killed or at least punished.'[6] If they do not view their suffering as just punishment, it is because 'the purposes of Zeus are inscrutable to mortals; only in the light of experience can men think over the past and trace out the working of the law of justice'.[7] This is all well and good for Agamemnon, Clytemnestra, and Aegisthus, but what of those victims to whom such a justification simply does not apply? If Zeus in the *Agamemnon* is just and does not punish the innocent, and if all that happens in the play is part of the working out of his divine plan, how does one explain the sacrifice of Iphigeneia, the murder of Cassandra, the destruction of the young and innocent at Troy, all of which Aeschylus is careful to emphasize repeatedly?

Thus, while some scholars simply assert that Zeus is just and does not punish the innocent, ignoring the apparent counter-examples, others, because they have not seen the issue clearly, lapse into conceptual incoherence. Thus, Robert Goheen maintains, on the one hand, the 'long range philanthropy in Zeus' rule'[8] yet characterizes Cassandra as a 'guiltless sufferer'[9] without, evidently, seeing any problems for what he calls '. . . the achievement of *personal* and civic justice . . .' in the *Oresteia*.[10] Many scholars, however, have perceived the problem that the divinely ordained destruction of the innocent poses for their conception of the justice of Zeus, and their attempts to reconcile these two features of the trilogy constitute the second variation of the traditional view which I mentioned above.[11]

The main strategy of this second approach to the trilogy is to argue (I put it crudely) that though there may be some victims along the way, the justice of Zeus is manifested in a progressive movement which finds culmination in the resolution of the trial as Athena's 'clear, persuasive reason'[12] brings about the establishment of a new and better order. This is, it seems, a type of progressive interpretation which sees the first two plays of the trilogy as presenting seemingly irreconcilable conflicts, which, through the agency of Zeus' justice, are resolved in the final play by the transformation of the Erinyes into the Eumenides, and the foundation of the new social and legal order of the democratic polis: 'It is a tour de force of reconciliation. . . . The Furies' *dike* of blood-for-blood has been shown to be inadequate. It has been superseded by a new conception, a legal *dike*, justice achieved through process of law, a human embodiment of the divine exemplar . . .'[13] This achievement of a new and better order is implicitly taken to justify the cost at which it has been achieved: 'Beside this, Orestes, Agamemnon, and Clytemnestra shrink to secondary import- ance. The human act—the murder of Agamemnon—has been dwarfed by its consequences.'[14] If this emergence of a higher political and moral order (assuming, for the moment, it is such) was achieved pursuant to a divine plan which encompassed the deliberate murder of the innocent, is this truly what Aeschylus meant to depict as the 'moral sense of Justice for which Zeus stands . . .'?[15] Before concluding that Aeschylus was, indeed, one of those who 'die Schlangenwindungen der Gluckseligkeitslehre durchkriecht',[16] it may be useful to approach the question of his intention from another perspective.

I would like to suggest an alternative view of the problem of justice in the *Oresteia*, taking as a starting point the rejection of the preconception that Aeschylus must be pious and Zeus must be just. This seems to me not unreasonable, in that if Aeschylus was intending to produce a theodicy of Zeus it is odd that he chose to emphasize so strongly the innocent suffering which the justice of Zeus produces. The *Oresteia* is not the Book of Job, and Aeschylus does not dismiss the question of innocent suffering with a Greek equivalent of the 'Where were you when I laid the foundation of the earth?' (Job 38:4), which challenged Job from the whirlwind. If he thought that the justice of Zeus, encompassing the destruction of the innocent, was simply incomprehensible to man and had to be accepted as a matter of faith, then the law of 'learning through suffering', the ending of the *Eumenides*, and, indeed, the movement of the trilogy as a whole, would all be rendered meaningless. Here too, we must give Aeschylus more credit than that, and, having rejected both crude utilitarianism and blind faith as his solution to the problem of evil, it is perhaps appropriate now to inquire more closely as to the nature of this 'Justice' of Zeus and as to whether or not Aeschylus regards it as the proper foundation of a theodicy. The three plays will be considered in turn.

Agamemnon

I cannot, in such a short space, hope to do justice to the enormous subtlety of a play as difficult and complex as *Agamemnon*; the following argument will merely attempt to demonstrate the centrality of the destruction of the innocent in the play, and the causal agency of Zeus in bringing it about.

As Benjamin Daube has brilliantly shown, the play is dominated by legal imagery.[17] In particular, from the very beginning the Trojan war is depicted as a lawsuit for the theft of Helen in which the Atreidae are 'the great adversary at suit' (*Ag.* 41). The significance of the war as a suit at law extends beyond *Agamemnon*, for the trilogy will be concluded by yet another lawsuit decided under the aegis of Zeus. Unlike an ordinary lawsuit, however, this one can only be won with the help of force (*Ag.* 47, στρατιῶτιν ἀρωγήν); in *Eumenides* Athena will fulfil a similar function. Further, in the prosecution of this lawsuit the Atreidae are the agents of Zeus:

[Like the Erinyes . . .] Even so the sons of Atreus are sent by the mightier one against Alexandros, by Zeus, guardian of guest-law, who over a woman of many husbands will bring about wrestlings many and wearying . . . for Danaans and Trojans alike.   (59–67)[18]

What is implied by this identification of the Atreidae with Zeus as the agents of his justice? It is clear that he sends them against Paris, who has wronged them and infringed his law of guest-friendship (*xenia*), but who are the victims? In the famous passage (110 ff.) concerning the omen of the twin eagles devouring the pregnant hare, which speeds the expedition 'with avenging spear and arm on its way' (111),[19] the eagles are identified as the Atreidae—but the eagle is also the bird of Zeus. This is, of course, appropriate, since they are the agents of Zeus' punishment, but it also means that Zeus is identified with the devouring of the hare with its unborn offspring (only original sin could mar the innocence of the unborn—the deliberate portrayal of the destruction of the innocent could not be clearer). Calchas, the seer, interprets the omen for the Greeks, naming the 'warlike devourers of the hare' (124) as the Atreidae laying waste to Troy. He goes on to pray that 'no envious grudge from the gods strike beforehand and overcloud the great bit for Troy's mouth, the army on campaign' (131–5), referring to Artemis, who halts the expedition at Aulis because she 'loathes the feast of eagles' (138). Artemis, the goddess who protects the young and the helpless, pities the future victims of the eagles (135) and demands an impossible sacrifice to turn them back. If Agamemnon wants to proceed he must himself sacrifice his offspring to the devouring eagles; the prosecution of Zeus' lawsuit demands yet another innocent victim. Rather than turn back,[20] Agamemnon applies the bit he had readied for Troy (134) to his own daughter, Iphigeneia, to stifle her curses (236–8). The parallelism between Iphigeneia and the Trojan victims is surely deliberate, and the same trope will be applied later to Cassandra (1066).[21]

Such is the cost of this suit 'for the loss of a woman' (225; and cf. 62 and 448), and, as is repeatedly emphasized throughout the play, it is also the justice of Zeus, whose agents the Atreidae are:

Zeus . . . thou who didst fling on the Trojan fortress a covering net, so that no one full-grown, *nor any of the young* could surmount the mighty drag-net of slavery, of all-catching doom. The great Zeus of Hospitality I hold in awe, him who has achieved this, long since bending his bow on *Alexandros*. . . (355–65; my emphasis)

Or again:

Agamemnon . . . [who] has dug down Troy with the mattock of Zeus the bringer of justice [τοῦ δικηφόρου Διός], wherewith the soil has been thoroughly worked and the seed perishes out of the land.[22] Such is the yoke which our king . . . has laid upon Troy.   (523–9)

This is the 'double penalty' for theft.[23] Paris 'has lost not only his plunder but has caused the house of his fathers to be shorn off and utterly destroyed together with the land' (534–7). This has been accomplished, we are told at 581, by the grace, the benevolence (χάρις) of Zeus the Fulfiller, and this phrase brings us back to the famous Hymn of Zeus, so important in the theories of Zeus' justice. Here (167–83) we learn that the divine order is also founded upon violence, crimes against kin, and the law of superior force: 'But anyone who gladly shouts "Hail to Zeus the victor!" shall hit full on the target of understanding' (174–5).

This is the Zeus 'who has put men on the way to wisdom by establishing as valid law "By suffering they shall win understanding"' (176–8). This is, again, his grace or benevolence (χάρις, 182), but it is, again, accomplished by force (βιαίως, 182), and we have already seen at what cost. It is fine for critics to speak of this great law of learning through suffering as it is applied in an 'ethical pattern'[24] to Agamemnon, Clytemnestra, and Aegisthus. But what of Iphigeneia, and the hare and her brood, the Trojan women and their infants; what did they learn of the moral order of Zeus through the operation of this great law of 'cosmic justice'?[25]

This, then, is Zeus' justice in *Agamemnon*: compulsion, the bit, the yoke, and the bridle, applied indiscriminately to guilty and innocent alike. This is Zeus' law, and the human order mirrors the divine, as expressed in the trope of the Trojan war as a law-suit with Zeus and the Atreidae as the co-prosecutors (811–26).[26] Agamemnon begins his first speech of the play:

For the gods, when they had heard . . . the parties' claims, cast with no wavering verdict into the urn of blood their votes for the death of men, the destruction of Ilion. . . . By the smoke the conquered city is easily recognized even yet. The gusts of destruction are alive but the embers are dying with the city and sending forth rich breaths of wealth. For this the gods must be paid with ever-mindful

gratitude, since we have exacted payment for a presumptuous robbery, and for a
woman's sake the city was laid in the dust. . . .   (813–24)

Agamemnon himself is a victim of this inscrutable justice, for as the
Chorus say when Clytemnestra justifies her act by reference to Iphigeneia,
'Hard is the case to judge. The plunderer is plundered; the slayer pays the
price. And it abides, while Zeus abides upon his throne, that to him who
does it shall be done: for so it is ordained' (1561–4; and cf. 1480, where
they again affirm that all that has happened is the will of Zeus). Critics
have found comfort in the ethical 'reciprocity'[27] of the operation of this law
of retribution, for at least those who are punished are guilty.[28] But what
have Iphigeneia, Cassandra, and the Trojan women and children done?
They are neither plunderers nor slayers, but they are murdered or sold
into slavery none the less, the victims of vengeful deities. And this we are
to comprehend as the benevolence by force (χάρις βιαίως, 182) of Zeus,
who has set the law of learning through suffering for men. This may be
Zeus' law, but it is neither moral nor just if it punishes the innocent as well
as the guilty. Instead, it is a law which provides that the ultimate
foundation of the human order, as of the divine, is superior force: 'he who
proclaims Zeus the Victor' has understood its operation. What other
lesson have the hare and her brood learned?[29]

Choephoroi

The foregoing analysis should be sufficient to refute those, like Lloyd-
Jones, who flatly assert that 'In Aeschylus Zeus never punishes the
guiltless . . .'[30] In *Agamemnon* Aeschylus is careful, as has been shown, to
emphasize the agency of Zeus in the repeated destruction of the innocent
and, if one is to view him as providing a theodicy through his portrayal of
the justice of Zeus, it is clearly to the other plays of the trilogy that one
must look for evidence. This is, of course, precisely the tactic of those who
adopt a progressive interpretation of the trilogy. Kitto, for example,
argues that *Choephoroi* represents a new, intermediate world, in which
Apollo, the vengeful god of *Agamemnon*, has become a god of light and
purity. Orestes and Electra want vengeance, but they too are pure, not
bloodthirsty and out for gain. Moreover, according to Kitto, Troy and the
old Agamemnon are forgotten, and the new portrayal of Agamemnon is as
the king who symbolizes the political order that must prevail over the
chaos of retributive justice.[31] This new world, according to the progressive
view, conflicts irreconcilably with the old order represented by the
Erinyes, and this conflict, portrayed in *Choephoroi*, can only be resolved
through the intervention of Zeus in the trial that concludes *Eumenides*. In

the following discussion of *Choephoroi*, what I would, in contrast, like to emphasize is not change, but continuity.

The play opens with Orestes and his prayer that Zeus grant him vengeance and act as his ally (18–19; recalling Zeus' alliance with the Atreidae in another act of vengeance). So far this sounds all too familiar. The Chorus, also in a well-known refrain, next recall the fate of the helpless and innocent in the divine plan that destroyed Troy, bewailing their life of slavery (75–83). They affirm that fear is the basis of the present order and that success is the god (and 'the more than god') which men worship (57–60). The law of Zeus of *Agamemnon* that the plunderer must be plundered, the slayer slain, is also established as the retributive maxim of this play when the Chorus instruct Electra to pray to the gods for revenge, for murder in response to murder (117–24; and cf. 66–74). This same verb (ἀνταποκτεῖναι, to kill in return) is used by Orestes in recounting Apollo's divine command to exact vengeance. It is hard to see that the crude retributive justice of *Agamemnon* is not fully present here.

This sense of continuity is explicitly affirmed, moreover, when Electra seeks to question the humanity and piety of such a law, asking how a prayer for vengeance against kin can be pious (122; she does not know to what sort of gods she is praying). The Chorus assure her that answering evil with evil is not impious (123), but her doubts will surface again later. At first, they seem to be resolved when, after the recognition scene between her and Orestes, she prays that in Orestes' quest for vengeance, Victory and Justice (Dike) and Zeus may be with him (224–5). The Chorus, as noted above, have already proclaimed success as the god of men, and here Electra invokes the Zeus of the *Agamemnon*, assuming, in her innocence, that Justice and Victory/Power (Dike and Kratos) are compatible (they are, if Justice is taken to be the right of the stronger, but I hardly think that this is what *she* had in mind). That Aeschylus intends this invocation of Zeus, Victory, and Justice to recall *Agamemnon* emerges from Orestes' response to Electra's words: 'Zeus, Zeus! Behold us and the deed we undertake. Behold the eagle's brood bereaved; *the eagle* killed, caught in a net of death, in a cruel viper's coils' (246–50; Orestes himself becomes the snake that in Clytemnestra's dream is born to her and kills her in 540–50, 928–30, reinforcing the sense of continuity).[32]

Electra's doubts recur, as she questions Providence, wishing that Clytemnestra and Aegisthus could have died earlier by fate's hand, sparing her and Orestes the anguish of revenge (345–52). She wonders further whether Zeus will in fact lend his hand to matricide (394–6), but the Chorus respond by appealing to the Erinyes and citing the law of retribution, that blood spilt upon the earth demands blood in return (400–4). This is the law which prevails, as Electra likens herself and Orestes to wolf cubs who have inherited their savagery from their mother (421–2) and they pray to the gods to assist them in their just revenge. This the gods seem to do, as the Chorus assert that Justice, daughter of Zeus, guided Orestes' hand (946–52). And when Orestes pauses before killing his mother, asking 'Pylades, what shall I do? Is it right to kill a mother?' (899), the answer that urges him on to matricide is clear: 'Where are Apollo's words, his Pythian oracles?' Where is Kitto's new order, and the Apollo of light and purity, as opposed to the dark, vengeful Erinyes?[33] If a change from the dark world of *Agamemnon* is to be found, it is not to *Choephoroi*, but to *Eumenides* that we must turn.

Eumenides

This final play of the *Oresteia* must be the real test of the progressive theory of Zeus. Accordingly, we must look to the famous trial of Orestes before the Areopagus to demonstrate the movement from darkness to light,[34] from the moral chaos of the *Agamemnon* to 'the new and higher morality of the *polis*'.[35] Since the divinely imposed suffering of the innocent cannot, as has been shown, be *justified* within the context of the first two plays, the progressive view would argue (I am trying to make the best possible case for it) that it is *transcended* through the establishment of a new moral and social order which is truly just, and which, through the imposition of the measured reason of legal process, will presumably prevent such occurrences in the future.[36] In discussing the play, I will once again attempt to demonstrate the continuity of *Eumenides* with the rest of the trilogy in certain essential respects. There may be a new political order at the end of the trilogy, but there is little reason to hope that it is either the product or the reflection of a just moral order in the universe or the polis.

The play opens at Delphi, where Apollo, depicted as the agent of Zeus' justice, has purified, and given sanctuary to, Orestes.[37] Apollo enables Orestes to flee from the Erinyes, who are pursuing him, and the angry goddesses of retributive justice rebuke him for tricking them (140–77). They accuse him of dishonesty and the defilement of justice in saving a matricide from their fury, and they extend their accusation to Zeus and his new Olympian order, which has, by violence, replaced the old. They say that the very throne of Zeus is stained with blood and gore (recalling the Zeus the Victor passage of *Agamemnon*). They confront Apollo directly (198 ff.) and blame him because his oracle 'bade him (Orestes) kill his mother' (202). The wording of Apollo's reply is significant, for in this setting he skirts the issue of matricide, replying equivocally that his oracle only 'sent him to avenge his father' (203). This is literally true, in that the oracle did not specify who, specifically, was to be killed. At the trial, however, Apollo will argue differently, testifying that he alone is responsible, since he directly commanded Orestes to kill his mother. Moreover, the ensuing dialogue reveals that Apollo (Zeus' agent, remember) has lied to Orestes in instigating the murder, for he had threatened Orestes with the horrors of the Erinyes if he did not avenge his father (*Choephoroi*, 275 ff.). Now, he rebukes the Erinyes because they had no interest in pursuing Agamemnon's murderer (because husband and wife are not blood relations, 210–24). Well has Orestes asked, 'Ought I to trust in oracles like these?' (*Choephoroi*, 297), and he concluded that even if he could not trust in them he must none the less take the responsibility on himself and do the deed (298 ff.). What is clear, at this point before the trial, is that Orestes is guilty, and that Apollo, who will try to get him off, is hardly to be trusted. He tells the Erinyes that the dispute must be settled by trial, and the scene shifts to Athens.

At Athens the stage is set for the entrance of Athena by the clash of opposing viewpoints: Orestes claims that he is guiltless, purified by Apollo and his suffering, but the Erinyes maintain that the blood of matricide cannot be washed away and must be avenged. Only Athena, as 'clear persuasive reason' and the agent of her father's justice, can provide for the resolution of this seemingly irreconcilable conflict. Before proceeding to an examination of the trial itself, however, one detail must be noted. What are the first lines with which Aeschylus chooses to mark Athena's entrance? She says that she has come from Troy, where she had gone to claim her portion of the plunder that had been allotted by the Achaean chiefs (397–402). Here Aeschylus deliberately connects Athena to the destruction of Troy, in which he shows her to have a share; the justice of Zeus in this play is not entirely distinct from the justice of Zeus (and its horrible consequences) in the *Agamemnon*. As the trial proceeds the connection will be deepened further.

Athena opens the proceedings by hearing the pleas of the two parties. The Erinyes claim that Orestes '*chose* to be his mother's murderer' (425). Athena asks them if he acted under compulsion (426), and they reply, 'What can goad a man to kill his mother?' (427). To this question she has no response, and she turns to Orestes' plea. After reassuring her that he is not polluted, Aeschylus has him introduce himself in a significant manner: 'I am of Argos and you know my father well, Agamemnon . . . with whom *you* made the city of Troy no city' (455–8, my emphasis). If the justice of Zeus in *Agamemnon* has been laid to rest, why does Aeschylus resurrect it here and again explicitly connect to it Athena, the agent of Zeus' 'new', 'impartial' justice in this play?

As the trial proceeds, Orestes repeatedly admits that he killed his mother, but shifts the responsibility to Apollo (459–69, 588–94), who now concurs that he is to blame (579–80, and note the technical expression of

legal liability, αἰτίαν δ᾽ ἔχω . . ., with which he seeks to exculpate Orestes).
To Orestes' plea the Erinyes reply, astounded (as at 202) at the impiety of
this suggestion, 'The god of prophecy commanded matricide?' Shortly
thereafter Orestes founders upon the preposterousness of his own sophistic argument that he was not the kin of his mother, and he calls upon his
divine protector for help in pleading his cause (610–14). Apollo understands the basis upon which this lawsuit is actually to be won, and his
arguments quickly reveal the nature of the principles of justice which will
prevail.

Apollo does not involve himself in the legal niceties of necessity, choice,
and responsibility; what would be the point since, as Gagarin rightly
remarks, 'Orestes has no case from a legal point of view'?[38] Accordingly,
Apollo comes straight to the heart of the matter: he explains that since all
his oracles are ordained by Zeus they are therefore necessarily just (615–
21). Like all circular arguments, this is difficult to refute as long as one
does not question the premise, namely, that Zeus is just. The Erinyes are
again aghast at the apparent impiety of this statement: 'Zeus, you say, was
the author of this oracle?' (622). Apollo, having successfully passed the
buck upwards, replies, and now, perhaps, the truth emerges. He explains
that Zeus so ordained because the deaths of Agamemnon and Clytemnestra are not to be compared. She was a mere woman, he a king, a
commander of men and fleets, wielding his sceptre by divine command.
Here, we are back in the world of *Agamemnon*, of the Atreidae as the twin
eagles of Zeus. Is this the 'just moral order'[39] of Zeus, or justice as the right
of the stronger?

Critics have recognized the problems for the progressive theory, inherent in Aeschylus' portrayal of Apollo, and have sought to explain away his
role, and to emphasize instead what they regard as the reasoned persuasion
of Athena.[40] This however is wishful thinking in an attempt to somehow
salvage 'the moral sense of Justice for which Zeus stands'.[41] In reality,
Athena has already been deeply implicated in the dark past, and, more
importantly, her argument is precisely that of Apollo. After he has ended
his plea with a last attempt to bribe the jury (678–83), Athena submits the
case for decision. As is well known, her vote must decide the issue, and she
votes for acquittal for the profoundly moral and just reason that no mother
gave her birth (734–43), and, hence, she too regards the male as supreme
and the death of Agamemnon as the worse crime (she does not explain how
the fact that one crime is worse than the other absolves Orestes of guilt).
The Erinyes, understandably, are somewhat irritated by this pronouncement of the voice of 'clear, persuasive reason'[42] and maintain that the
result is unjust. Athena, in what is regarded as the triumph of reason and
persuasion over force, offers two main arguments why the Erinyes should

compromise and accept the deal she offers them. The first is that it is the will of Zeus (they have already heard this), and the second is a bribe: the benefits and honours of a seat of worship in Athens (851ff.). To overcome their reluctance she offers an additional incentive in the form of a threat: 'I rely on Zeus ... and I alone of the gods have access to the keys of the chamber where his thunderbolt is stored' (826–9). These arguments may not respond to the Erinyes' objection of injustice, but they are compelling none the less, and the Erinyes, yoked by the power of Zeus, reconcile themselves to their incorporation into the new order. As Thomas Rosenmeyer, perhaps the only critic who fully portrays the arbitrariness of the trial without attempting to explain it away as somehow still reconcilable with the justice of Zeus, puts it, 'Athena is an adroit politician; but her success is qualified by the thought that, unlike human persuaders, she cannot fail'.[43] As Athena herself sums up the trial (968–75), she says that 'Zeus the Advocate was victorious', but the preceding prayer of the Erinyes, that the Athenian maidens may know the joys of wedded life, recalls the unwedded fate of Iphigeneia and Cassandra and reminds us of the character of Zeus the Victor (959–60).

Thus, as Athena makes all too clear, fear (681–710) and force underlie the transformation of the social order. There is a new order, that is not to be denied, but its character is the question. Aeschylus, like Sophocles and Thucydides, recognized that no political order is, or can be, based upon the morality of absolute justice. In the *Oresteia* the human order mirrors the divine, and every character in the trilogy, from Agamemnon, Clytemnestra, Aegisthus, and Orestes, to Apollo and Athena, justifies his or her actions by reference to the justice of Zeus. And if they prevail they are right; this is the lesson of Zeus the Victor (see above p. 49) and the violent transformation of the divine sphere which brought him to power. Thus the justice of Zeus does prevail, but it is the arbitrary justice of the right of the stronger: persuasion and compulsion, backed by fear and force. Thus Orestes, the self-confessed matricide, goes free. Agamemnon is honoured as the great king who made the city of Troy no city, the Erinyes are bought off, and Iphigeneia, Cassandra, and the hare and her brood, have the consolation of having learned through suffering that their fate has been ordained by the justice of Zeus. Though Aeschylus is supposed to be a great Athenian patriot, he surely realized the implications of this theory of justice in the paeans to the armies, the wealth, and the might of Athens with which the trilogy closes. As Thucydides would show, this Athenian/Olympian conception of justice as the right of the stronger would soon serve for the enlightenment of Melos, Plataea, Scione, and many other parts of the Greek world. 'By the smoke the conquered city is easily recognized even yet' (*Ag.* 818).[44]

NOTES

1. All references to *Agamemnon* are to E. Fraenkel's edition (Oxford, 1974). All references to *Choephoroi* and *Eumenides* are to the *OCT*, ed. D. Page.

2. *Studies in Aeschylus* (Cambridge, 1983), p. 155.

3. See D. Cohen and E. Inoue, *CJ* (1978), 26–33.

4. These three plays are notoriously difficult, and it would be presumptuous of me to attempt a full discussion of a major aspect of them in such a limited space. What I will do is simply to suggest a direction for a different kind of reading of the trilogy in regard to the issue of justice.

5. *The Justice of Zeus* (Berkeley, 1971), pp. 86–7, 90.

6. Michael Gagarin, *Aeschylean Drama* (Berkeley, 1976), pp. 60–1.

7. Lloyd-Jones, op. cit., p. 88. See also A. Lebeck, *The Oresteia* (Washington, D.C., 1971), pp. 137–8.

8. R. Goheen in M. H. McCall (ed.), *Aeschylus* (Englewood Cliffs, 1972), p. 113 n. 2.

9. Ibid., p. 118.

10. Ibid., p. 119 (my emphasis). See also the similar confusion in Gagarin, op. cit., p. 61, and in J. Jones, *On Aristotle and Greek Tragedy* (London, 1962), pp. 128–37.

11. N. G. L. Hammond, in McCall, op. cit., has attempted to explain away the problem of innocent suffering. But it is simply conceptually incoherent to argue that because the punishment of the innocent is part of cosmic necessity it somehow thereby becomes compatible with a just moral order. The problem is that few scholars like to face the intractability of the problem of evil; they would rather explain it away and believe that justice triumphs, that divinity is ultimately benevolent. As Kant showed with devastating finality, however, in his *Über das Misslingen aller Philosophischen Versuche in der Theodicee* (Leipzig, 1921), v. 4 of *Immanuel Kant's Werke*, no such comfort is rationally possible. This is, I am convinced, precisely the way in which Aeschylus wished to present the problem of innocent suffering, and easy explanations should not be sought to defuse the force of his argument.

12. G. Thomson, *The Oresteia of Aeschylus* (Cambridge, 1938), p. 56.

13. A. Podlecki, *The Political Background of Aeschylean Tragedy* (Ann Arbor, 1966), pp. 77–8; Gagarin, op. cit., p. 83; Lebeck, op. cit., pp. 136–40; B. Otis, *Cosmos and Tragedy* (Chapel Hill, 1981), p. 90. Winnington-Ingram (op. cit., pp. 171–2) and H. D. F. Kitto, *Form and Meaning in Drama* (London, 1969), pp. 82–6, offer more complex interpretations, but the fundamental assumption that Aeschylus was seeking to portray and explain a just and moral divine order seems to be the same. T. Rosenmeyer, *The Art of Aeschylus* (Berkeley, 1982), pp. 343–4, 355 ff., is far more careful in pointing out the unresolved ambiguities.

14. Otis, op. cit., p. 93.

15. Hammond, op. cit., p. 101.

16. Kant, *Die Metaphysik der Sitten*, op. cit., v. 5. 455.

17. *Zu den Rechtsproblemen in Aischylos' Agamemnon* (Zürich, 1941).

18. Fraenkel's translation, as for the other quotations from *Agamemnon*.

19. Note the use of the legal πράκτωρ.

20. See Hammond, op. cit., pp. 96–7.

21. Note also the use of ἀρωγή as applied to the lawsuit/war (47) and the sacrifice of Iphigeneia (226).

22. The very seed perishes, like the unborn offspring of the hare.

23. In Athenian law the penalty for simple theft was a double fine, a very light penalty by Athenian standards (see my *Theft in Athenian Law* (München, 1983)), Ch. 3.

24. Gagarin, op. cit., Ch. 3.

25. Podlecki, op. cit., p. 71.

26. See Fraenkel, op. cit., commentary pp. 371–4.

27. Gagarin, op. cit., Ch. 3.

28. Ibid.; Lloyd-Jones, op. cit., pp. 86–7, 90.

29. See Rosenmeyer's acute discussion, op. cit., p. 355.

30. Lloyd-Jones, op. cit., p. 90 and cf. p. 91.

31. Kitto, op. cit., pp. 39–53.

32. Cf. 421–2 where Electra acknowledges that they have inherited the savage heart of a wolf from their mother.

33. See Rosenmeyer, op. cit., p. 245 on Apollo as Zeus' agent.

34. The trilogy begins and ends in darkness.

35. Podlecki, op. cit., p. 78.

36. Such is the approach of Kitto, op. cit., pp. 84–6 and Winnington-Ingram, op. cit., pp. 165–74, and it is preferable to the crude utilitarian view that the suffering of the innocent was necessary for the fulfilment of the plan of Zeus, and thus is somehow justified. Such a view hardly deserves consideration as a theodicy.

37. See Winnington-Ingram, op. cit., pp. 154 ff.

38. Gagarin, op. cit., p. 76, and note the implicit contradiction at pp. 77 and 83.

39. Winnington-Ingram, op. cit., p. 155.

40. Ibid., p. 168 ff.; Podlecki, op. cit., pp. 74 ff.; Kitto, op. cit., 82 ff.

41. Hammond, op. cit., p. 101.

42. Thomson, op. cit., p. 56.

43. See Rosenmeyer, op. cit., pp. 350 ff. Cf. Lebeck, op. cit., pp. 137–8.

44. I wish to thank Sir Moses Finley, Dr. Peter Garnsey, and Professors John Crook, David Daube, Mark Griffith, and Arthur Quinn for their helpful comments and criticisms.

CHARACTER IN SOPHOCLES

By P. E. EASTERLING

Critics are always reminding us that character-drawing in Greek tragedy
was a very different thing from what we meet in the modern theatre,
different and (it is implied) perhaps more limited or rudimentary. But this
contrast between ancient and modern is too vague to be illuminating: we
need to define exactly what kind of difference it is before we can decide
whether it is important. In drama meant for live performance it can hardly
be a difference of *technique*, since every playwright is limited to two basic
means of character-drawing, what his figures say and do and what other
people say and do to them and about them. Nor can there be much
significance in differences of *convention*. Of course convention counts for
something: a dramatist writing for three masked male actors, who must
take all the speaking roles in his play, male or female indiscriminately,
using a highly formal and declamatory style of acting in a large open-air
theatre, will create characters which can be rendered in these circumstances. But there is no reason why the particular conventions of his time
should limit his portrayal of character in any serious way: Lady Macbeth,
after all, was written to be played by a teenage boy. Surely the differences
that really demand attention are those of *attitude*.

Modern audiences, brought up on post-Romantic literature with its
overwhelming emphasis on the individual, and conditioned by modern
psychological terminology, expect a dramatist to be primarily concerned
with the unique aspect of each man's experience, with the solitary focus of
consciousness which, as John Jones puts it, is 'secret, inward, interesting'.[1] When they first read a Greek play they are naturally inclined to
interpret what the characters say and do as if the ancient dramatist shared
their preoccupation with idiosyncratic detail. But closer study soon makes
plain that this is an anachronistic prejudice, which can all too easily lead us
to irrelevant or absurd conclusions.

The prologue of *Trachiniae* will perhaps illustrate my point. The first
forty-eight lines are a careful presentation of Deianira, full of significance
for the rest of the play. She begins by recalling her past, how she was
courted by the terrifying river god Achelous who came to her in the guise
of bull, snake, and bull-headed man. Heracles appeared and challenged
him, and there was a duel; but she could not bear to watch: 'I sat apart
terrified lest my beauty should bring me pain one day' (ἐγὼ γὰρ ἥμην
ἐκπεπληγμένη φόβῳ | μή μοι τὸ κάλλος ἄλγος ἐξεύροι ποτέ, 24–5). Then she
describes Heracles' victory and their subsequent life together, or rather
apart: Heracles always away from home performing his Labours, herself

waiting in lonely anxiety. Here we have a speech of the greatest importance for our understanding of Deianira, establishing her history as the
princess who was the object of violent passion and showing how her life as
wife of Heracles has brought her nothing but fear, pain, and loneliness.
What of the detail at line 25? In a modern writer it would certainly have to
be interpreted as a glimpse of an idiosyncrasy: Deianira talking about her
own beauty would be revealing her self-absorption, even her narcissism
... But the tone in Sophocles is so clear that the 'modern' interpretation
does not even occur to us, and we take the line quite straightforwardly as
an unselfconscious statement of the situation: it is Deianira's rank and
beauty that make her a fitting battle prize for the great river god and the
great hero. The phrase is picked up in a telling way later, when Deianira
sees the captive princess Iole and pities her 'because her beauty has
destroyed her life' (ὅτι | τὸ κάλλος αὐτῆς τὸν βίον διώλεσεν, 464–5). Deianira
does not yet know that, like her, Iole has been fought for by Heracles; for
the audience there is irony and pathos in the echo, which links the two
women as victims of Love. The idea is further developed in the lyric which
follows this scene (497 ff.): the Chorus recall the duel of Achelous and
Heracles and the beautiful Deianira sitting apart (ἁ δ' εὐῶπις ἁβρὰ |
τηλαυγεῖ παρ' ὄχθῳ | ἧστο, 523–5) as an analogy to the case of Iole.

So the apparently rather incidental detail at 24–5 turns out to have an
important function, which we are in no danger of failing to recognize; but
later in the same prologue there is a passage which it is much easier to
misinterpret, Deianira's response to the Nurse's advice. Deianira has
ended her long speech with an account of her present anxieties: Heracles is
still away, no one knows where, but there is reason to fear that he is in
danger. The Nurse suggests sending one of his sons to find news: Hyllus,
as the eldest, is the obvious choice, 'if he is concerned for his father's
safety' (εἰ πατρὸς | νέμοι τιν' ὥραν τοῦ καλῶς πράσσειν δοκεῖν, 56–7). Hyllus
opportunely rushes in; Deianira at once acts on the Nurse's advice,
paraphrasing her words in a rather striking way: 'She says it is a disgrace
that you are not trying to find out where your father is, as he has been away
so long' (σὲ πατρὸς οὕτω δαρὸν ἐξενωμένου | τὸ μὴ πυθέσθαι ποῦ 'στιν αἰσχύνην
φέρειν, 65–6). The Nurse has in fact said nothing of the kind; why does
Deianira rephrase her words like this? Because Sophocles wants to give
her a suitably dignified and queenly response (this is also the effect of her
preamble at 61–2, 'Son, even the lowly can speak noble words . . .'), and it
is dramatically important to create a sense of urgency: Hyllus must be
stirred to act straight away.

Editors and critics commonly ignore these details, which give a
purposeful tone to Deianira's words, and instead make much of the fact
that she has failed to take action earlier and even now has to be prompted
by the Nurse. Does not this mean that she is irresolute, weak-willed,

helpless, timid? But it is easy to see why Sophocles leaves the decision to
look for Heracles till now: the play must open at the most critical moment;
and the sending of Hyllus must take place within the play, not before the
action starts. Hyllus himself gives the reason why nobody has taken steps
to look for Heracles before: in the past he was always successful (88–9).[2]
When the greatest of Greek heroes is away on an expedition his family
expect to wait patiently at home, not to go running after him. Why make
the *Nurse* suggest sending Hyllus, though? We may guess that Sophocles
chose to do it like this partly because the Nurse would have greater impact
in the scene where she reports Deianira's suicide if she had already been
introduced to the audience early in the play, partly because she can convey
expository information about Hyllus (at 54 ff.) more appropriately than
Deianira herself; and in any case it is more interesting for the audience if
the action starts with someone else's response to Deianira's account of her
anxieties. I suggest that, having decided to use the Nurse for these or
whatever other reasons, Sophocles gave Deianira the rather dignified
words at 65–6 precisely to avoid an impression of weakness.

Suppose, then, that we agree to be wary of our natural pre-occupation
with idiosyncrasy and to distrust the modern view of what constitutes an
'interesting' character, what is there to be said positively about character
portrayal in Greek tragedy, or more particularly, in Sophocles? For the
ancients, at any rate, Sophocles was one of the great masters of the art, as a
famous passage in the *Life* attests: 'He knows how to arrange the action
with such a sense of timing that he creates an entire character out of a mere
half-line or a single expression. This is the essential in poetry, to delineate
character or feelings' (οἶδε δὲ καιρὸν συμμετρῆσαι καὶ πράγματα, ὥστ᾽ ἐκ
μικροῦ ἡμιστιχίου ἢ λέξεως μιᾶς ὅλον ἠθοποιεῖν πρόσωπον. ἔστι δὲ τοῦτο
μέγιστον ἐν τῇ ποιητικῇ, δηλοῦν ἦθος ἢ πάθος, 21). And Sophocles himself,
according to Plutarch (*De prof. in virt.* 7), described his mature style as
'the best and most expressive of character'.

Perhaps it will be helpful to start by making a distinction between
idiosyncrasy and individuality. For it is a striking feature of Sophocles'
characters that although we are given so little circumstantial detail about
them they are all clearly distinct from one another, and it does not seem to
be enough to say that he is just a brilliant depictor of *types*. One might
argue that in the *Tyrannus*, for example, Sophocles does indeed make us
believe in Oedipus' intense experiences of fear and hope and pain, but that
is as far as it goes: Oedipus could be any noble sufferer finding out the
truth about himself. But I suspect that most of us when reading or
watching the plays are conscious of a significant difference between
Oedipus and, say, Ajax or Philoctetes, which goes beyond the basic
observation made by G. H. Gellie[3] that 'these people are different because
their stories are different'. Of course the stories are important; and in any

case all the main and many of the minor characters had a certain pre-existing mythological identity which helped to give them individuality. It is also true that Sophocles deals in dramatic formulas, particularly that of the intransigent hero or heroine whose passionate refusal to compromise is set off by the sympathetic ordinariness of an associate.[4] But he finds ways of making the formulas work differently in different plays, so that Chrysothemis, for instance, is quite distinct from Ismene, though both have the same functional role, and Tecmessa, Deianira, and Jocasta are all sharply individualized.

This impression of individuality derives, I think, from the dramatist's ability to seize on significant detail. Much must depend on the intensity with which he explores the situations he takes from the myths; if he can recreate them in dramatic form with the fullest understanding of what happens to people and what they do and feel in real life, then he will be able to present his readers with the significant details that force them to suspend disbelief and accept his characters as individuals. This demands of us as critics that we use our imagination, as actors do when they are trying to understand a part: in other words, we have to be open to psychological insight in the dramatist's observation.

Consider the notorious scene early in *Oedipus Tyrannus*, where Tiresias tells Oedipus the whole truth about himself; but Oedipus responds only to the accusation that he is Laius' murderer (apart from giving just a fleeting hint of uncertainty at 437 and 439, when he tests the seer about his parentage). How do we explain this failure to react to the rest of Tiresias' denunciation, particularly his speech at 447 ff.? 'Fortunately', says Tycho von Wilamowitz,[5] 'it cannot be explained in terms of Oedipus' psychology, because the Chorus reacts in the same way and can talk ... only about the murder of Laius. ... The poet's intention is a far cry from all psychological refinements, and the effect of this scene, which is still powerfully felt, does not depend on the presentation of so-called characters.' The dramatic power, he goes on, is in the contrast between the knowing seer and the unsuspecting Oedipus, with Oedipus forcing the full revelation of his guilt out of Tiresias. The characters understand only what is necessary for the action and do not hear the rest. Can one doubt that Sophocles knew he was being implausible?

The essential point left out of this analysis is Sophocles' insight. Tiresias accuses Oedipus of killing a man he *knows* he has never met, a king what is more, whom he could hardly expect to meet and kill without realizing it in some casual skirmish.[6] Oedipus knows, therefore, that the accusation is false; but false as it must be it comes as a shattering challenge to his sense of his identity, and there is nothing at all surprising in the fact that he is unable to take in the rest of the seer's words, which suggest even more outrageous and unthinkable guilt. No wonder, either, that the

Chorus are unable to grasp their significance. Thus, although the scene may indeed have little directly to do with character-portrayal, it does deepen our sense of the reality of Oedipus' experiences.

This impression of depth, of a solid individual consciousness behind the words, is often conveyed by the ambiguity with which Sophocles treats people or episodes. Take Antigone. A great many details of her motivation are left inexplicit, but from what we are given most of us have a full and vivid picture of that role and know how we would want it acted. But we should not all agree—and I think this is quite an important point. It seems to be true of most great roles that they offer scope for varying interpretation (I mean of course something more serious than mere producer's gimmicks, like putting on Hamlet in a space-suit). When Antigone rejects Ismene's claim to share the guilt of burying Polynices (536 ff.), how do we interpret her motives? No doubt it is too sentimental to say that she is using these cruel words as an attempt to shield Ismene; some of her retorts recall the harsh way she spoke to her sister in the prologue, when there was no third party present (one thinks particularly of 69–70: 'I won't ask you again, I won't accept your help if you change your mind'). On the other hand, it would be too trivial to narrow down Antigone's reaction to simple petulance or doctrinaire martyrhood: is it not a more whole-hearted sentiment than that? Certainly the picture is complicated by Ismene's reiterated claim that life without Antigone is not worth living (548, 566) and by her remark at 570 about the love of Antigone and Haemon. Critics will go on disagreeing; but at least Sophocles has given us something real in this ambiguous little scene.

What I am trying to suggest is that a dramatist with a delicate sense of the complexity of experience will often give his characters words and actions which are susceptible of varying shades of interpretation, for in so doing he will be imitating life. Behaviour that can be variously explained has great dramatic potential; what bores us is either motiveless, totally inconsequential behaviour which we cannot relate to our observation of life, or its opposite, the over-simple, too predictable behaviour we meet in soap-opera. We welcome an intimation by the dramatist that 'character' is not a static thing detachable from people's words and actions, but a dynamic phenomenon not ultimately to be separated from what they say and do. Sophocles' extant plays abound in examples of this kind of ambiguity: the Deception Speech in *Ajax* (646 ff.); Clytemnestra's reaction to the false news of Orestes' death in *Electra* (766 ff.); Odysseus' threat to Philoctetes that he is to be left behind on Lemnos: 'We're leaving you here, we don't need you now we have the bow. There are plenty of expert archers at Troy . . . Enjoy yourself pacing Lemnos' (1054 ff.). This can be seen as a bluff designed to force Philoctetes off the island, or as a genuine threat: readers react differently, but the important point is that

Sophocles creates a situation—as in life—in which both interpretations are plausible, and he thereby gives a certain depth to his portrait of Odysseus.

One of the finest examples of Sophocles' sustained use of ambiguity comes in this same play. When Neoptolemus is carrying out the plan to trick Philoctetes, almost everything he says can be interpreted in two ways, either as direct deceit or as an indication of his growing reluctance to take part in the trickery at all. So at 431 ff., where he is talking of the Greek heroes at Troy, we know he has been instructed by Odysseus to tell whatever slanderous stories he likes about him as part of the deception ('vilest of vile reproaches', 65), and this makes it hard to know how to take his denigration of Odysseus. He could just be leading Philoctetes on when he agrees with him that Odysseus is one of the wicked who survive, by contrast with the good, like Ajax and Antilochus, who die (426 ff.); but the audience knows that he was reluctant to use deceit in the first place, that he is after all the son of Achilles; and this scene shows him and Philoctetes forming a bond based on shared heroic attitudes. So at 431, for example, when he slightingly calls Odysseus a 'clever wrestler' ($\sigma o \phi \delta s \ \pi \alpha \lambda \alpha \iota \sigma \tau \eta s$) and adds that even clever schemes are often thwarted, or at 441, when he again insults him, we cannot help wondering whether this hostility is not seriously meant. Certainly the pitiful appearance and dignified behaviour of Philoctetes affect the audience's feelings: one is bound to wonder, as one watches the scene, how far they are affecting Neoptolemus' feelings too. How long will he be able to sustain the deception?

The stage action itself is often used to contribute to the depth of the situation the dramatist is exploring. I argue elsewhere[7] that the breaking point for Neoptolemus comes when he supports Philoctetes physically, raising him to his feet after his attack of the disease (893 ff.). Sophocles puts the visual action to equally powerful use in *Electra*, when Orestes tries to make Electra set down the urn so that he can convince her that her brother is not dead after all but alive and standing beside her (1205 ff.). In the *Coloneus* there are two great moments when the stage action greatly deepens our sense of Oedipus' consciousness. The first comes at 1130 at the end of his speech of gratitude to Theseus for rescuing Antigone and Ismene from Creon. Oedipus is overjoyed; he wants to take Theseus' hand and embrace him—but then he suddenly holds back. 'What am I saying?' His sense of his own pollution prevents him from touching Theseus or allowing Theseus to touch him; and yet one of the most insistent themes in this play has been Oedipus' passionate assertion of his innocence (e.g. 266 ff., 966 ff.). This instinctive feeling of pollution is a touch of great psychological nicety; it is worth considering the possibility that the whole sequence—Creon's kidnapping of Antigone and Ismene, and their rescue by Theseus—is designed to lead up to this dramatic moment. The second example is the famous climax at 1540 ff. when the blind Oedipus leads the

way off stage, in striking contrast with his helplessness shown all through
the play so far, and particularly in the prologue, where he has to be led step
by step.[8]

I have said little so far about language, though this is surely one of the
most important means of creating an impression of depth: if a character
talks with the power of the Deception Speech in *Ajax* or Electra's opening
anapaests (86 ff.) or her lament over the urn (1126 ff.) we are forced to
recognize the reality of the person portrayed. I am not of course suggesting that Sophocles consistently gives each character a style of his own.
There are habits of style that any character will use in certain circumstances—in an *agon*, or a narrative, or stichomythia—in response to what
A. M. Dale[9] called 'the rhetoric of the situation', which reminds us of the
dangers of over-interpretation I mentioned at the beginning. However,
one can detect some degree of characterization by style, for example in
contrasts between noble and lower characters: in *Trachiniae* the differences between Deianira, the rather grand herald Lichas, and the crude
old man who comes as messenger, show that it can be a fairly complex
matter too. But beyond this use of style to differentiate there is a more
pervasive use of language, inextricable from the poet's development of a
play's themes and structure, which deepens our awareness of the particular individual at the centre of the action. This is one reason why I think we
can go further than Gellie in his claim that 'the people are different
because their stories are different'. What I want to suggest is that
Sophocles' conception of his central character or characters influences his
choice of words and images in a quite fundamental way.

Philoctetes is a clear-cut example, though each of the plays illustrates the
same technique. Not only is Philoctetes given a series of magnificent
speeches, full of subtle detail; he is also the focus of almost everything in
the lyrics, and the play's leading images are all associated with him: the
desert island with its lonely rocks and its wild beasts, the wound, the bow,
the dead man. The theme of his loneliness is explored in terms both of
being cut off from civilization (as in the lyric at 676 ff.: he has no
neighbours, no one to heal him, no crops, no wine) and of having only the
wild creatures and the rocks of Lemnos for companions—and the birds
and beasts that are his prey will prey on him in turn if he is abandoned
without the bow. All this, which is both literal and symbolic, creates a
highly individual impression of Philoctetes, which distinguishes him
sharply from other great sufferers in Sophocles. Of course he is cast in the
same mould as Electra and Oedipus, but the poetry which defines him is
uniquely his.

Finally, can we agree with the ancient *Life* that Sophocles captures a
character in a 'half-line or single expression'? If one can allow a whole
verse there is Antigone's famous 'It is my nature to join not in hating but

in loving' (οὔτοι συνέχθειν, ἀλλὰ συμφιλεῖν ἔφυν, 523); or there is Philoctetes' brief and ordinary-seeming question at 923–4: 'Stranger, what have you done to me?' (τί μ' ὦ ξένε | δέδρακας;). This depends for its powerful impact on the cumulative effect of all Philoctetes' generous and trusting words to Neoptolemus up to this point. All through the play he has called him 'my child', 'my son' (ὦ τέκνον, ὦ παῖ), but the moment when he realizes that Neoptolemus has been deceiving him and his trust evaporates is precisely defined with ὦ ξένε.

I have perhaps been implying in these notes that in the matter of characterization the differences between Sophocles and modern drama-tists are ultimately unimportant, that there is nothing in modern drama that does not have its counterpart in his plays. In a qualitative sense I believe this to be true: his insight into human behaviour and his gift for expressing it in dramatic form remain unsurpassed; but it would be absurd to argue that he covers all the same ground as his modern successors. There are times, if we are honest, when we are made uneasy by the extremely public nature of his characters, as indeed by that of all characters in Greek tragedy. This is no doubt because the Greeks were interested in individuals as part of a community much more than in the individual's unique private experience, a difference of attitude which is sometimes hard for us to share or appreciate. For example, in Sophocles the loneliness and isolation of the suffering hero is a major tragic theme, but his heroes are quite unlike outsiders in the modern sense, men and women who can only define themselves meaningfully in terms that cut them off from society for good. There are many things that his characters simply do not talk about and that he and his contemporaries presumably never thought about. But that is a historical matter, something to be discussed in a quite different sort of paper.[10]

NOTES

1. *On Aristotle and Greek Tragedy* (London, 1962), p. 33.
2. Reading εἴα at 88 with Vauvilliers. There is no justification for bracketing these two lines as in the *OCT*.
3. *Sophocles: A Reading* (Melbourne, 1972), p. 209.
4. See in particular B. M. W. Knox, *The Heroic Temper* (Berkeley and Los Angeles, 1964), chs. 1 and 2.
5. *Die dramatische Technik des Sophokles* (Berlin, 1917, repr. 1969), p. 78.
6. Sophocles later explains Oedipus' failure to recognize Laius as a king by emphasizing that Laius was on a visit to the oracle, with only a modest retinue (750 ff.).
7. *Illinois Classical Studies* 3 (1978), 27–39.
8. Jebb has a sensitive note on this passage.
9. Euripides, *Alcestis* (London, 1954), p. xxvii.
10. See further p. 28 n. 38 for the author's latest thoughts on character in Greek tragedy.

THE BACKGROUND TO POLYNEICES'
DISINTERMENT AND REBURIAL

By JOHN WHITEHORNE

Why should Antigone in Sophocles' play want to return to Polyneices' body, after apparently successfully burying it, if we may judge from the guard's report to Creon at lines 245 ff.? Ever since it was first raised by Jebb in his note on *Antigone* 429, this question has given scholars almost as much trouble as the original burial gave Antigone herself.[1] Basically, there are two opposed views on the problem. Firstly, that both burials were performed by Antigone and their duplication is to be explained primarily in terms of the play's dramatic organization.[2] Secondly, that not only is it impossible within the framework of the play's chronology for Antigone to have performed the first burial but that, had she done so, there would have been no need for her to return to the body after sprinkling the symbolic dust. Therefore it was not Antigone, but the gods, who first buried Polyneices.[3]

Putting aside for the moment the matter of Antigone's motive in returning to the body, and concentrating instead on the fact of the second burial, the simplest question we can ask is 'Why did Antigone cover Polyneices' corpse with dust again at this time?' The simplest answer possible is 'Because Creon's guards had uncovered it.' If we then ask 'Why did they uncover it?', I think we can go some way towards understanding why Antigone undertook its reburial.

This final question, like the other two, may seem absurdly obvious. Yet, as far as I can see, it has never been squarely put (although it has been half-answered in passing several times). The significance of the disinterment, I believe, can help to reveal the significance of the second burial.

I

I begin with a brief outline of my own position on the burial question.

Firstly, it is sometimes claimed that by symbolically sprinkling the body with dust Antigone had fulfilled her obligation to Polyneices' spirit, and therefore had no need to return to the body. However, this distinction between a symbolic and a real burial is a modern illusion.[4] In the ancient world covering a corpse with dust was a duty incumbent on any passer-by who happened across a dead body.[5] This act constituted the bare minimum necessary to allow the deceased rest, and equally if not more importantly it removed a source of pollution from the living community.

It was not a symbolic act, any more than stopping by the roadside to give first aid in the event of a car accident is symbolic, while giving the victim medical aid at a hospital is somehow a more real act. In both cases, the difference is in degree, not in kind.

Scattering dust did not preclude the later performance of more elaborate rites of burial, particularly as a full Greek burial was not a single action. Nor was it an unbroken series of continuous actions. A full burial took place intermittently over a period of days, even weeks.[6] Indeed it is difficult finally to draw a firm dividing line between burial and cult, for the dead always remained a part of the *oikos*.[7] They received offerings, had the anniversaries of their deaths commemorated, and joined in festivals like the Genesia and Apaturia along with the living.[8] They shared the hopes and aspirations of their living relatives, and might rise up to help them in times of trouble, like the two gigantic soldiers who chased the Persian invaders away from Delphi (Hdt. 8.36), or, as Orestes and Electra hope he will, the spirit of Agamemnon in the *Choephoroi*.

It is Antigone's expressed intention at the play's beginning to give her brother a full burial of this type. That is why she first approaches Ismene, for help in uplifting the body (43).[9] When her sister declines to help, Antigone does not depart from her original plan any more than she has to. She cannot now physically move the body, so she will raise a tomb over it where it lies (80–1). Ismene suggests that even this may be a physical impossibility, to which Antigone retorts that she will go on as long as her strength holds out (90–1).

The contrast between these fighting words, and the bare sprinkling of earth and pitifully few rites which are all she eventually manages to carry out, is meant to arouse our pity for Antigone's girlish physical weakness contrasted to her great strength of purpose. It is not meant to imply any further off-stage modification of her plan for such changes of plan demonstrably do not take place unannounced off-stage in Greek tragedy. Her intention is always to do everything she can to give Polyneices full burial, with all which that implies, and it is this intention which is the main motivation for her return to the body. This does not of course exclude the second burial from having an important place in the mechanics of the play, for there can be no doubt about the dramatic impact which the discovery of Antigone in the very act of reburying Polyneices has at this point in the play, immediately after the first *stasimon*. Human daring, man's inventiveness, the dangers of reaching too far—all the themes of this justly famous ode find an immediate illustration in what has just happened.

Secondly it is argued by proponents of the divine burial theory that Antigone had no need to return to the body because all necessary rites of purification had already been carried out, as we are told by the guard at line 247. But the words in question—καφαγιστεύσας ἃ χρή—do not of themselves carry the implication that the rites were complete. What ἃ χρή means is 'necessary', 'appropriate', at that stage of the burial. It is not equivalent to 'complete',[10] which would be πάντα ἃ χρή. Nor does the verb itself imply completion.[11] The phrase means rather that all the rites of purification which were *appropriate* at that time had been *duly* carried out, not that a complete burial had been accomplished so that it was now unnecessary to return to the graveside.

Thirdly it is argued, particularly by McCall, that chronological difficulties within the play make it impossible for Antigone to perform the first burial. If the prologue between Antigone and Ismene takes place immediately before the chorus enters and welcomes the rising sun (100 ff.), there is simply no time for Antigone to get out of the palace, bury Polyneices, and get away before the first guard of the day watch (253–4) comes along and discovers the burial.

It does not matter for our purposes whether we believe that the first burial took place at night under the cover of darkness, or that it was performed very early in the morning while the watch was being changed.[12] The chronology in the latter case is tight, but it is not impossible, and like most dramatic chronology it cannot be pressed too hard. We have no idea how far from Thebes Polyneices' body was lying, but it cannot have been far from the city's walls. The legend was that both brothers fell fighting before one of Thebes' seven gates. Furthermore the entry song of the chorus, referring to the famous story of Capaneus, one of the seven attacking champions, who had his foot on the very ramparts before he was overwhelmed by a lightning bolt from Zeus (131–4), serves to underline how physically close the attack came to the city, as well as establishing the mood for Creon's initial 'state of emergency' speech.

Yet another argument is that, had Antigone performed the first burial, she must surely have been seen and apprehended by the guards whom Creon states (217) he has already had posted over the body. The burial was discovered and reported to his colleagues by the first guard of the day watch (253–4). Unless we want to take πρῶτος as 'chief' and not 'first' in a temporal sense—and no translation that I have seen does—it is surely legitimate to deduce from the singular that up to then there had only ever been one guard at a time watching over the corpse.[13] Moreover there would have been none of the mutual recriminations described in lines 259–63, if the night guards had been watching as a group, and not sleeping on the job.[14]

The final point adduced in favour of the first burial's divine nature, and the one which causes the chorus to ask 'Isn't this act perhaps wrought by the gods?' (278–9), is that the burial seems to be surrounded by such mysterious circumstances. There is no sign of human activity, nor is there any indication that wild animals, or dogs from Thebes itself, have disturbed the corpse (249–58). This is highly unusual, as anyone who has left out food while camping or put a garbage bin out overnight would probably agree. We are certainly justified then in seeing the hand of the gods at work here, just as we are in the dust storm of the second burial.

Yet Antigone too is involved as the human agent, who has scattered the dust and carried out the other rites. When she returns to the body at midday and sees it uncovered, she screams like a bird finding its nest robbed of young and curses those who have done the deed (423–8). The guard's comparison and Antigone's curse are alike meaningless, if Antigone has had no part in the first burial. If she had not already been to the body, she could not have known that it had ever been covered in the first place.[15] Under such circumstances it might have been appropriate for her to have screamed like a bird finding its nestling *dead* in the nest for example, and to have cursed Creon for his edict, or her fellow citizens for their failure to carry out their basic civic duty and to cover a source of pollution. She would not have cursed 'those who have perpetrated the crime' (428), using the same word which the guard used at line 262 of the original, criminally defiant act of burial.[16] What Antigone sees before her in the exposed corpse of Polyneices is the result of a sin of commission, not of omission.

Divine involvement and human action are not mutually exclusive, however.[17] We know that well from Homer and Aeschylus. In Sophocles this link between the intentions of the gods and men's actions may be presented much less overtly. Nevertheless it is a theme which is present throughout his drama, so that in this play I would certainly want to accept divine involvement in both the burials of Polyneices. The absence of footprints, the miraculous preservation of the body from scavengers, and later the choking dust storm, going on and on, described by the guard with unconscious irony as 'a divine scourge' (421), all point that way. But I do not accept the notion of a first divine burial and a second human burial,[18] or the line of thought that if the gods were involved, then Antigone must have had some knowledge of their involvement when she acted as she did.

To sum up, Antigone set out to perform as full a burial as she could, as soon as she could, after finding out that Ismene would not assist her. She covered the body where it lay, probably near one of the city's gates, and performed all due rites appropriate at that stage of the burial. Later she returned in order to continue the next stage of the interment. She found the body uncovered and cursed those who had uncovered it. She started the burial again from scratch, by sprinkling more dust before pouring her libations. Sophocles' language suggests that the gods may have had a hand in both acts of burial, but if they did Antigone herself reveals no knowledge of it.

II

A number of writers on the *Antigone* have referred to the need felt by the Greeks to give their dead proper burial.[19] However a passing reference does scant justice to the full strength of contemporary fifth-century attitudes towards a subject which is of central concern in this play, and on which everyone not excluding the chorus and even the unseen Theban population, as reported by Haemon (691–700), has an opinion to express.

Nowadays the wonder of television ensures that unburied bodies are set before us practically every day as we sit down to our evening meal. This makes it doubly hard for us to comprehend the importance of the cult of the dead in ancient Greek thought, and to appreciate fully the significance of leaving a body without burial. Or worse, deliberately mutilating a corpse or denying even an enemy his right to be buried. A few examples will serve to elucidate that significance.[20]

Homeric heroes often threaten their foes with denial of burial, or boast that they are going to leave their bodies to rot as food for vultures and dogs.[21] Indeed this horrid image of putrefying corpses and feasting scavengers is conjured up in the first few lines of the *Iliad*, in an early form of what nowadays would almost certainly be challenged as deliberately misleading advertising. For in fact no bodies at all are left on the battlefield as carrion prey.[22] Furthermore, out of all the warriors on both sides, there is only one hero in the whole epic who ever manages to put his threat into practice and deny his enemy due burial, and then only for a strictly limited period of time.

Achilles' refusal to render up Hector for burial, and his desecration of the dead hero's body, represent the depths of degradation to which Achilles, the best of the Achaeans, has been brought by his fury. Yet it is the events leading up to, and following on from, the death of Hector which illustrate most clearly the Homeric attitude towards the denial of burial.

In *Iliad* 21 the fighting has moved to the banks of the Scamander. There Achilles comes upon first Lycaon (*Il*. 21.34 ff.), and then Asteropaeus (139 ff.). He kills both of them in short order and throws their bodies into the river for the fish to feed upon. As a result the Scamander, which first stirred in anger at lines 136–8, is fully enraged by line 212. When Achilles then refuses to stop polluting its waters with corpses, the river itself rises against the hero. The passage which follows is one of the finest in Homer, but its beauty should not obscure its moral, that nature itself will refuse to have anything to do with the dead who are unburied.

The Scamander spews out the Trojan corpses onto the plain (235–7) and attempts to drown Achilles. It is only the divine intervention of Hera, assisted by her son Hephaestus, which saves him. Nevertheless it is significant that when Hephaestus does intervene at Hera's request (342 ff.)

his first action is not what Hera had instructed him to do, which was to burn the trees on the river's bank and to hurl fire at the river itself (337–8). Nor are his flames ever fanned up by the west and south winds for Hera to carry against the living Trojans, as was her original intention (334–7). The fire god's first action is to burn the dead (343–4). Only then does he turn on Scamander.

Fire and water are opposed elements, but each in its different way has rejected Achilles' impious act of denying burial to his enemies. Scamander, it is true, had appeared to be trying to drown Achilles but in reality the river had intended to entomb him properly (316–23), albeit underwater. Hephaestus was asked to help destroy the living. Instead he chose to use his flames to give the dead their due rights.

Just as there is only one hero in the *Iliad* who ever manages to deny burial to his enemy, so there is only one who ever publicly expresses his fear that his corpse will be mutilated. Hector had made the return of his body, if he was to be bested by his opponent, a condition of the single combat he proposed at *Il.* 7.76–91, and at 22.254–9 he attempts to make a similar covenant with Achilles. This repetition of his concern for the correct treatment of his corpse, like Homer's tidy and unobstrusive disposal of every other dead body in the poem except for Hector's own, has the purpose of highlighting the enormity of Achilles' final act of desecrating the body of his fallen enemy. The act is inexcusable, even though this is the body of the man who had killed Patroclus.

The effect upon the gods themselves of Achilles' outrageous conduct towards Hector's dead body is strikingly presented at the beginning of the final book of the epic. The corpse is already under the continuous protection of Aphrodite and Apollo (*Il.* 23.185–91) so that it cannot really be defiled. Nevertheless a bitter drawn-out quarrel has erupted among the immortals over the body's desecration. The majority of the Olympians are filled with compassion and want Hermes to steal the body away to protect it (*Il.* 24.23–4), but Hera, Athena, and Poseidon, the three main enemies of the Trojans, have opposed them for nine of the twelve days that Hector has been dead (107). The plan for Hermes to steal the body is dismissed by Zeus on the grounds that Thetis will see what is happening (*Il.* 24.73) and he is still bound by the promise he gave her in *Il.* 1.500 ff. to guard Achilles' honour (*Il.* 24.110–11). This would obviously be impugned, were the body to be taken away in a clandestine manner. However Zeus himself is even more deeply enraged than all the other gods (113–16), and it is his personal intervention which resolves the impasse, ensuring the body's return and eventual burial.

The significance of this for our understanding of what happens in the *Antigone* is twofold. Firstly, in refusing burial to Polyneices Creon is starting off from the lowest point that Achilles, with far greater provocation, ever reaches in the *Iliad*. Secondly, apart from the few pro-Greek Olympians who are motivated by an over-riding personal malice, all the gods in the *Iliad*, and most especially Zeus himself, detest the wrongful treatment of the dead. Just as it takes the intervention of Zeus himself finally to force Achilles to lay aside his anger in the *Iliad*, so in the *Antigone* it is Teiresias' reading of the omens (998 ff.) as a sure sign of the gods' rejection of Creon's impious and offensive conduct which finally convinces Creon to change his mind and relent.

Coming to Sophocles' own time, we find very much the same beliefs and attitudes prevailing about the proper treatment of the dead. The examples of the mass trial and condemnation of the victorious Athenian generals for their failure to pick up the dead after the battle of Arginusae, or the distress which the Athenians in Sicily felt on leaving their unburied dead behind after the decision to withdraw from Syracuse, are too well known to need further comment.[23] There are however several lesser known examples from the earlier Archidamian War which illustrate contemporary Athenian attitudes towards burial, and which are worth study.

Among the most shocking results of the plague in Athens in 430 B.C., according to Thucydides 2.52.3–4, were that the dead were left where they had died in temples, and that all the customary funeral rites were thrown into confusion. Men had to bury their dead as best they could. These are the first items to which Thucydides draws attention in his account of the breakdown of law and order under the plague's impact. The practice which he notes of disposing of more than one corpse at a time on a pyre would be elementary sanitary practice for a public health authority confronted by similar circumstances in modern times, but it is something 'abominable' in the fifth-century historian's eyes.

Concern for the dead is highlighted, too, a few years later by the story told by Plutarch, *Nicias* 6.5, that Nicias was willing to forgo victory against the Corinthians in 425 B.C. in order to make sure of the recovery of two Athenian dead whose bodies had not been accounted for. Plutarch may have embroidered the story to emphasize his subject's piety, but the detail of the two missing corpses is there in Thucydides too (Thuc. 4.44), so that there can be no doubt that it is contemporary.

The final example provides an instructive parallel from real life for the situation in the *Antigone*. This is the refusal of the Boeotians in the winter of 424/3 B.C. to render up the Athenian dead after the battle of Delion until the Athenians should withdraw from the temple which they had fortified and were using as a stronghold (Thuc. 4.97–101). Even granted that the manœuvres of both sides were dictated as much by political motives as by any moral or religious scruples, we find in this incident the same conflict of interest, between honour for the gods above and honour for the dead, which lies at the heart of the *Antigone*. The Boeotians claimed that the Athenians were still committing a sacrilegious act by remaining in possession of the temple. They were therefore justified in withholding burial from the Athenian dead, until such time as the Athenians withdrew from Delion. The Athenian reply was that their sacrilege was involuntary, since they had been forced to fortify Delion against the threat of Boeotian invasion. Their right to receive back their dead was not something to be impiously traded off, by swapping the temple for the corpses. It was a basic and time-honoured right which the Boeotians should respect by granting a truce for taking up the dead 'according to ancestral custom' (Thuc. 4.97.8).

Gomme found this whole argument 'highly sophistical (and unnecessarily drawn out)', and Thucydides' interest in it hard to understand.[24] There can be no denying the first part of his charge, but the whole incident reflects once more the great importance which the cult of the dead held in Greek thought, and the intense interest which contemporary Athenians showed in these matters. I say 'contemporary Athenians', and not 'Thucydides' or 'Sophocles' at this point for two reasons. First, because Thucydides himself was of course absent in Thrace during the Delion campaign, and therefore his account of this squabble and the inordinate amount of space (at least in our estimation) which he devotes to it may reflect the views of his informants, and therefore public concern over the affair, as much as his own feelings on the matter.[25] Then because we can see another writer, Euripides, trying to capitalize, as it were, on this interest in death and proper burial soon afterwards in his version of the story of the attack on Thebes. There can be no doubt that the Delion incident provided the inspiration, however loosely, for certain parts of the *Suppliants*,[26] in which the white knight of Athenian mythology, Theseus, after proclaiming that he is 'upholding a universal Greek law' (*Suppl.* 526–7) and that withholding burial is 'a concern of all the Greeks' (*Suppl.* 538), leads his army against Thebes to recover the bodies of all those dead heroes whom Creon had refused to bury.

A final point to be made about the burial of Polyneices is that to bury the dead was properly the duty of the immediate male next of kin.[27] As he was usually also the heir, in some inheritance cases from the next century we find speakers basing their claim to an estate on the fact that it was they who had performed the last rites while their opponents had done nothing.[28] The act of burial is therefore held to indicate, if not actually to determine, succession. So in performing an act which Creon himself, as the nearest surviving kinsman, should have undertaken, Antigone is directly challenging Creon's position as head of the household (cf. 525, 659–79), and in the final analysis (although it is not a point made in the play) his position as

king of Thebes, the legal successor to the political estate of Eteocles and
Polyneices, its co-rulers.

III

As we have seen, to deny burial, even to one's worst enemy, was regarded
as utterly abhorrent. That is why it was adopted as the ultimate penalty
which the state could inflict, depriving the criminal not only of life itself
but of family and native land for all time. In many Greek states it was for
this reason the punishment reserved for those guilty of sacrilege, treason,
or attempted tyranny.[29] At Athens it seems to have remained as the fixed
penalty for these most serious of crimes until at least as late as 406 B.C.[30]

Many scholars have seen that it is for one, or perhaps all, of these alleged
crimes that Creon denies Polyneices the right to be buried. All three
charges appear to be included in Creon's initial edict in lines 199–202, and
they recur in lines 285–9. It is in reaction to the infliction of this
punishment that Antigone performs her initial act of burial, so defying
and denying Creon's charges.

In life itself the full penalty consisted of a combination of denial of
burial and what may be termed posthumous exile, with the corpse thrown
beyond the country's frontiers there to lie unburied. For dramatic reasons
this cannot be done in the *Antigone*. Antigone has to be able to slip out of
the palace to bury Polyneices, and return undetected. Young princesses
cannot travel far unsupervised. Therefore the body must be nearby. So
Polyneices is left lying where he fell, before Thebes' seventh gate, and the
play's chronology is adjusted accordingly. The battle is represented as
having ended only a few hours before the play's action begins, and the
remnants of the invading forces are still in retreat as dawn breaks (106–7).
In the entry song of the chorus Sophocles is therefore giving us not only a
context for Creon's dictatorial manner in his 'state of emergency' speech
(162 ff.). He is also indirectly explaining why Polyneices' dead body
happens to be still lying nearby, polluting Theban soil. Clearly there has
been no time yet to think about such niceties as the *ekbole* of a traitor's
corpse.

While such a variation of the penalty, having Creon refuse burial but
leave the body lying on Theban territory, may be necessary dramatically
in the *Antigone*, it is nevertheless highly artificial. Any Greek, however
driven by personal hatred, would have thought twice about leaving the
pollution of a dead body on his own land. Yet it is more than simply a part
of the play's mechanics, or something in the legend which Sophocles has
inherited and cannot alter. By deliberately excluding any possibility that
friends of Polyneices beyond Thebes' borders might find his body and

give it burial, the dramatist concentrates the audience's attention fully on the hideous nature of the punishment, even at the risk of creating a situation which the onlookers may reject as artificial.

We can see the same device being used again when Sophocles emphasizes the familial relationship between Antigone and Polyneices, by temporarily glossing over the fact that Creon has also refused burial to the other heroes who attacked Thebes along with Polyneices. It is only when the 'family' theme is no longer the play's foremost concern, and attention has shifted to the downfall of Creon, that Sophocles unobtrusively works in this important detail at the climax of Teiresias' denunciation at lines 1081 ff. Similarly in *Ajax* 1052–90 and 1326–7, the full horror of the threats of Menelaus and Agamemnon to leave Ajax unburied, for the same alleged crime of treachery, is underlined by omitting any mention of the second part of the penalty, that the dead hero will also be exiled for all eternity from his native land.

A notable feature of the punishment of those found guilty of treason, sacrilege, or attempted tyranny was that the same penalty—denial of burial and posthumous exile—could also be applied long after the man himself was dead and buried. The remains of the individual, or sometimes the whole family, could be exhumed and cast out into exile. We see an example in the case of the Alcmaeonidae, twice banished for the sacrilege of Megacles.[31] The whole clan, living and dead, were sent into exile, with the bones of the Alcmaeonid ancestors being disinterred and banished along with the living. Although the living members of the clan were not immediately put to death and denied burial, as they might well have been for sacrilege, their banishment effectively meant a delayed sentence of posthumous exile, and both living and dead were denied the right of burial in Attic soil. The other side of the coin is seen in the case of Themistocles, whose bones were brought back from Magnesia, where he had died in exile, and secretly interred in Attic ground,[32] so denying long after his death the sentence of banishment passed upon him during his lifetime by the Athenians.

It is this notion, that it is possible to punish a dead man just as effectively as a living one,[33] which lies behind the disinterment of Polyneices and his subsequent reburial. Antigone has denied Creon's charges against her brother by her initial defiant act of burial. Yet Creon's edict still stands and it must be reimposed. This is why the guards exhume Polyneices. They are not acting from any personal whim, or seeking to gratify Creon, or trying to tempt a tiger back to its kill.[34] The careful manner (409–10) in which the disinterment is carried out points to its ritual significance. It also excludes the possibility that the action should be seen primarily as a trap for the unknown perpetrator of the first burial. Naturally there may be an expectation on the part of the guards that, if they uncover the body, then whoever had buried the dead man may return and attempt to rebury him. But the trap (if it is a trap) is never set by making any announcement that they have exhumed Polyneices, nor does the text give us any reason to suppose that Antigone's return to the body is motivated by anything she may have heard or suspected to this effect.

Creon does not repeat his edict denying burial, for he does not need to. If a prisoner escapes during the course of his sentence and is later recaptured, it is not necessary for the trial judge to reconfirm his original sentence or direct the warders before the man can be put back into his cell, nor is the warders' action in putting him back under lock and key done with a view to gratifying either the judge or themselves, although this may well be a by-product of their action. So in the *Antigone* Creon's edict has not been specifically cancelled (this is not done until lines 1108 ff.), and therefore it must still be enforced.

Faced with the evidence of the punishment's reimposition when she returns to continue the next stage of Polyneices' burial, Antigone reacts in the only way she can. Starting with its initial act she repeats the burial again from the beginning. Polyneices' spirit found release at the first sprinkling of dust, but that is now irrelevant and does not obviate the need to rebury his mortal remains. In the Sophoclean *Electra*, to take the most obvious example, when Orestes and Pylades gain entrance to the palace by pretending to be bringing Orestes' ashes back to his homeland, the expectation that his remains will be reburied in his native soil is clearly expressed.[35]

So too with the remains of Polyneices. The penalty has been reimposed by exhuming his corpse. He is again dishonoured and deprived of his rightful place in the *oikos*, and the focus of his due rites in the tomb. Antigone came prepared to continue one burial ceremony from the point at which she had left off at dawn. Now she finds she must begin the process all over again. In a sense Norwood was right when he wrote that 'this gruesome contest (of disinterment and reburial) could continue indefinitely'.[36] But the dust storm abates, Antigone is revealed, and the drama can progress.

In this way we can account for Antigone's motive in returning to the body, and for her further action in performing the so-called second burial. We can also explain the troublesome detail which originally led Jebb to raise the problem. 'The only answer (for the two burials) which I can suggest', wrote Jebb in his note to line 429, 'is that, at her first visit she had not brought the *choai*.' In fact, Antigone was now bringing the *choai* not because she had forgotten them earlier, but in order to perform a further stage of the full burial which she had always intended her brother to have. It does not affect the issue whether her actual pouring of the libation after the reburial is counted, like the sprinkling of dust itself, as a repetition of the original rites, or is seen instead as a continuation of the first burial. At least part of her action may certainly be counted as a true second burial. Yet if a member of the original Athenian audience had been asked whether Antigone had performed one burial or two, he might well have expressed puzzlement at such a question. As far as he and his fellow spectators were concerned, neither action would have included the full sequence of those rites which the ancient Greeks themselves associated with a proper burial ceremony. This fact in itself would probably have added to the effect which the *Antigone* had upon its first audience for the play touches deep-rooted beliefs about death and burial, which nowadays we can perhaps only just begin to appreciate, but which we should nevertheless not ignore.

NOTES

1. I have benefited most, even in disagreement, from the discussions of A. T. von S. Bradshaw, *CQ* 12 (1962), 200–11, J. S. Margon, *CJ* 64 (1968/9), 289–95 and 68 (1972/3), 39–49, D. A. Hester, *Mnemosyne* 24 (1971), 11–59 (esp. 19–29), G. H. Gellie, *Sophocles: A Reading* (Melbourne, 1972), pp. 38–9, and M. McCall, *YCS* 22 (1972), 103–17. Margon, Hester, and McCall all give very full reff. to earlier discussions of the double burial.

2. Gellie (supra n. 1), pp. 38–9.

3. McCall (supra n. 1); J. Ferguson, *A Companion to Greek Tragedy* (London and Austin, 1972), p. 198.

4. M. Pohlenz, *Die griechische Tragödie.² Erläuterungen* (Göttingen, 1954), p. 82.

5. E. Rohde, *Psyche*⁸ (tr. W. B. Hillis) (New York, 1966), i. 163 and 187 n. 29; cf. Aelian, *V.H.* 5.14.

6. Rohde (supra n. 5), 162–6; D. C. Kurtz and J. Boardman, *Greek Burial Customs* (London, 1971), pp. 142–61.

7. Rohde (supra n. 5), 166–82; W. K. Lacey, *The Family in Classical Greece* (London, 1968), pp. 148–9; S. C. Humphreys, *JHS* 100 (1980), 96–123.

8. F. Jacoby, *CQ* 38 (1944), 65–75; H. W. Parke, *Festivals of the Athenians* (London, 1977), pp. 53–4 and 88–92.

9. Jebb, on *Ant.* 43; *contra*, T. von Wilamowitz-Möllendorff, *Die dramatische Technik des Sophokles* (Berlin, 1917), pp. 17–18 n. 1.

10. As Wilamowitz (supra n. 9), p. 31, McCall (supra n. 1), 104–5.

11. See A. M. Dale's note on Eur. *Alc.* 1146.

12. Night: Bradshaw (supra n. 1), 203, Margon (supra n. 1), 295. Morning: Jebb, note on lines 253 ff., McCall (supra n. 1), 108–9.

13. *Pace* Bradshaw (supra n. 1), 203 n. 1 ('. . . the detail has no dramatic significance').

14. Margon (supra n. 1), 300.

15. A point well made by A. O. Hulton, *Mnemosyne* 16 (1963), 283–5.

16. The word is also used in *Ajax* 315 and 377 of Ajax's 'massacre' of the Greek leaders; by Clytemnestra of her acknowledged crime in killing Agamemnon (*Ag.* 1379); by Darius at *Pers.* 759 of what he now recognizes as Xerxes' criminal folly. The theory of McCall (supra n. 1), 115–16, that the guard is unconsciously editing his report of events to give the impression that Antigone was responsible for the first burial whereas it was in fact performed by the gods, seems to me oversubtle.

17. See especially, on this aspect of the *Ant.*, K. Reinhardt, *Sophocles* (tr. H. and D. Harvey, Oxford, 1979), pp. 72−7 = 82−6 in German ed.

18. As originally proposed by S. M. Adams, *CR* 45 (1931), 110–11, *Phoenix* 9 (1955), 47–62, and *Sophocles the Playwright* (Toronto, 1957), ch. 3, followed most recently by McCall (supra n. 1) and Ferguson (supra n. 3).

19. e.g. D. W. Lucas, *The Greek Tragic Poets* (London, 1950), pp. 22–3 and 125–6, Brian Vickers, *Towards Greek Tragedy* (London, 1973), pp. 527–8, R. P. Winnington-Ingram, *Sophocles: An Interpretation* (Cambridge, 1980), pp. 120–1.

20. This excursus is prompted by the view that, because there is evidence that denial of burial was common in heroic times (reff. in Hester (supra n. 1), 55), it was also common in Homer, and by such comments as those of Margon (supra n. 1), 48 ('We do not have sufficient knowledge, extrinsic to the play, of the fifth-century attitude toward burial to specify its nature in the *Antigone*'), or W. R. Connor, *The New Politicians of Fifth-Century Athens* (Princeton, 1971), p. 51 ('It would be perfectly all right to leave an enemy unburied but kin, Polyneices, must not be treated in this horrible way').

21. See C. P. Segal, *The Theme of the Mutilation of the Corpse in the Iliad* (*Mn.* Suppl. 17, Leiden, 1971), J. Griffin, *CQ* 26 (1976), 161–85, and *Homer on Life and Death* (Oxford, 1980), ch. 4.

22. A point noted by M. M. Willcock, *Companion to the Iliad* (Chicago, 1976), p. 4, n. on *Iliad* 1.4–5.

23. Lysias 12.36, Thuc. 7.75, and see Lacey (supra n. 7), p. 270 n. 188.

24. A. W. Gomme, *Historical Commentary on Thucydides* (Oxford, 1956), notes on Thuc. 4.98. 1 and 5.

25. See Gomme (supra n. 24) on Thuc. 4.99 and 101 2.

26. The play is dated to *c.* 423? on metrical grounds: C. Collard (ed.), *Euripides. Supplices* (Groningen, 1975), i. 8–14.

27. Lacey (supra n. 7), p. 148, Kurtz and Boardman (supra n. 6), p. 143.

28. See M. A. Hardcastle, *Prudentia* 12 (1980), 13; Humphreys (supra n. 7), 98–101.

29. Fullest reff. in G. Glotz, *La solidarité de la famille dans le droit criminel en Grèce* (Paris, 1904), pp. 460–1 and nn. Surprisingly C. M. Bowra, *Sophoclean Tragedy* (Oxford, 1944), p. 70 only cites its recommendation by Plato, *Laws* 9.873C, 10.909C, 12.906B.

30. When Euryptolemus proposed that the generals of Arginusae be tried individually under the law relating to sacrilege and treason: Xen. *Hell.* 1.7.22, and see A. R. W. Harrison, *Law of Athens* (Oxford, 1971), ii. 59 and 82. I am not convinced by the arguments of G. Cerri, in G. Gnoli and J.-P. Vernant (edd.), *Les morts dans les sociétés anciennes* (Paris and Cambridge, 1982), pp. 121–31, that the decree of Cannonus, the alternative suggestion of Euryptolemus for dealing with the generals in accordance with the law (*Hell.* 1.7.20, preserving the MSS reading), also involved a denial of burial.

31. Thuc. 1.126.11–22, and Gomme's note ad loc.

32. Thuc. 1.138.6, and Gomme's note ad loc.

33. On the aspect of Polyneices' 'honour' as Antigone's motivation see B. M. W. Knox, *The Heroic Temper* (Berkeley and Los Angeles, 1966), pp. 91–3. Cf. Aegisthus' abuse of Agamemnon's tomb in Eur. *El.* 326–31.

34. As suggested by Hester (supra n. 1), 28, and Bradshaw (supra n. 1), 207.

35. Sophocles *El.* 760, 1098 ff. On the Athenian practice of bringing home for burial the ashes of those killed in battle abroad see F. Jacoby, *JHS* 64 (1944), 37–66. On the date of its introduction see Gomme (supra n. 24) on Thuc. 2.34–6.

36. *Greek Tragedy* (London, 1920), p. 140.

ADDENDUM: THE DOUBLE BURIAL QUESTION SINCE 1983

The problem of the so-called double burial of Polyneices in Sophocles' *Antigone* is one which continues to interest writers on Greek tragedy. I include here only those studies known to me which deal specifically with the question.

The year in which this paper first appeared (1983) was a particularly fruitful one for different approaches to the problem. G. F. Held argued that Sophocles' motive in including the double burial was to distinguish Antigone's two primary motives for burying her brother. The first burial and Antigone's first speech (450–70) underline the motive of religious duty. The second burial and her second speech as it is reported by the guard (891–928, with their imagery of the mother bird screeching for the loss of its young) serve to emphasize the motive of Antigone's personal love for her brother. It also paves the way for the dramatist's presentation of the more feminine side of her character in the second half of the play.[1]

V. J. Rosivach surveyed both earlier literary and contemporary fifth-century instances of the ancient Greeks leaving the dead unburied and concluded that in the *Antigone* Sophocles has conflated two distinct types of non-burial—deliberate exposure, which remained acceptable as a civil punishment for treason, and refusal of burial as an 'epic' act of vengeance which was no longer acceptable in the more enlightened fifth century. By conflating these two types Sophocles is able to show in the course of the play's denouement that unacceptable acts done for personal 'honour' remain unacceptable even when it is claimed, as by Creon, that they are motivated by civic concerns.[2]

Finally that year Robert Parker, in his book on ritual pollution in the ancient Greek world,[3] drew attention to the unique nature of the picture which Sophocles draws in *Antigone* 999–1015 of the terrible consequences which arise for Thebes when Creon denies burial to Polyneices. The threat of pollution is never mentioned, for example, in the extended debates about burial in the *Ajax* or in Euripides' *Supplices*, although characters in both plays freely appeal to divine law. Parker's conclusion is that non-burial did not always cause pollution and that even in the fifth century the obligation to grant burial was never absolute. On the other hand prolonged public exposure as visited by Creon on the corpse of Polyneices was not practised by any Greek state and was always regarded as outrageous. Polyneices, who is an enemy who has fallen in defeat and not a traitor, deserves to be treated justly.

In the following year Ruth Scodel discussed two groups of passages in epic which, she argued, may help us to understand what is happening in the *Antigone*.[4] Epic type-scenes of god-assisted appearances and disappearances (e.g. *Il.* 3.380 ff., 24.333 ff.) help to explain the mysterious and numinous circumstances surrounding the two burials of Polyneices. Even if the assistance of the gods is not made explicit by the dramatist as it is by the epic poet, the need for dramatic motivation is reduced by our recognition that the action has been stage-managed by the gods. Furthermore epic doublets, in which an action is repeated (e.g. the three repetitions in *Od.* 5.298–382), are similar to Sophocles' device of the double burial in that they also often provide a new beginning or offer an alternative outcome for the narrative action. Scodel has also given a brief account of the question of the double burial in her book on Sophocles.[5]

Although they do not address the double burial question as such, two other works deserve mention here. Robert Garland's study of ancient Greek burial customs now makes even more clear the extended nature of Athenian funerary rites and the great importance which was placed upon the proper observance of tomb-cult.[6] R. G. Lewis has argued (not entirely convincing, I feel) that the *Antigone* was first produced in 438 B.C. rather than the late 440s B.C. His suggestion is that the theme of Eteocles' honourable burial versus the dishonour shown to the corpse of Polyneices was inspired by the barbaric treatment (including denial of burial) allegedly meted out by Pericles to Samian prisoners of war after the fall of Samos in spring 439 B.C. as compared to the grandiloquence of his eulogy for the Athenian dead of that war.[7]

Finally, although the theory of M. McCall[8] that the first burial was the work of the gods has generally found little support,[9] is is only fair to mention that there are still those who take it as a point of departure for other arguments about the play.[10]

NOTES

1. 'Antigone's dual motivation for the double burial', *Hermes* 111 (1983), 190–201.
2. 'On Creon, *Antigone* and not burying the dead', *RhMus* 126 (1983), 193–211.
3. *Miasma: Pollution and Purification in Early Greek Religion* (Oxford, 1983), pp. 43–8.
4. 'Epic doublets and Polynices' two burials', *TAPhA* 114 (1984), 49–58.
5. *Sophocles* (Twayne's World Authors Series 731; Boston, 1984), pp. 55–7.
6. *The Greek Way of Death* (London and Ithaca, 1985), chs. 4 and 7.
7. 'An alternative date for Sophocles' *Antigone*', *GRBS* 29 (1988), 35–50.
8. Op. cit. (p. 77 n. 1).
9. See e.g. D. A. Hester, *Ramus* 15 (1986), 77 ('This is, in dramatic terms, plain nonsense').
10. e.g. J. Shelton, *Ramus* 13 (1984), 102–23, esp. 113; R. W. Minadeo, *Arethusa* 18 (1985), 133–54, esp. 143–5.

A MISUNDERSTOOD SCENE IN SOPHOKLES,
OIDIPOUS (*O.T.* 300–462)

By DAVID BAIN

Just as (*pace* Blaydes and Dawe) ὕβρις φυτεύει τύραννον, Sophokles' *Oidi-pous* continues to beget misunderstanding. One can guarantee that any conversation about the play will soon produce any one of at least four large-scale misconceptions regarding it. One of these is discussed here, not so much for the purpose of dispelling it, as in the hope that such discussion will lead to some general conclusions about the dramatic technique of the Greek tragedians.[1]

First, however, since *four* misconceptions have been mentioned, brief notice should perhaps be afforded to the other three. Little time need be spent on discussion of whether the 'Oedipus-complex' is relevant to the interpretation of Sophokles' play. It is sufficient to note with J.-P. Vernant[2] that Oidipous never had a son–mother relationship with Iokaste and then to quote 794 ff. Far from desiring to sleep with his mother and remove the rival for her affections from the scene, Oidipous, on being told by the Delphic oracle that he would sleep with his mother and kill his father, immediately strove to put as great a distance as possible between himself and Merope, the lady he believed to be his mother. 'I fled, henceforth to guess at the location of Korinth by the stars' expresses, perhaps colloquially, his firm resolve never again to visit his parents' home.[3] Later in the play (973 ff.) we find him expressing the same fear and the same determination never to visit Korinth while his mother lives. It is in fact this expression of his determination that leads to the revelation that he is a foundling and to the terrible consequences of this discovery.[4]

There are two misconceptions about the play which being more relevant and more tenacious than the Freudian one would certainly require a more extended rebuttal were it not that they have already been answered in an accessible and most elegant form. Professor E. R. Dodds's 'On Misunderstanding the *Oedipus Rex*', a work rightly regarded as a classic,[5] deals a devastating blow to two[6] views of the play which have had a seemingly relentless grip on the minds of readers of Greek tragedy. One is the notion that Oidipous is punished for actions that take place during the course of the play, his irascible behaviour towards Teiresias and Kreon, behaviour that corresponds to his hot-tempered reaction years ago when he was confronted by Laios. The terrible fate that befalls him is alleged to be the consequence of a flaw in his character and here appeal is made to Aristotle and to the concept μεγάλη ἁμαρτία, which is taken to mean 'tragic flaw'.

The other is the view which sees the play as a tragedy of destiny with fate inexorably tracking down its victim, Oidipous, who has neither freedom of action nor way of escape. The first view produces a play that is morally trivial, the second a play that is morally repellent. Dodds demonstrates with great clarity that neither suits the play which Sophokles actually wrote.

Oidipous the guilty and Oidipous the puppet have been discredited along with the Oidipous who should have consulted a psycho-therapist. There remains, however, another pseudo-Oidipous who will be examined here with reference to a particular scene. This is the Oidipous who is slow on the uptake, 'Oidipous the stupid'.

Since antiquity it has been asserted that Oidipous' conduct was in some way or other foolish. Many of these assertions were tendentious or else humorous like the unusual angle on the topic which the cynic Diogenes is given by Dio Chrysostomos in his tenth oration (Dio Chrys. 10.29 f.) which was scarcely meant as a serious criticism of Sophokles' play. Criticism of the improbability of Oidipous' behaviour in the play multiplied in modern times, its most eloquent exponent being Voltaire. The contrast has often been made between the clever man who outwitted the Sphinx and the man who, on starting a murder inquiry about the death of Laios, does not think of summoning the only surviving witness to that murder. Oidipous learns of this man in line 118, but does nothing about him until half-way through the play (754 ff.) when he has at last realized that he himself might be the murderer.

This is a problem which will be returned to later, but first one must examine the scene which above all has given rise to the view of Oidipous mentioned above, a scene in which critics have found the conduct of Oidipous incredible and unrealistic and from which far-reaching conclusions have been drawn. This is of course the confrontation between Oidipous and the seer Teiresias (300–462).

After Oidipous has learned that the plague at Thebes has been brought about by the polluting presence of Laios' murderer in the town, he undertakes to track down the murderer. He does not, as has been noted, immediately send for the one surviving witness. Instead he begins by cursing the murderer and anyone who may have complicity in the act or may be hiding him. The chorus then advises him to send for the seer who has clairvoyance like Apollo: he will certainly reveal the murderer. Oidipous replies that he has already sent for Teiresias at Kreon's suggestion—this incidentally gives him some basis for the suggestion he later makes about a conspiracy—and that he is surprised that he has not yet arrived (284–9). After a little delay the chorus announces the arrival of the seer. Attendants bring in 'the divinely inspired man in whom alone of mortals the truth is implanted'. There follows an extremely respectful address of him by Oidipous and a request that he reveal who are the killers of Laios. Oidipous here uses the language of the supplicant (303, 312 ff.), thus reversing the situation of the play's opening where the priest supplicated him.

From now on the emotional content of the scene builds up until both characters explode with anger. Oidipous is calm at the outset, but is soon reduced to blind rage. Teiresias is emotionally upset right from his entrance. He starts by wishing that he had not come and demands to be taken home, persistently hinting that he has knowledge which he does not wish to divulge, knowledge which will harm Oidipous (320 f., 324, 329, 332). This refusal to co-operate in the inquiry provokes Oidipous and leads him to suggest that Teiresias is a party to the murder (346 f.). This in turn angers Teiresias and he begins to make accusations in reply. Oidipous is liable to the penalties of the curse he has just invoked: *he* is the polluter of the land (350 ff.). More specifically, in reply to questioning, he states: 'I say that you are the murderer whom you seek' (362). In what has now become a slanging-match he throws out accusations in response to charges from Oidipous: 'I say that you have escaped notice, associating in the most disgusting way with those most dear to you and that you do not see in what a state of evil you are' (366 f.). Provoked further by Oidipous' τυφλὸς τά τ' ὦτα τόν τε νοῦν τά τ' ὄμματ' εἶ (371), Teiresias turns to prediction: 'You are nothing but a poor wretch and the abuse you direct at me will *soon* be directed by everyone at you' (372 f.), going on a little later (376 ff. as emended by Brunck) to say, 'it is Apollo's concern to destroy you'. After these short, sharp exchanges, single lines answering single lines or a pair of lines answering a single line, the two contestants deliver extended speeches.

Oidipous (380–403) accuses Teiresias of being in league with Kreon in a conspiracy to oust him from his tyranny. He abuses him, saying that Kreon has hired for this purpose 'this false prophet, manufacturer of tricks, this charlatan', and ends by threatening him, 'you and Kreon will not get away with this'.

In reply, Teiresias foretells a terrible downfall for Oidipous: 'You have sight and yet you are blind to the evil in which you live, not knowing where you live or with whom you live. Surely you realize whose child you are? You have become without realizing it the foe of your dear ones, both below and upon the earth. The two-forked curse of mother and father, terrible in its approach, will drive you from this land ... You have no perception of other disasters which will make you equal both to your self and to your children.'

The argument is then resumed in shorter exchanges and, charged with folly, Teiresias says that he did not seem foolish to Oidipous' parents (436). Oidipous asks about his parents and receives as answer a riddle, 'this day will give you birth and will destroy you'. At line 444 Teiresias announces his intention of leaving, but before departing (or as he departs) delivers another extended speech. This time what he says is no longer mysterious or vague. The man whom Oidipous seeks is in Thebes. He is reputedly an incomer, in fact a Theban. He will be blind though now he sees, a beggar though now a wealthy man. He will go into exile, feeling his way with a stick. 'This man will be revealed as father and brother at the same time, son and husband of the woman who gave him life and at once fellow-sower to and murderer of his father.'

There is no reply from Oidipous. The old man is led away and the chorus begins to sing on a stage where they are by now alone.

If one reads this scene bearing in mind all the while the rest of the Oidipous-legend, it is not difficult to find the behaviour of Oidipous during the scene and in the scene that follows (532 ff.) past comprehension. Oidipous after all, we know, has been told that he is to kill his father and marry his mother. Soon after being told this, when on his way to Thebes, he killed an old man. These events he presumably remembers, yet here, in the face of charges that he is the murderer of Laios, that he is a party to some disgusting form of intercourse and that his father's *and* his mother's curse will drive him from the land, he sees no connection between this and his past life, scarcely bothering to cross-examine the seer at all. Mention of Oidipous' parents in line 436 provokes a flicker of interest, but for the rest it is all abuse of the seer and counter-accusation. The most explicit of Teiresias' predictions, the ones contained in his exit-speech—admittedly they are expressed about him in the third person—evoke no response at all. In the following scene Oidipous proceeds on the assumption that Teiresias has been suborned by Kreon and spends the first part in angry debate with Kreon. Later when Iokaste has calmed both of the combatants and Kreon has left the stage, the possiblity of Oidipous having killed Laios is indeed raised, but it is raised without reference to Teiresias; it is Iokaste's mention of the place where three ways meet that calls it to Oidipous' mind. There is no mention of Teiresias' allusions to Oidipous' incest either, not even when Oidipous tells Iokaste of the predictions of the Delphic oracle (790 ff.).

Critics who take all this into consideration and are loath to convict Oidipous of a lack of intelligence have recourse to two escape routes. Neither bears close inspection. The first consists of supposing that Oidipous does not hear—or hear properly—what Teiresias says to him. Asides are indeed possible, if not particularly frequent, on the Greek tragic stage, but there is no question of the Oidipous–Teiresias confrontation containing any.[7] For one thing Teiresias' utterances are formally addressed to Oidipous: 'I say to you . . .' (350 ff., 362, 366 ff.). For another, Oidipous is depicted as reacting to them. To lines 350 ff. which contain the charge that he is the polluter of the land, he replies with an angry threat. Similarly he answers the explicit statement that he is the killer (362). To the oblique charge of incest made in lines 366 f., he responds by asking whether Teiresias thinks he can say such things with impunity. He has a similarly irate response to the more extended charges and predictions of lines 413 ff., exclaiming 'who could bear to listen to such words from this man?' (429).[8]

Oidipous of course does *not* reply to Teiresias' clearest statements, those contained in his exit-speech (447–62). Again, however, there can be no question of an aside-convention being employed. Teiresias is haranguing Oidipous and clearly means what he says to be heard by him: 'I tell you this' he begins in line 449. The possibility has been raised that, while the lines are indeed intended for Oidipous' ears, he does not hear them because he rushes off the stage in high dudgeon before Teiresias begins to speak.[9] The subsequent action does in fact show that Oidipous must leave the stage at some point before the first stasimon (the chorus announces his re-entry at line 531), but a moment's consideration shows how unacceptable it is to have him exit around line 447. What point would there be in having Teiresias address fifteen lines into thin air in the belief that he was addressing Oidipous? The effect of having a blind man harangue an absent interlocutor would be grotesque, suitable for the black comedy of Bunuel or Joe Orton, not for the tragedy of Sophokles. The scene ends surely with a victory for the blind seer who is given the last word; Oidipous is dismissed from the stage with Teiresias' final command: 'Go inside and think this over, and, if you find me a liar, then say I have no art of divination.'[10]

An alternative to supposing that Oidipous was afflicted with temporary deafness is to suppose that Oidipous hears and fully comprehends everything that Teiresias says and that his lack of reaction is explicable because he is concealing his guilt, being aware throughout the play that he has killed his father and is married to his mother (and presumably as content with this state of affairs as Diogenes would have him be). This interpretation involves composing a play somewhat different from the one Sophokles actually wrote. Apparently there are those who enjoy such rewriting.[11]

While the belief that Oidipous is stupid and the events of the play are totally incredible is in my view a misinterpretation, it is at least supportable from the text and therefore being somewhat more tenable than the two theories just discussed requires a more extended refutation. It is the kind of mistake which would never be made by a spectator of the play, but which a reader or student of poetic drama always finds hard to avoid. It is not, incidentally, a mistake that the first great critic of tragedy, Aristotle, shows any signs of having made. The irrational element which he detected in regard to the play, the ἄλογον, lay not in the play itself, but in the events reported as having happened before the play and thus ἔξω τῆς τραγῳδίας.[12]

The 'Oidipous is stupid' heresy springs from the reader's concern with the mind of Oidipous. If for the moment we forget Oidipous' mind and concentrate on the mind of the spectator attending the first performance of Sophokles' play, the spectator without benefit of Jebb or Kamerbeek, the spectator who does not have time to stop and turn pages back and forth, the Teiresias scene will be found to be less remarkable.

That the play proceeds on a tack different from that apparently demanded by logic and probability, that Teiresias' dark hints which become ever clearer are not taken up immediately or even subsequently by Oidipous and taken up only in part by the chorus is far more troublesome to the reader than to the spectator. The reader, and particularly the reader who is coming to the play a *second* time, is disturbed by the character's failure to react on several crucial occasions because through reading he is aware of the outcome of the play and approaches each scene, not to say each line, with all the relevant facts about Oidipous in his head. The spectator, on the other hand, does not have time for leisurely reflection on Oidipous' state of mind. He can take note only of what the dramatist emphasizes and draws to his attention.[13] In this instance it is possible to argue that Sophokles has deliberately arranged things so that the spectator does *not* experience the kind of reaction we have just been attributing to the reader. This can be seen most easily if one compares the sequence of events in the myth with the order in which they are alluded to in the play. The following tabulation is designed to show most clearly the divergence between the two sequences, the left-hand column showing the antecedents of the drama reconstructed from the play and put in the 'correct' order, the right-hand column the points at which each event is first mentioned in the play. The numbers in brackets in the right-hand column indicate the sequence of these mentions.

Event in myth	Allusion in play
1. Apollo's prophecy that Laios will be killed by his son.	(4) 711 ff.
2. Exposure of Laios' child.	(5) 717 ff.
3. Child rescued by herdsmen and	(11) 1039 ff. (confirmed at 1171 ff.)
4. received by Polybos, king of Korinth.	(10) 1022 ff.
5. Oidipus brought up in Korinth as son of Polybos and Merope.	(7) 774 ff.
6. He hears the suggestion that he is illegitimate and	(8) 780

7. consults the Delphic oracle which tells
   him that he will kill his father and marry
   his mother.   (9) 787 ff.
8. He meets an old man at a place where
   three roads meet and in self-defence kills
   him.   (6) 716, 723 ff.
9. Death of Laios is reported at Thebes by a
   single surviving attendant who says he was
   killed by a band of robbers.   (3) 106 ff., 118
10. Oidipous arrives at Thebes and deals with
    the Sphinx.   (1) 35 f.
11. He becomes king and marries Iokaste.   (2) 70

Before the Teiresias-scene only one of the relevant facts about Oidipous' early career has been presented and that only in an oblique way. From lines 103 f. the audience is in a position to infer that Oidipous is a latecomer to Thebes. The incident at the place where three roads meet and the reply of the Delphic oracle are only presented as part of Oidipous' consciousness much later in the play (723 ff., 774 ff.). If Sophokles had alluded to them *before* Oidipous' encounter with Teiresias, doubtless the audience would then have found Oidipous' failure to react to what Teiresias was saying extremely strange. As it is, when they are eventually presented with this information, the scene is long gone by and they are not given time to think back to it.

Even so Teiresias' exit-speech might be felt (and often has been felt) to be going too far, as giving the game away. Sophokles, however, has arranged it so that the audience is not allowed time to ponder on Oidipous' failure to make the necessary connections and to act accordingly. Oidipous disappears from sight immediately after the speech and the chorus begins to sing, not about what they and the audience have just seen, but about the curse Oidipous pronounced on the murderer over 200 lines before. This immediately distracts and draws the attention away from Teiresias' last utterance, his instruction to Oidipous to go in and ponder over what has just been said (460 f.). Later, in the second strophic pair, the chorus does revert to Teiresias, but only in the most general terms. They cannot believe in a dispute between Oidipous and the family of Laios. Significantly they express no doubt about Oidipous' parentage, referring to him as the son of Polybus (490) and quite ignoring Teiresias' hints about Oidipous' incest.

At this point it might be objected that, however much the poet rearranged the sequence of events of the story by revealing them out of order in the play and however much he manipulated his actors, the audience would still react as a reader is liable to do because the story of

Oidipous was simply too famous. Here one hesitates to use the famous passage of the *Poetics* where Aristotle states that few people in the Athenian audiences knew the stories of the tragedies they went to see (*Poet.* 1451^{b}25). The Oidipous-legend does seem to have been extremely well known in antiquity. One may infer this from the way it is alluded to in Aristophanes' *Frogs*. In a passage where Aischylos is criticizing Euripides' prologues, Euripides recites the opening of his *Antigone*: 'Oidipous was at first a lucky man . . . but became in turn the most wretched of mortals.'[14] 'Lucky at first?' exclaims Aischylos. 'How could he have been lucky when even before he was born, Apollo said he would kill his father? Even before he was born. How could this man have been "lucky at first"? "Became the most wretched of mortals"? He never stopped. In the first place when he was born they exposed him in the middle of winter in a broken jar . . . then he made his way to Polybos somehow or other with his swollen feet. Then though a young man he married an old hag and his mother to boot. Then he blinded himself' (*Frogs* 1180–95). This account, told from a standpoint quite different from that of a tragedian, but corresponding essentially with the story as presented by Sophokles is narrated in such a way as to suggest that Oidipous' life story was common currency by 405 B.C. Essentially it reflects the ordinary man's view,[15] reducing the story to an everyday level, not worrying about the moral consequences of Oidipous' acts, but concentrating instead on his physical discomforts, not the least of which was the misfortune of having to marry a woman who not only was his mother, but was actually old enough to be his mother (the age difference between Oidipous and Iokaste is a topic which Sophokles scrupulously avoids). The form of the narrative supports this suggestion: it is surely meant to resemble that of a person with no great cultural pretensions even if the speaker happens to be the great Aischylos. This is a good example of the 'καί-style'.[16] Aristophanes is putting into the mouth of Aischylos a comic version of the ordinary man's reactions to Oidipous. It is perhaps significant that this is the only one of Euripides' prologues handled (or manhandled) in this scene where discussion centres on the legend involved.

In the prologue of a play by the fourth-century comic poet Antiphanes we meet further testimony to the notoriety of the Oidipous story. The speaker of this prologue contrasts the tasks that confront the writer of tragedy and the writer of comedy. The tragic poet has it easy. All the stories of tragedy are already known to the audience, before the play begins. 'I've just got to mention Oidipous and they know all the rest. Laios was his father, Iokaste his mother, who his daughters were and who were his sons, what will happen to him, what he has done' (fr. 191.5–8 Kock).

Both of these comic passages come from plays written after Sophokles' classic treatment of the story, and in the second passage the speaker is pleading a special case and is therefore liable to be unscrupulous in his argumentation. Even so, it would be perverse not to believe that practically everyone in the first audience of Sophokles' *Oidipous* was at least aware before the play started that Oidipous was the man who killed his father and married his mother. Sophokles surely counted on this. Otherwise how are we to explain the sinister ambiguities put into the character's mouth from early in the play (note particularly lines 260 ff.)? To admit this, however, is not to say that the audience was aware of *every* detail in the story. Indeed one is scarcely justified in talking of 'the' story. There are a great many variations and contradictory features in any given Greek myth and this is particularly true of the Oidipous legend. Because Sophokles' play became the classic treatment of the story it is generally assumed that it represents *the* story, the one an Athenian would have expected to see every time he went to the theatre or the account he would necessarily give if asked what he knew about Oidipous. But we know of many details or variants known to have existed before Sophokles which Sophokles has chosen to omit (or of which he may not have been aware). Some of these apply particularly to the scene in question. The rescue of Oidipous from the mountainside of Kithairon for instance is not an inevitable ingredient of the story. In some versions the baby is put to sea in an ark. Nor were Merope and Korinth canonical. Polybos is certainly the figure who receives Oidipous, but sometimes he is king of Sikyon and his wife is not always Merope. There is also considerable variation in the tradition as regards the place where Laios and Oidipous met, where each was going at the time, and what was the aftermath of the killing (there are versions where Oidipous drives Laios' horses back to Korinth and gives them to Polybos, which implies a sequence quite different from Sophokles', no oracular pronouncement preceding the encounter). Nor is Oidipous' self-blinding invariable. In Euripides' play he is blinded by the servants of Laios (at what stage in the story we cannot be sure).[17]

We have no right to assume that there was before Sophokles an 'authorized version' of the story which each spectator would transport mentally into the theatre with him and which would condition his reaction to the behaviour of the characters in Sophokles' play. When we recall the multiplicity of the legend and also bear in mind that the Greek dramatic poets enjoyed considerable freedom in the way they shaped any given story, even to the extent of innovation, we will be less inclined to believe that an audience would have been puzzled by Oidipous' behaviour towards Teiresias in the way that critics have been. We cannot be sure that an audience will at that stage in the play take it for granted that Sophokles is using the version he is using or that they will be aware of all the details Sophokles is later to reveal about Oidipous' early life.

Even if what has been said about the likelihood of the audience being only partially aware of the story is not accepted, there is another factor which must be taken into consideration with regard to our scene. One should never underestimate the manipulative power of dramatists and the capacity of audiences for being willing victims.[18] A great dramatist can get away with a great deal. On paper the motivation of characters may appear questionable; in the theatre the audience does not pause to question it, trapped by some other aspect of the dramatist's art. When this simple truth is propounded with reference to Greek tragedy it often meets with dogged resistance and the angry accusation that great authors are being accused of cheating when one talks of them manipulating the audience. In fact such manipulation is characteristic not only of the great ancient tragedians but also of Shakespeare. What ancient tragedy and the trage-dies of Shakespeare have in common, amongst other things, is that they were written above all to be seen rather than read. For this it is instructive to refer to a passage written by the eminent Shakespearian scholar, John Dover Wilson: 'The dramatist had his own perspective, his own restric-tions, and his own liberty. Like the musician, while depending on the memory of his audience, he was free to avail himself of its limitations. So long as he could preserve the illusion of consistency, he was not obliged to adhere to it in any historical or logical sense.' This was written of the Elizabethan stage, but it would also make an admirable description of the kind of theatrical milieu in which Sophokles worked. Dover Wilson's remarks about plays being actions and not books are particularly apposite:

I use the past tense, because the dramatic art of which I write belongs to the past and is now dead. Its decease was not due to any improvements in dramatic skill or deepening of dramatic appreciation ... It was killed, like so many of the old art-forms, by mechanical invention. The printing-press brought about the multi-plication and cheapening of books, and, as the reading habit became general, dramatists took more and more to writing with publication in mind, until today plays with any pretension to literary merit appeal quite as much to the reader as to the spectator. This is one, perhaps even the chief cause of the decline of the poetic drama; for, directly a dramatist begins to keep one eye upon a reading public, he is obliged, or at least feels himself obliged, to conform to the rigid consistency which the novelist must observe nor dare he leave points in doubt or intentions obscure.[19]

This again hits the nail on the head. I am not so sure that the present-day theatre or even the theatre of forty years ago, the time at which Dover Wilson was writing, are or were quite so devoted to realism and literary pretensions as he makes out (indeed much present-day 'theatre' seems to be moving away from literature at an alarming rate). However that may be, most interpreters of drama find themselves the slaves of the kind of drama they saw in their youth. In the case of 'modern' interpreters of Sophokles that drama was the literary drama of the late nineteenth and early twentieth centuries, the type Dover Wilson was alluding to, drama meant to be read as well as seen. Brought up on such a diet it was natural that they should be puzzled by apparent loose ends in Sophoklean drama and occasions where his intentions seemed obscure. Instead of accepting such phenomena as a concomitant of the kind of drama Sophokles was writing and in no way detracting from his capacity as a dramatist, such critics attempted to save his reputation and get rid of the difficulties by resorting to elaborate 'psychologizing' explanations for the behaviour and motivation of characters. Such explanations derived from a treatment of plays as documents, records of facts rather than actions meant to be performed. Those of us brought up on a more varied theatrical diet should be less prone to fall into such a trap.

Sophokles was not a policeman reporting the Oidipous-case and leaving the file to posterity: he was a writer of poetic drama who hoped to shock and move an audience of his fellow-citizens on a particular occasion in the Theatre of Dionysos. For this purpose he selected material from an unwieldy and far from coherent body of legend and organized this material to create an effective sequence of scenes. If in doing this he left some loose ends or on occasion made his actors' behaviour appear improbable for someone with the opportunity to read ahead, it is not altogether surprising, nor, to my mind, a matter for assigning blame. The real Oidipous should, it cannot be denied, have summoned the surviving witness to Laios' death as soon as he heard of his existence. It is as well that Sophokles' Oidipous did not do so otherwise the play would have been an extremely short one, since this man not only knew that Oidipous was the killer, but happened himself to be the very herdsman who rescued the exposed child of Laios and Iokaste (we have no reason to suppose, however, that Sophokles' audience knew or would have guessed that this was the case).

Similarly, the real Oidipous should have been more put out than he was as a result of his confrontation with Teiresias, should even perhaps have arrived at the horrible truth by combining what Teiresias had told him with his own recollections of the time before he came to Thebes. Again this would have considerably shortened the play. Once Sophokles decided on a confrontation between Teiresias and Oidipous early in the play, he was inevitably faced with difficulties. The seer knows the truth and must be forced to reveal it (otherwise why bring him on at all?). Oidipous must not accept what he says. By arranging his material in the way that has been described here Sophokles skates on thin ice, but with a triumphant outcome. The audience is left free to concentrate on the confrontation itself and its brilliant contrasts, on the man who sees but does not know the truth and the blind man who does know; on its imagery, the play on light and darkness used literally of sight and blindness and metaphorically of knowledge, ignorance, and the darkness of Oidipous' acts;[20] and finally on the psychologically convincing depiction of a quarrel between two angry men. Here Sophokles uses all his linguistic resources, here as elsewhere showing extreme boldness in allowing tragic characters to lapse or appear to lapse into the language of everyday speech.[21] What Sophokles has achieved in the Teiresias-scene may not in the strictest sense be described as realistic: no one I hope would seek to deny that it is dramatic.

NOTES

1. I have discussed this scene more briefly in *Actors and Audience* (Oxford, 1977), pp. 73 ff. I did not then know of the treatment in Brian Vickers, *Towards Greek Tragedy* (London, 1973), pp. 496 ff., to which I am much indebted. My debts towards the pioneering work of Tycho von Wilamowitz, *Die dramatische Technik des Sophokles* (Berlin, 1917), should also be obvious. For a chalcenteric bibliography of the various heresies treated in the text see now D. A. Hester, *PCPhS* n.s. 13 (1977), 49 f., 51 ff., 59 f.

2. 'Greek Tragedy: problems of interpretation' in *The Language of Criticism and the Sciences of Man: The Structuralist Controversy*, edited by E. Donato and R. Macksey (Baltimore, 1970), p. 293 (a reference I owe to Vickers). See also the chapter 'Oedipe sans complexe' in J.-P. Vernant and P. Vidal-Naquet, *Mythe et tragédie en Grèce ancienne* (Paris, 1973), especially pp. 91 ff.

3. I am sorry that Dr. Dawe who in his Teubner edition of the play is normally generous in mentioning conjectures does not take note in the apparatus of Nauck's τεκμαρούμενος in 795. The conjecture as explained by A. E. Housman (*The Classical Papers*, Cambridge, 1972, p. 1096) seems to me to belong in the text. The most recent editors of Sophocles, H. Lloyd-Jones and N. G. Wilson, accept Nauck's conjecture and in their companion volume to the text (*Sophoclea* (Oxford, 1990), p. 98) treat Housman's discussion as decisive.

4. I will not go into the suggestion that Oidipous was repressing an unconscious desire or the arguments put forward by Freudians to explain why non-Freudians are not convinced by Freudian explanations. For an attack on 'the olympian glibness of psychoanalytic thought' see P. B. Medawar, *The Hope of Progress* (London, 1972), pp. 63 ff. Medawar's essay has been reprinted in *Pluto's Republic* (Oxford, 1982), pp. 62 ff.: the phrase in question is found on p. 67.

5. *G & R* 13 (1966), 37–49, reprinted in Dodds's collection of essays *The Ancient Concept of Progress* (Oxford, 1973), pp. 64–77, and in other places.

6. I am not sure that Dodds has been quite so successful in dealing with what Hugh Lloyd-Jones (*The Justice of Zeus*, Berkeley, 1971, pp. 106 ff.) terms the 'third heresy of interpretation', that which claims the play conveys no particular 'meaning' or 'message' but merely exploits the terror of coincidence.

7. On asides in tragedy see Bain, op. cit., p. 56 (Euripides) and pp. 82 f. (Sophokles).

8. For argument against the transposition of lines 404–7 to precede this line (readvocated by Dawe, *Studies on the Text of Sophocles* (Leiden, 1973), p. 230, but not adopted in his text), see Bain, op. cit., p. 72 n. 3.

9. Against this see Bain, op. cit., p. 74, Kamerbeek on 449–62, and O. Taplin, *The Stagecraft of Aeschylus* (Oxford, 1977), p. 91 n. 1.

10. Regarding Oidipous' silent exit here compare Taplin, op. cit., p. 310 on the significance of characters having the last word.

11. For an attack on them see Vickers, op. cit., p. 547 n. 9.

12. See *Poetics* 1454ᵇ7 and 1460ᵃ30. The second passage makes it clear that he was thinking of the improbability of Oidipous not knowing how Laios was killed.

13. It is this consideration that prevents me from accepting P. E. Easterling's explanation of Oidipous' failure to react to Teiresias' final predictions (*G & R* 24 (1977), 125 = pp. 61–2 of this volume) which seems to me a case of 'reading between the lines'. If Sophokles had wanted the

audience to believe that Oidipous did not think the man he killed was a king, Oidipous would have said so.

14. Ar. *Frogs* 1182 = Euripides fr. 157N. εὐτυχής must be preferred to εὐδαίμων here. See Ed. Fraenkel, *Beobachtungen zu Aristophanes* (Rome, 1962), pp. 142 ff.

15. I differ from C. Robert, *Oidipus* (Berlin, 1915) I. pp. 257 ff., who believes that Aischylos is here using Euripides' own *Phoinissai* as a stick with which to beat him. I cannot accept that here Iokaste is old because the Euripidean character is old: Oidipous is no longer young in Euripides' play so that the contrast is no more made there than in Sophokles' play. The one significant variation from the Sophoklean version in the narrative, ἐν ὀστράκῳ, might be an allusion to Aischylos' *Laios* where the child was exposed in a jar (see the scholion on Ar. *Wasps* 289 explaining the word ἐγχυτριεῖς, but it may simply be a reference to the most common way of exposing babies at the time of writing). See also U. von Wilamowitz-Moellendorff, *Aischylos Interpretationen* (Berlin, 1914), p. 81 n. 2, and compare G. O. Hutchison, *Aeschylus, Septem contra Thebas* (Oxford, 1985), p. xxiii n. 3: 'Aristophanes may (but need not) have Aeschylus in mind.'

16. N.B. εἶθ' 1192, ἔπειτα 1193, εἶτ' 1195. See S. Trenkner, *Le Style καί dans le récit attique oral²* (Assen, 1960), p. 13, with n. 4, and K. J. Dover, *Lysias and the Corpus Lysiacum* (Berkeley, 1968), pp. 84 f. Surprisingly Trenkner, who notes that Aristophanes uses the style to characterize vulgar persons, discounts this possibility here (op. cit., p. 78) and because Aischylos is the speaker argues for an affinity with somewhat more elevated passages in prose writers. This is to ignore the vulgar treatment of the subject matter.

17. For all this see Robert's great work. Since its publication more evidence has come to light on Euripides' *Oidipous*, a play whose structure and plot remain mysterious. See J. Vaio, *GRBS* 5 (1964), 43–55, J. Dingel, *MH* 27 (1970), 90–6, and R. Kannicht, *WJb* n.f. 1 (1975) (*Festschrift Ernst Siegmann*), 71–82. On Euripides' *Oidipous* see now R. Parker, *Miasma: Pollution and Purification in Early Greek Religion* (Oxford, 1983), pp. 385 f., and M. Hose, *ZPE* 81 (1990), 9–15.

18. Compare the remarks of Taplin (op. cit., p. 292) on how the spectator has his sense of time manipulated by the dramatist.

19. J. Dover Wilson, *What Happens in Hamlet* (Cambridge, 1935), pp. 230 ff. Cf. also P. Walcot, *Greek Drama in its Theatrical and Social Context* (Cardiff, 1976), pp. 1–21.

20. For these and other aspects of the scene not dealt with here, see K. Reinhardt, *Sophokles³* (Frankfurt, 1947), pp. 115 ff., H. Drexler, *Maia* n.s. 8 (1956), 3 ff., and S. Lattimore, *California Studies in Classical Antiquity* 8 (1975), pp. 86 ff.

21. Note ἄληθες 350 (see P. T. Stevens, *CQ* 39 (1945), 99 and *Hermes*, Einzelschrift 38 (1976), 23); οὔ τι χαίρων 363 (Stevens (*CQ*), 100); εἴπω τι 364 (cf. Ar. *Frogs* 1); ὁ . . . ὁ 385 (cf. Ed. Fraenkel, *Glotta* 41 (1963), 285–6); κλαίων 401 (see Fraenkel on Aes. *Agamemnon* 1148 and Stevens (Einzelschrift), 15); third-person address of 429 (D. J. Tarrant, *CQ* 8 (1958), 159 and Bain, op. cit., p. 72); οὐκ εἰς ὄλεθρον 430 (cf. A. Platt, *CQ* 4 (1910), 158); σχολῇ γ' 434 (see Stevens (*CQ*), 99 f.).

ADDENDA

Pages 84–5

I now believe that in my discussion of Teiresias' final speech insufficient attention is paid to the fact that it is presented as a kind of riddle for Oedipus to solve. See on this O. Taplin, *Greek Tragedy in Action* (London, 1978), pp. 43 f. who produces further arguments against the views that Oidipous has already exited before Teiresias begins or is in the process of exiting as Teiresias begins. Bernard Knox has argued (following Vellacott) that 446 ff. is an address to Oidipous' 'retreating back', Teiresias being fully aware that Oidipous is leaving since he can hear Oidipous' footsteps ('Sophocles, *Oedipus Tyrannos* 446: Exit Oedipus?', *GRBS* 21 (1980), 321–32). This at least has the merit of removing the grotesque effect I objected to when attacking the staging that removes Oidipous from the view of the audience by line 447, but I remain firmly convinced that Oedipus is present throughout the speech.

Page 85

An analogous example of how a literary work can be distorted and misinterpreted if one approaches it with methods inappropriate to its genre, dwells upon insignificant detail at the expense of the obvious overall interpretation, and scrupulously ignores the absurdity of the consequences the distorted interpretation would entail can be found in the amusing short piece by James Thurber, 'The Macbeth Murder Mystery'. In it Thurber relates how, confronted by a fellow hotel guest who had acquired a paperback edition of *Macbeth* in the mistaken belief that she was buying a crime novel and expressed her doubts about the identity of Duncan's killer, he proved to his own satisfaction that the murder was the work of Lady Macbeth's father.

Pages 89

For the general issues raised in this part of the paper compare now M. Heath, *The Poetics of Greek Tragedy* (London, 1987), pp. 111 ff.

BOW, ORACLE, AND EPIPHANY IN SOPHOCLES' *PHILOCTETES*

By CHRISTOPHER GILL

There are certain puzzling features about Sophocles' *Philoctetes*, notably concerning the oracle of Helenus that is the mainspring of the whole action. What were the exact terms of Helenus' prophecy? Did he state simply that Troy was to fall to Neoptolemus and the bow of Heracles; or did he also stipulate that the bow was to be used by its present owner, Philoctetes, that Philoctetes was to come willingly to Troy, and that his wound was to be healed there? By the end of the play, we may well think that the prophecy made these further stipulations; but the references to the prophecy earlier in the play (and the actions of Odysseus, who should be familiar with its conditions) do little to make this plain. It is also difficult to determine exactly how much Neoptolemus knows about the prophecy. In the opening dialogue with Odysseus, he seems to know nothing about the oracle, not even the role of the bow in the capture of Troy (112 ff.). But, as the play proceeds, he gives an increasingly precise account of its conditions; although the source of his expanding knowledge is by no means clear. A further problem is posed by the epiphany of Heracles that concludes the play. Why has Sophocles constructed his play in such a way that the natural conclusion of the human characters' interaction is in direct contradiction both to the divine plan and the traditional myth, and needs (as it may seem) to be awkwardly reversed by a *deus ex machina*?

These puzzles have been much discussed in recent years,[1] but there is scope, I think, for a further attempt at clarification. It may be useful to begin by making the general point that (whatever is true of Sophocles' other plays) this seems to be a play which is concerned not only to represent a human situation, and to do so with great psychological subtlety, but also to unfold a pattern of moral and religious ideas. These ideas are conveyed partly through the characters' behaviour, but partly through other dramatic means: the messages of the gods (both in the form of reported messages and a direct announcement) and the visible object that stands at the centre of the play, the bow of Heracles. In this article, it is the significance of these additional dramatic means I wish to examine; they disclose the underlying unity of the play and, by explaining the 'logic' of the action, enable us to make sense of much that is puzzling in the development of the plot.

The significance of the bow is the easiest to unravel; but it can help us in turn to understand both the oracle and the epiphany. The bow is the

special instrument of ἀρετή, that is, of heroic achievement;[2] but in this play
the bow (and heroic achievement) is inseparable from genuine friendship.[3]
Philoctetes inherited the bow by an exceptional act of friendship. He was
prepared to do something Heracles' own son could not bring himself to
do: to light the funeral pyre that would end Heracles' mortal life, and so
free him from the agonies of the poisoned robe of Nessus (801–3).
Philoctetes compares this act of friendship with the favour he begs of
Neoptolemus: he asks the young man to put up with the repulsiveness of
his sickness, and to end his wretched solitude by taking him home to
Greece (468 ff.).[4] Neoptolemus' consent to this (which seems genuine to
Philoctetes, though it is not sincerely meant) earns him the right to handle
the bow of Heracles. Philoctetes stresses the uniqueness of this privilege:
'Have confidence; you are allowed to touch it, and return it to the giver,
and boast that you alone of men have handled it, in return for your
goodness (ἀρετή). It was by doing a good deed (εὐεργετῶν) that I myself
gained possession of it' (667–70). Neoptolemus, who had shown a proper
reverence for the 'famous bow' (654 ff.), expresses a proper respect for
Philoctetes' gesture of friendship. 'I am not sorry to have met you and
taken you as a friend. For a man who knows how to do a favour when he
has received one is likely to be a friend more valuable than any possession'
(671–3). A little later Philoctetes goes further: attacked by the periodic
spasm of his sickness, he entrusts the bow to Neoptolemus for safe-
keeping, twice reminding him that he is showing the same trust to
Neoptolemus as Heracles (in his physical extremity) showed to him (776–
8, 801–3). But his trust is—temporarily—betrayed. Under the influence of
Odysseus' advice (and then Odysseus' authority in person), Neoptolemus
retains the bow when Philoctetes asks for its return, and thus becomes the
'thief' of the bow that has been taken by trickery.[5] When the two other
men leave with the bow, Philoctetes, brooding on the theft, dwells on the
fact that the bow has been taken out of its proper context of trustworthy
friendship; he imagines it in the hands of the duplicitous Odysseus. 'My
own dear bow, wrenched by force from the hands that owned and loved
you, if you have any consciousness, you must be looking with pity at the
friend of Heracles who will never use you any more. In an exchange of
masters, you are being wielded by a man of many tricks, and you see low
deceits as you look at my hateful enemy' (1128–37).

But, in fact, Neoptolemus has kept his word not to hand over the bow
(774–5), and he returns, having rejected Odysseus' stratagems in favour of
his natural honesty, to give the bow back to its rightful owner. This act
places their friendship on a genuine basis; and Philoctetes now demands
from his friend the fulfilment of the promise formerly given insincerely,
that he be taken home (1397 ff.; cf. 526 ff.). Philoctetes had compared this
favour to that which he did for Heracles (667 ff.), and the two acts have

this in common, that the friend does what he is asked, even though he seems to be bringing about the other's destruction. (For, if Philoctetes goes home, he will lose the chance of curing his wound, which he can only obtain at Troy, 1329 ff.) The two actions have something else in common. Philoctetes' consent to light Heracles' funeral pyre and so destroy his mortal life enabled the hero finally to escape from pain; for it triggered the divine intervention that made Heracles into a god. Here also, Neoptolemus' acquiescence in Philoctetes' self-destroying wish triggers (in a way I shall examine later) the divine intervention that releases Philoctetes from his pain. For, once Neoptolemus has given his consent, the deified Heracles appears and commands that Philoctetes do what his new friend had tried to persuade him to do: to go to Troy and be healed. But he does more than this. In sanctioning the partnership of Philoctetes and Neoptolemus in the capture of Troy with his bow (telling Philoctetes that 'like two lions that hunt as a pair, he must guard you, you him', 1436-7), he sums up the significance of the bow as we have seen it in this play: that heroic achievement depends on authentic friendship. And, in stressing Philoctetes' continuing debt to him for acquiring the bow (and, in another way, his debt to his new partner, Neoptolemus), Heracles implies that possession of the bow—the visible symbol of the capacity for heroic action in partnership—carries with it the obligation to exercise that capacity in action.[6]

Understanding the significance of the bow brings us closer to the meaning of the oracle which refers to the role of the bow in taking Troy. I am not sure that we are ever in a position to spell out the exact wording of the oracle,[7] but I do think the play gradually discloses both the essential content and the character of Helenus' prophecy. The oracle, however it was worded, seems to have constituted (like Apollo's famous oracle to Socrates) a kind of riddle, or test, to those who heard it.[8] And it was a riddle whose inner meaning was inspired (as oracles sometimes were) by a higher than conventional moral code.[9] Its underlying message, I think, is identical to the significance of the bow: that, for the Greek army, strength, and heroic achievement, can only come through friendship. In particular, the strength to take Troy can only come through a restoration of friendship with the mistreated ally, Philoctetes, a friendship that can only be re-established through the uncompromised new entrant to the war, Neoptolemus. References to the prophecy imply that the healing of Philoctetes' emotional wound, his bitter grievance against the Greek army, is a precondition of the healing of his physical wound; and that both acts of healing are preconditions of the use of the bow by Philoctetes against Troy, on the Greeks' behalf.[10]

The oracle constituted a kind of test to its hearers, but a test of moral courage and compassion rather than intellect. For the fulfilment of the oracle depends (as we shall see) not so much on mechanical adherence to its exact terms[11] as on the adoption of the attitude of mind it recommends. Odysseus is stimulated to action by the oracle, but he fails totally in his attempts to bring about the results predicted by Helenus. His failure reflects not so much his neglect of the oracle's precise conditions but rather a complete misunderstanding of its spirit. Instead of urging Neoptolemus to form a genuine friendship with Philoctetes, he advocates deception and manipulation; and, when this fails, he threatens force and compulsion.[12] It is hard to tell whether he is confused or deliberately ambivalent about whether the oracle predicts the fall of Troy to the bow alone, or to the bow handled by Philoctetes. But, in either case, his words show his inability to see Philoctetes as a person, not simply the instrument of his plans, and as the rightful owner, not simply the present holder, of the bow.[13] The bow itself he regards (with none of Neoptolemus' reverence) solely as an instrument of destructive force, not one that must be given freely to another as a token of trust.[14] It is appropriate that, when Neoptolemus (who has come to understand the bow's true character) returns it to its proper owner, Odysseus nearly finds himself destroyed by what he takes to be solely an instrument of destruction.[15] Odysseus' misunderstanding of the meaning of oracle and bow is certainly not a consequence of inadequate intelligence,[16] or of his personal fear of Philoctetes and the bow.[17] It is a natural result of his general philosophy (which he states repeatedly) that the end always justifies the means, that the end to be pursued is the good of the state, and that individuals are to be regarded as instruments to that end, without independent value.[18]

In Neoptolemus' case, Sophocles does not make plain, in factual terms, how much he knows about the oracle at the start of the play, or how his knowledge seems to increase as the play proceeds. But what is absolutely clear is that, when he is influenced by Odysseus' policies (and his interpretation of the oracle), he shows the least understanding of the oracle's terms and intentions; and when he follows through his own natural intuitions, he comes progressively closer to the spirit of the oracle, and gives an ever clearer account of its exact conditions. In other words, Sophocles does not allow Neoptolemus to state the terms of the oracle until he responds, in action as well as feeling, to its spirit. And in this way he indicates that understanding the oracle is a matter of response to a moral challenge rather than just adherence to a precise verbal formula.[19] In the opening conversation, Neoptolemus is misled by Odysseus into focusing on the bow as the object which 'must be hunted' (116), though even here (and despite Odysseus' lack of clarity on this point) Neoptolemus recognizes that Philoctetes too must be brought to Troy.[20] When left on his own, he soon shows his awareness that the divine plan presupposes that Philoctetes, the owner of the bow, will himself fire the arrows that will take Troy (195–200). None the less, as he adopts Odysseus' policy of deceit and manipulation, he also adopts the other's narrow (and poorly defined) conception of their aim. The object of their quest is the bow, and perhaps also Philoctetes, but only because he is the present holder of the bow. It is understandable, then, that when Philoctetes lies unconscious with disease, and the bow is left in Neoptolemus' hands, the chorus covertly advocate its theft (827 ff.). But, in response, Neoptolemus re-states, in more emphatic terms, his realization that the divine plan requires that Philoctetes, as archer, take Troy. And his reply shows, by its sentiments as well as its oracular metre, his increasing grasp of the spirit of the oracle. 'I see that we hold in vain this bow as our prize, if we sail without him. The crown [of victory] is his; it was him the god said we must bring. It would be a source of disgrace to boast about a job half done—and even so done by lies.'[21]

What leads Neoptolemus to this strengthened insight is not so much the report of Odysseus' agent, the pseudo-merchant, that Helenus' prophecy stipulated that Philoctetes come to Troy—and do so willingly (610 ff.);[22] Neoptolemus knows (if Philoctetes does not) the unreliability of such a witness. What activates Neoptolemus is his growing moral repulsion at his pursuit of the 'prize' of the bow through the deceit of its owner.[23] This feeling is intensified by vivid personal experience of the disease ignored for nine years by men like Odysseus, and the consciousness that the sick man is only now the object of interest because of the bow he holds. This combination of moral unease and 'terrible compassion' (965–6) leads Neoptolemus to abandon the policy of deceit and to deal openly with Philoctetes for the first time. This shift of direction brings him into closer conformity with the spirit of the oracle; and it is consistent with this that he becomes better able to state its terms, indicating Philoctetes' possible reconciliation with the Greeks and healing of his wound.[24] But Neoptole-mus' conversion is partial. He remains partly subject to Odysseus' authoritarian attitudes,[25] and to the personal authority of Odysseus himself, and leaves with his superior, retaining the bow (1078–80), in spite of Philoctetes' passionate pleas for its return. A little later, however, he gains the confidence to throw off both the values and the authority of Odysseus, to follow through his own moral intuitions, and to return the bow to its rightful owner (1222 ff.). In doing this, he acts in complete accord with the spirit of the oracle, and is correspondingly enabled to articulate fully the conditions he has formerly stated only in part. As he acts in conformity with the oracle, and as he solves its 'riddle', so Sophocles allows him to speak with its voice.[26] Philoctetes is moved by this utterance, and the friendship with which it is spoken, and comes close to responding to the oracle's intent (1350 ff.). But Neoptolemus' signal act of friendship is not enough to outweigh the bitterness created by the persistent failure in friendship of Odysseus and the Atreidae. Philoctetes not only rejects the offered reconciliation with the Greeks but makes a request that will make Neoptolemus too become their enemy (1398 ff.). Sophocles seems to have framed this final request to Neoptolemus so as to constitute the supreme demand of friendship. Not only is Neoptolemus asked to surrender his own interests to that of his friend,[27] he is also asked to respond to a claim of a kind hardly recognized in the Greek theories of friendship, the claim that he respect his friend's wishes rather than act for what seems to him his friend's good.[28] His consent to this claim apparently makes it impossible for the oracle to be fulfilled; and yet, paradoxically, his consent is in the fullest possible accord with the oracle's message that genuine reconciliation with Philoctetes is an essential precondition of the Greek capture of Troy.

It is in exact response to this paradoxical situation that the deified Heracles now makes his intervention. He turns the two men back from the road they had started on (the road to Philoctetes' home, 1416); but, in a deeper sense, he confirms the personal 'road' they have taken (the establishment of true friendship), and associates the continuation along that road with the fulfilment of the oracle (1423–4, 1434–7). Heracles' own authoritative prophecy confirms the intimacy of connection we have seen between the significance of oracle and bow. He makes it plain that for Philoctetes, ἀρετή, the heroic use of the bow, is inseparably linked with his two bonds of friendship, both to Heracles and to Neoptolemus (1423–40). As well as stressing his own bond of friendship with Philoctetes, symbolized by their common possession of the bow, Heracles maintains they have similar destinies: Philoctetes, like himself, will win lasting glory as a result of his troubles (1418–22). We have already seen the well-marked analogy between Philoctetes' act of friendship to Heracles (his consent to light the funeral pyre) and Neoptolemus' act of friendship to Philoctetes (his consent to take the sick man home to die). Heracles' speech confirms this analogy by emphasizing Philoctetes' twin bonds of friendship; but his intervention—and at this crucial moment—adds a further dimension to the analogy. Philoctetes' act had been the trigger that had released Heracles for the ἀθάνατον ἀρετὴν Zeus intended for him (1420); and Heracles' intervention here implies that Neoptolemus' act similarly releases Philoctetes to exercise the ἀρετή and win the εὐκλεᾶ βίον the gods have intended for him (1422 ff.). Neoptolemus' self-sacrifice has essentially healed the wounds that separated Philoctetes from other men and held him back from co-operative heroism.[29]

Neoptolemus' friendship was a necessary, but not, however, a sufficient condition, of Philoctetes' rehabilitation. Another kind of friendship was needed. Aristotle notes that the friendship of men for gods, like that of children to parents is 'as to something good and superior', for they have received the greatest benefits from them. Elsewhere, he describes the relation of gods to men as 'of the benefactor to the benefited, and in general of the natural ruler to the natural subject'.[30] The relationship of Heracles to Philoctetes embodies this type of friendship in a heightened form (since Heracles is a personal, as well as general, benefactor). And this quasi-parental relationship gives to Heracles the right (allocated to parents at Plato, *Ly.* 207–8)—a right unavailable to the more 'childlike' friend, Neoptolemus—of telling Philoctetes to do what is for his own good in place of what he wishes.[31] As a god, Heracles is also in a position to make plain to Philoctetes something that has not always been obvious to him: that it is the divine wish both to cure and to compensate Philoctetes for the pains he has suffered.[32] Philoctetes' reply expresses not simply submission to divine will but a deeply-felt response to a personal friend (1445–7). His concluding words show also that he has understood the integral connection Heracles has made between the divine plan and the establishment of friendship (and that he now accepts that friends can advise as well as consent). He asks his island's blessing on his voyage 'where a great destiny conveys me, and the judgement of friends, and the all-conquering Spirit, who brought these things to pass' (1466–8).

The *deus ex machina*, then, does not have the function of wrenching human will into conformity with an impersonal divine plan (or of forcing the organic development of the plot into the alien mould of the myth).[33] It is the final revelation of the underlying theme of the play, the truth finally recognized by Neoptolemus (though so long obscured by Odysseus) that the gods respect openness not manipulation, and the procedures of friendship (persuasion and consent) not of compulsion, and regard such procedures as a precondition of heroic achievement. In contemporary Greek terms, presenting the gods in this way is by no means conventional; indeed, it is a view of striking originality.[34] It was, I think, Sophocles' concern to convey this view that led him to give the play the structure it has: that of Neoptolemus' slow and faltering growth in understanding of, and response to, the moral challenge of the oracle, rewarded by direct revelation of divine will by Heracles.[35] On the printed page, this sequence of events may strike a modern reader as peculiar or even unclear at some points (in the ways I mentioned at the start of this article). But in its original performance[36] (and under the author's own direction) the gradual disclosure of a profound idea could have had intense dramatic power.[37]

NOTES

1. e.g., by C. M. Bowra, *Sophoclean Tragedy* (Oxford, 1944), pp. 261 ff., C. E. Whitman, *Sophocles, A Study of Heroic Humanism* (Cambridge, Mass., 1951), pp. 182 ff., H. D. F. Kitto, *Form and Meaning in Drama (FM)* (London, 1956), pp. 95 ff.; cf. *Greek Tragedy, (GT)* (3rd

edn., London, 1961), pp. 297 ff., G. M. Kirkwood, *A Study of Sophoclean Drama* (Ithaca, 1958), pp. 79 ff., B. M. W. Knox, *The Heroic Temper* (Berkeley, 1964), pp. 126 ff., A. E. Hinds, *CQ* 17 (1967), 169 ff., W. Steidle, *Studien zum antiken Drama* (Munich, 1968), pp. 169 ff., D. B. Robinson, *CQ* 19 (1969), 45 ff., O. Zweierlin, *GGA* 222 (1970), 206 ff., D. Seale, *BICS* 19 (1972), 94 ff. Recent work on the *Philoctetes* is surveyed in a perceptive article by P. E. Easterling, *ICS* 3 (1978), 27 ff. (I am grateful to Oliver Taplin for drawing my attention to this and other recent articles.) These works are referred to below by author's name alone.

2. Cf. 1418–40, esp. 1425–33, and P. W. Harsh, *AJPh* 81 (1960), 408 ff.

3. O. Taplin, *Greek Tragedy in Action* (London, 1978), pp. 90–3, C. Segal, *QUCC* 23 (1976), 67 ff. (hereafter, Segal, *QUCC*), esp. 76 ff.

4. The connection between the two acts is underlined by the fact that Philoctetes wants Neoptolemus to take him home to Oeta, which is famous for being the location of Heracles' funeral pyre (664 ff., 725–9, 1430–3).

5. Cf. Odysseus' advice in 54–5, 77–8, 100 ff., and Philoctetes' accusations in 927 ff.

6. Note esp. 1421–37. ὀφείλεται (1421) implies both that glory 'is owed' to Philoctetes in return for his labours and that he is 'obliged' to accept the chance of glory that his labours have given him.

7. Cf. Robinson, 49, and Zweierlin, 210. The content of the oracle is expounded at 1329 ff.; cf. 1421 ff., and (perhaps) 604 ff.

8. Cf. Plato, *Ap.* 21a–23b. For Sophocles' special interest in riddling prophecies, see Kirkwood, pp. 73 ff., and Knox, *Oedipus at Thebes* (New Haven, 1957), pp. 33 ff.

9. Cf. H. W. Parke and D. E. Wormell, *The Delphic Oracle* (Oxford, 1956), i. 378 ff.

10. See 915 ff., 1326 ff., 1423 ff., and cf. P. Biggs, *CPh* 61 (1966), 231–5, Segal, *QUCC*, 72, and Segal, *Hermes* 105 (1977), 133 ff. (hereafter Segal, *Hermes*), esp. 150–2.

11. As Bowra seems to suggest, pp. 265 ff.

12. See 54 ff., 100 ff., 981 ff., 1241 ff., 1293 ff.; cf. Bowra, pp. 267–8. In the pseudo-merchant's account of Odysseus' response to Helenus' prophecy (whether or not this account is a true one), Odysseus shows a similar indifference to the question of Philoctetes' willing co-operation; see 617–8 (contrast 612); cf. Zweierlin, 206 ff.

13. See 68–9, 77–8, 113–15, 1055 ff.; cf. Bowra, p. 268, Whitman, pp. 182–3, Knox, pp. 126–7, Segal, *Hermes*, 140–1. On Odysseus' possible reasons for being ambivalent, cf. Hinds, 180.

14. 68–81, 105, 113, 1055 ff.; contrast 654 ff., 774–5, 1232 ff.

15. 1293–1304; cf. Segal, *QUCC*, 76–7.

16. He is, perhaps, over-clever (431–2, 1244; cf. Bowra, p. 269).

17. As Robinson seems to suggest, 49.

18. 50 ff., 79 ff., 109 ff.; cf. 980 ff., 1049 ff., 1241 ff. Cf. M. Nussbaum's interesting article in *Phil & Lit* 1 (1976–7), 29 ff.

19. Cf. Zweierlin's criticism of Steidle's view, 209 ff., Segal, *Hermes*, 145, Easterling, 34.

20. Neoptolemus talks of bringing Philoctetes (ἄγειν, 90, 102) and of his coming to Troy (112). Odysseus talks of 'taking Philoctetes by a trick' (δόλῳ ... λαβεῖν, 101; cf. 103, 107), but this may simply mean 'tricking' Philoctetes to make him give up his bow (cf. 77–8); cf. Knox, p. 187 n. 20, Hinds, 171.

21. 839–42; cf. Whitman, p. 183, Knox, p. 131, Nussbaum, 36.

22. As Kitto seems to suppose, *GT*, p. 302, *FM*, pp. 117 ff.; cf. Steidle, p. 173. For a better account of the function of the pseudo-merchant's speech, see Zweierlin, 206 ff., Easterling, 30.

23. 902–3 and ff.; cf. 79–80, 86–9, 100 ff.

24. The phrase σῶσαι κακοῦ ... τοῦδ᾽ hints at this; the idea is spelled out more fully at 1329 ff., 1423 ff.

25. 925–6; cf. Odysseus' authoritarianism at 52–3, and 994 ff., 1241 ff.

26. 1329 ff., incl. his first reference to Helenus himself, 1336 ff.; for the account, cf. Heracles' own, 1421 ff.; cf. Segal, *Hermes*, 147.

27. Aristotle describes this as characteristic of a good man and good friend, *EN* 1168a 32–4.

28. Cf. Nussbaum, 47.

29. Cf. C. Campbell, *Theoria to theory* 6 (1972), 81 ff. (I am grateful to Philip Vellacott for drawing my attention to this article.) See further J.-P. Vernant, P. Vidal-Naquet, *Mythe et tragédie en Grèce ancienne* (Paris, 1973), pp. 161 ff., esp. 177–9, P. W. Rose, *HSCP* 80 (1976), 49 ff., esp. 77.

30. *E.N.* 1162a4–5, *E.E.* 1242a32; cf. Bowra, pp. 302–3, who also mentions these passages.

31. Heracles' epiphany is sometimes seen as essentially an externalization of Philoctetes' change of mind (e.g., by Whitman, pp. 186–9), but Philoctetes' realization that he should pay attention to the opinions of others, beside himself, is an important part of his 'cure' and rehabilitation with men and gods; cf. Segal, *Hermes*, 153.

32. For Philoctetes' comments on the work of the gods in the world, see 446–52; cf. 1197–1201, but also 1035–9 and 1466–8. The theological implications of the play are treated convincingly by Segal, *Hermes*, esp. 153 ff., unconvincingly by J. P. Poe, *Heroism and Divine Justice in Sophocles' Philoctetes* (Leiden, 1974).

33. Cf. Segal, *QUCC*, 79; and contrast, for instance, the *deus ex machina* of Eur. *Or.* 1625 ff., presented one year after the *Philoctetes*, in 408 B.C.

34. Plato gives a similar view of the gods at *R.*378–83, but he presents his view as being unconventional, and in contradiction with traditional accounts.

35. Cf. Easterling, 31–4, who emphasizes that Sophocles need not have made the oracle of Helenus so important to the plot, nor have included the epiphany of Heracles, if he had not some reason for doing so. (Easterling does not, however, see the play as religious in quite the sense I do, 33–4, though Segal, *Hermes*, 153 ff. comes closer to my view.)

36. Campbell, 81 ff., discusses a production in which she was involved, which set out to represent the epiphany as the natural climax of the human action.

37. I would like to acknowledge the perceptive comments and criticisms of Tim Chilcott on an earlier draft of this article.

ADDENDUM

Relevant work on Sophocles' *Philoctetes* since the original publication of this article includes: R. P. Winnington-Ingram, *Sophocles: An Interpretation* (Cambridge, 1980), pp. 280–303; C. Segal, *Tragedy and Civilization: An Interpretation of Sophocles* (Cambridge, Mass., 1981), pp. 293–361; R. G. A. Buxton, *Persuasion in Greek Tragedy: A Study of Peitho* (Cambridge, 1982), pp. 118–32; and M. W. Blundell, *Helping Friends and Harming Enemies: A Study in Sophocles and Greek Ethics* (Cambridge, 1989), pp. 184–225.

THE *PHUSIS* OF NEOPTOLEMUS IN SOPHOCLES' *PHILOCTETES*

By MARY WHITLOCK BLUNDELL

In the opening lines of *Philoctetes*, Odysseus addresses his companion Neoptolemus as his famous father's son (3 f.). This is the first indication of an important theme: *phusis*, in the sense of inherited human qualities or capacities.[1] Although Achilles has died before the dramatic action begins, he hovers in the background of the play, and no one challenges his claim to the highest admiration.[2] Neoptolemus is closely associated with his father, and is repeatedly addressed or referred to as his father's son. In one particularly striking passage he describes to Philoctetes his own reception at Troy, where the welcoming army swore that they saw the dead Achilles alive once more (356–8). These lines conjure up a vivid physical likeness between father and son, but their descriptive context ironically questions the identification, and it remains to be seen how deep the resemblance really lies. Neoptolemus has the potential, in virtue of his inherited *phusis*, to be as admirable as Achilles.[3] But two questions remain to be answered in the course of the play: Will he prove to be his father's son in character as well as birth? If so, how will this excellence be manifested?

Odysseus is faced with the task of convincing Neoptolemus that he must deceive Philoctetes in order to get him and his invincible bow to Troy. Neoptolemus will reap great glory from the sack of Troy—a prospect which we might expect to attract the son of Achilles (cf. 352, 1344–7). But the use of deceit is unquestionably alien to the Achillean *phusis*. As commentators have observed since ancient times, Achilles in the *Iliad* declares his hatred of duplicity, addressing none other than Odysseus (9.312 f.). It is thus only natural that Odysseus should anticipate difficulty in convincing Achilles' son to carry out his plan. He therefore resorts to subtle persuasion.

Before even mentioning the need for deception, he urges Neoptolemus as his father's son to be *gennaios* or 'noble' (50 f.). This is an aristocratic term of approval, rooted in the faith in inherited excellence most clearly enunciated by Pindar, for whom the *gennaios* spirit passes by nature (*phuē*) from father to son (*Pyth.* 8.44).[4] Aristotle explains *gennaios* as 'abiding by one's *phusis*', in contrast to *eugenēs*, which refers merely to excellence of lineage (*Rhet.* 1390b 21–3).[5] By using such language, Odysseus is appealing to Neoptolemus' pride in his birth and desire to live up to his *phusis*. He exploits the language of *phusis* to anticipate the objections prompted by Neoptolemus' true nature. He will end by admitting that such duplicity is alien to Neoptolemus' *phusis*, underlining the point by his repetition of the root *phu-* (79 f.; cf. 1068).[6] But he urges Neoptolemus to disregard the promptings of *phusis* in order to reap the pleasure of victory (81).

Neoptolemus' first reaction is an unequivocal rejection. He invokes his father Achilles, the source of his *phusis*, closely echoing Odysseus' language (86–9). He goes on to suggest instead that they take Philoctetes by force (90–2). Here is the instinctive response of the Achillean *phusis* at its crudest: honest action, however brutal, is preferable to deceit.[7] This repugnance for deception must compete with Neoptolemus' sense of loyalty (93 f.), and his respect for the authority of Odysseus (whom he addresses as 'lord', 26, 94). But he ends with a statement of principle expressed in terms of his general moral goals or wishes: 'I wish, lord, to fail acting nobly (*kalōs*) rather than conquer wrongfully (*kakōs*)' (94 f.). He has the advantage of a promising *phusis*, with certain feelings and principles to match. But he has yet to order these and apply them to the dilemmas of life, to make a decisive choice and confirm his moral intuitions with action. As Aristotle says, it is by performing just actions that we become just people (*E.N.* 103b 1). Neoptolemus' admirable convictions have yet to be translated into admirable deeds, and so into a firm and settled disposition (cf. ib. 105a 28–33).

This ethical immaturity enables Odysseus to take advantage of his superior age and experience. Neoptolemus has never met the father whom he is so concerned to emulate (351).[8] Odysseus exploits this absence of paternal guidance, addressing Neoptolemus for a third time as his father's son (96). He invokes the commonplace that age brings wisdom (96–9), thus hinting that he himself may now take on the advisory role of the dead Achilles.[9] He will adopt an overtly paternal tone when he addresses Neoptolemus as 'child' (130). Neoptolemus is addressed this way throughout the play, above all by his other moral 'teacher' Philoctetes.[10] Along with the many references to him as his father's son, this contributes to the impression of a young and untried moral agent.

The turning point for Neoptolemus comes with Odysseus' promise not only of success and profit (111–15), but of a reputation as both *agathos* or 'good' and *sophos* or 'clever' (119). The first of these epithets is especially appropriate to the son of Achilles. The second better suits Odysseus himself (cf. 1244), but need not be scorned by one who has been brought up like Achilles to be a speaker of words as well as a doer of deeds (cf. *Il.* 9.443). These inducements succeed in outweighing Neoptolemus' instinctive sense that lying is shameful (108). When he finally capitulates, declaring that he will discard his sense of shame (120), we can be confident that in dismissing it he is also betraying his *phusis*.

His task accomplished, Odysseus departs, and the chorus of Neoptolemus' sailors enters. Ironically, their opening words express a pious faith in a divinely sanctioned and aristocratic inherited excellence. They attribute to their young master the inborn judgement and 'craft' (*technē*) of the hereditary ruler, on which they depend to guide them in their loyal support (138–42). 'Craft' recalls Odysseus' plot (cf. 80, 88), about which they betray no scruples. But it remains to be seen whether this kind of skill is really appropriate to the ancestral role which they assign to their master.

With their help, Neoptolemus succeeds in convincing Philoctetes that he is sailing away from Troy after a violent quarrel with Odysseus and the Atreidae. This sets the scene for Philoctetes in turn to exert moral pressure on Neoptolemus. Addressing him as 'child' he supplicates for help, in the name first of all of the young man's father (468–70). Then, like Odysseus, he supports his plea by appealing to the behaviour of those who are *gennaios* (475–8). But where Odysseus induced Achilles' son to dismiss the instinctive promptings of his *phusis*, Philoctetes is exhorting him to obey them by avoiding something 'shameful' (476), which will bring an 'ignoble reproach' (477). Having praised Achilles as *eugenēs* (336), he is urging the son to live up to his father by being *gennaios*. When Neoptolemus does deceptively agree to help, his acquiescence is expressed in the aristocratic language of honour, shame, and noblesse oblige (522–5). The very moment of betrayal thus ironically echoes Philoctetes' appeal to be *gennaios*. This marks the nadir of the sensitivity to shame which is the hallmark of Neoptolemus' *phusis*.

They are on the point of departure, when Philoctetes is overcome by an attack of his disease. Twice, in the extremity of his pain, he calls the young man *gennaios* (799, 801). After waking to find that Neoptolemus has still not abandoned him, he attributes this to a *phusis* which is *eugenēs* and from a *eugenēs* line (874). As far as he is concerned, Neoptolemus is now living up to the standard of excellence set by Achilles, and proving his noble *phusis* in action (904f.). But this confidence is based upon a lie. Moreover the values which underlie his approval harmonize with the principles enunciated by Neoptolemus himself in the prologue (94 f., 108). Philoctetes' misconceived praise is a repeated reminder that the young man has failed to live up to his own words. Accordingly he falters under Philoctetes' influence, failing to put aside his sense of shame as he previously resolved (120).

The first sign of his re-emerging sense of shame appears when the chorus exhort him to abscond with the bow while Philoctetes sleeps. Neoptolemus summarizes his dual motivation for staying: if he quits now, he will not only fail in his mission but incur the 'shameful reproach' of deceit (842). But it is not until the moment comes for departure that Neoptolemus starts to crack. He is reduced to bewilderment (897–9), the condition of a Socratic victim (cf. Pl. *Meno* 80a). For him as for Socrates' interlocutors this results from ethical confusion. His general moral desires have come into conflict not only with self-interest, but also with the obligations of loyalty and obedience.

But the means by which he regains and confirms his original intuitions is not the Socratic path of rational argument. It is not reason, but feelings which alert him to the demands of his *phusis*.[11] His first reaction to Odysseus' suggestion was expressed in terms of a pleasure and pain associated closely with his *phusis* (86–9). After meeting Philoctetes, he resorts to repeated expressions of mental pain, at first in reaction to Philoctetes' pitiful condition (759 f., 806). This emotional response is a powerful force in his moral education. Before meeting Philoctetes he was willing to advocate violence (90 f.), and blithely ascribed Philoctetes' sufferings to the divine plan (191–200). But the actual sight of these sufferings inspires a 'terrible pity' which brings him to the point of returning the bow (965 f.). Similarly, when this first moment of weakness is thwarted by Odysseus, he will leave the chorus with Philoctetes out of a pity which he associates with his *phusis* (1074).

As his *phusis* reasserts itself, Neoptolemus more and more decisively rejects shameful deeds. His sympathy for Philoctetes' physical suffering helps to prompt moral pain at his own behaviour. He is distressed not by the physical discomfort of witnessing Philoctetes' disease, but by the discomfort of betraying his *phusis* and being shown up as shameful and *kakos* (902–9).[12] He therefore determines to avoid at least the shame of deceit by revealing their true destination. In effect, he is now turning to force (cf. 921 f.), the method he proposed at the outset (90 f.). But he no longer defends violence as acceptable *per se*. The emotional impact of his encounter with Philoctetes has made this simplistic form of Achillean honesty untenable.

The distraught Philoctetes attacks Neoptolemus' most sensitive point: 'Are you not ashamed?' (929). In expressing his outrage he emphasizes Neoptolemus' paternity (940). He urges him once more to avoid incurring 'reproach' (967 f.), and implicity appeals to *phusis* when he begs him even at this stage to return to himself (950). For he still believes that Neoptolemus fundamentally shares the same values as himself: 'You are not *kakos*. But you seem to have come here after learning shameful things from men who are' (971 f.). He anticipates Aristotle's distinction between one who acts wrongly from a settled disposition, and one who does bad deeds but is not yet a bad person (*E.N.* 134a 17). As long as Neoptolemus remains hesitant, Philoctetes refrains from blaming him for his actions (961 f.). Philoctetes' enemies, by contrast, are not only *kakoi* (984, 1369), but intrinsically and incorrigibly so. They have been educated in evil not by some external corrupting source, but by their own judgement (*gnomē*)

(1360 f.).[13] They have reached Aristotle's stage of settled vice. Neoptolemus should henceforth leave bad and shameful deeds to such as these, to whom they are fitting (972 f.).

The pivotal nature of Neoptolemus' decision is brought out by his vain wish that he had never left home (969 f.). He cannot return to childhood, but must face up to his dilemma and make an adult choice. He appeals to the chorus, but both advice and decision are forestalled by the intervention of Odysseus (974). Philoctetes now knows who the 'teacher' is who has corrupted Neoptolemus against the grain of his *phusis* (1013–15). He has already seen direct evidence for the claim that Neoptolemus wants to be true to his *phusis* (902 f.). Moreover Neoptolemus' moral sensitivity is still in operation, even if it has been misdirected (925 f.). Even Philoctetes recognizes that his behaviour has been prompted in part by the obligation of obedience (1010). But these excuses apply only to one too inexperienced to defy his commander. When Neoptolemus seems to have made an informed decision in Odysseus' favour, Philoctetes once more blames him fully for his deeds (1282 f.), condemning him in the strongest terms as a disgrace to his illustrious father (1284).

But Philoctetes is unaware of the real nature of the choice which Neoptolemus has made. When the young man returns, his earlier hesitation has been replaced by decisive action. He has made the kind of informed and purposeful choice which is a reliable indicator of moral character—in Aristotelian terms, a *prohairesis* (*E.N.* 111b 3–12a 17). Although we do not witness him reaching this decision, it is represented as a deliberate choice in contrast to his earlier hesitancy.[14]

Odysseus' attempts to interfere are now totally ineffectual. With the decision to return the bow, Achilles' son has finally rejected his quasi-parental influence and adopted his own birthright of authority.[15] He has also regained his sense of shame, which he uses to justify his decision (1228, 1234, 1249). At last he is acting on the instinctive feelings, wishes, and principles he expressed at the outset. As Aristotle rightly saw, his action results not merely from a victory of principle over pleasure, but from the compelling influence of a different kind of pleasure and pain: 'He is praiseworthy for not standing by what he was persuaded to do by Odysseus, because he felt pain at lying . . . And yet it was through pleasure that he did not stand firm, but a noble (*kalos*) pleasure' (*E.N.* 146a 20 f., 151b 19–22). He has thus displayed not merely self-discipline but the true virtue that is distinguished by the feelings that accompany it.[16]

Philoctetes now addresses Neoptolemus with paternal affection (1301), and declares that he has displayed his true *phusis* as Achilles' son (1310–12). Neoptolemus acknowledges his pleasure at this praise, which unites him with his father (1314 f.), then tries to persuade Philoctetes to come willingly to Troy. But Philoctetes refuses. Instead, he sets Neoptolemus a still more stringent test of his concern for principle, by begging him to keep his originally deceptive promise and take him home (1398–1401). When Neoptolemus agrees to do so, he earns once more Philoctetes' seal of ethical approval: his words are *gennaios* (1402).

But is Philoctetes correct in the belief that Neoptolemus has now fulfilled his inherited *phusis*? Let us return to the moment when Philoctetes first supplicates Neoptolemus to take him home (475–8). He uses the language of heroic values, appropriate to their shared admiration for the *phusis* of Achilles, language of shame and reproach, nobility and glory. Later he will treat Neoptolemus' compassionate assistance as evidence of his *aretē* (662–9), and commend it in terms of Achilles' *phusis* and the claims of a good (*esthlos*) man (904f.). And as we have seen, both he and Neoptolemus freely use the aristocratic language of nobility and shame in evaluating the behaviour proper to the son of Achilles.

But the behaviour which Philoctetes urges, and Neoptolemus eventually agrees to, is rather different from a deed of Achillean heroism.[17] Heroic language is being used to commend a course of action which conforms to intrinsic moral standards rather than the approval of the community at large, and to humane cooperative values rather than the glory of martial accomplishment. However much honour and glory Philoctetes may personally bestow upon Neoptolemus for his action, it will not benefit him in either heroic or practical terms. The price he must pay for Philoctetes' 'prize of renown' (478) is the renown he hoped to win at Troy by following in his father's footsteps. Moreover keeping his promise will put him at odds with the rest of the Greeks and expose him to charges of disobedience and treachery. This becomes clear when, after agreeing to take Philoctetes home, Neoptolemus asks how he is to escape the blame of the Achaians, who may come and lay waste his territory (1404 f.).[18]

Achilles' son has thus displayed an almost Socratic willingness to sacrifice personal advantage to the demands of justice (cf. 1246).[19] Socrates also provides a parallel for the play's use of heroic language. In the *Apology* he imagines an interlocutor asking if he is not ashamed at pursuing a way of life for which he now risks execution (28b). He replies that life and death are insignificant compared to whether one does 'just or unjust acts . . . and the deeds of a good (*agathos*) or bad (*kakos*) man'. He then points to the example of Achilles, who risked death rather than do something shameful (28c). The point of comparison is that both would rather die than live as a *kakos* man (28d). But in support of the parallel Socrates revealingly misrepresents Achilles' motivation. In Homer he acts out of remorse for the death of Patroclus: 'May I die at once, since I was not there to defend my comrade as he was killed' (18.98 f.). In Plato's version this becomes: 'May I die at once . . . after exacting justice (*dikē*)

from the offender (*adikōn*)' (28d). Achilles does regard his pursuit of
Hector as a just revenge (cf. e.g. 18.93), but this motive is absent from the
lines Plato purportedly quotes. Socrates ignores the egoistic aspects of
Achilles' behaviour, and exploits one salient feature of Achillean heroism—courage in the face of death—to support his own conception of the
agathos man, with its fundamental emphasis on an utterly different kind of
justice.

Like Socrates, Neoptolemus lays claim to the moral inheritance of
Achilles. But how far has he really proved to be his father's son? He does
resemble the Achilles of the *Iliad* in important ways, especially in his
initial predilection for violent action, his hatred of deception, and his
desire to avoid disgrace and reap military glory. Neoptolemus' presence at
Troy, like that of his father before him, is essential for a Greek victory, and
the fictitious tale of his quarrel with Odysseus and the Atreidae closely
resembles Achilles' quarrel with Agamemnon.[20] This pattern is echoed
and confirmed when, like Achilles, Neoptolemus defies an authority figure
with a threat of violence in what he considers a just cause (1255 f.).[21] Like
Achilles, he temporarily abandons the war at Troy. And like Achilles in
Iliad 24, his preference for raw violence succumbs to compassion for the
wretched (965, 1074).

But the differences between them are equally significant. Pity is a
powerful force in inducing Neoptolemus to live up to his *phusis*. But
Achilles is generally conspicuous for his pitilessness (11.664 f., 16.33–5,
24.44).[22] He is eventually moved to compassion for Priam (24.516), but
only after divine intervention, and even then with great difficulty (cf.
24.568–70). Neoptolemus, though he cares about military glory, is willing
to sacrifice it and ruin his reputation with the rest of the Greeks. But
Achilles withdraws from battle to increase his own ultimate glory by
making his absence felt. Like Neoptolemus, he does briefly turn his back
on the heroic ideal, intending to sail for home (9.356–63). But he does so
out of wounded personal pride, whereas Neoptolemus reluctantly sacrifices personal accomplishment to the claims of another. Both make a
choice which will damage the cause of their allies. But Neoptolemus does
so out of respect for a personal friend, whereas Achilles' intransigence is a
violation of friendship caused by the indulgence of his wrath against an
enemy (9.628–48). Neoptolemus is open to a friend's persuasion, allowing
Philoctetes to convince him not to go to Troy. But Achilles, though
conscious of the claims of friendship (9.645), rejects the appeals of the
embassy and also of his closest personal friend, Patroclus.[23] Neoptolemus
prevents Philoctetes from killing Odysseus, refusing to adopt his new
friend's unqualified hostility towards his enemies (1300). But Achilles tells
Phoenix to love and hate in harmony with him, and not to befriend
Agamemnon lest he become hateful to Achilles himself (9.612–15). Both

remain loyal to one close personal friend, but Neoptolemus defers to his friend Philoctetes, while Achilles pursues a selfish policy which leads to the death of his friend Patroclus.[24] Finally, Neoptolemus is moved by a disinterested concern for justice (1246), whereas Achilles undermines the justice of his cause by refusing Agamemnon's offer of compensation (cf. 9.515–23).[25]

Philoctetes, rather than Neoptolemus, is the Achillean figure in this play.[26] Both he and Achilles value honesty and care about renown.[27] Both believe in loyalty to friends, but only on their own terms. Both are sorely needed, but refuse to cooperate out of revenge for dishonour, preferring temporarily to return home rather than fight (1367 f.; cf. 1363–5). Both regard vengeance as beyond price, and reject offers of compensation. Each is prepared to avenge an insult by thwarting his personal enemies, at the cost of many innocent Greek lives, his own ultimate glory, and the best interests of a personal friend. Each is on the point of killing his enemy when a more prudent friend intervenes (1.188–221; 1299–1304). Each is induced only by the appearance of a divine messenger from Zeus to abandon his intransigent wrath and accept recompense for a grievance (24.139 f.; 1447). Finally, each will ultimately help to bring about a Greek victory at Troy and his own ultimate glory as *aristos* amongst the Greeks (1344 f.).[28]

It is thus only to be expected that in diverging from his father, Neoptolemus also departs from the values of his new father-figure, Philoctetes. They agree on the central moral issues of justice and honesty, yet their values are not identical. For Philoctetes allows hatred for his enemies to outweigh all other considerations, including the obligation to help a friend. But Neoptolemus has different priorities. When Philoctetes tries to kill Odysseus he intervenes, rejecting, at least in this instance, the ethic of revenge (1300–4). Instead of rigidly pursuing hostility, he is concerned to involve Philoctetes in the constructive, mutually beneficial enterprise of conquering Troy.

This gulf between their values re-emerges after Neoptolemus' final attempt at persuasion has failed. Philoctetes begs Neoptolemus to take him home instead and so not seem, by helping *kakoi*, to be like them in *phusis* (1371 f.). But Neoptolemus remains unmoved. For him, it is no violation of his *phusis* to cooperate even with *kakoi*, if this is to the mutual advantage of himself and his friends. To Philoctetes, any such suggestion is disgraceful (1382). Neoptolemus' *phusis* requires him too to avoid disgrace, but in his view, the obligation to help friends outweighs the obligation to harm enemies, and brings no shame (1383).[29]

It seems, then, that to do justice to his *phusis* a son need not duplicate his father's character. *Phusis* is a potential, and a noble *phusis* may manifest itself in various ways. The way in which Neoptolemus actualizes his

potential, confirming his *phusis* in action, is identical with none of the
models available to him. He lives up to his noble *phusis* in a distinctive
manner, combining the best of Achillean honesty and Odyssean persuas-
iveness, while avoiding the concomitant vices of recalcitrance and treachery. His father's forthright pursuit of honour is tempered in him by an
unselfish concern for pity, justice, and friendship.

The contrasting figure of Odysseus shows that aristocratic birth alone
does not guarantee an admirable *phusis* or the corresponding behaviour.[30]
Moreover even the son of a truly admirable father may fail to manifest his
phusis (cf. Arist. *Rhet.* 1390b 23–31). If the son succeeds in inheriting his
father's potential, then he starts off at a distinct advantage. But this
potential may still be nipped in the bud by evil 'teaching', as the prologue
of *Philoctetes* vividly illustrates.[31] Even the most promising *phusis* must be
fortified by proper education and practice, or it may never reach fruition.[32]
Neoptolemus is led astray despite his inherited nobility, and to some
extent because of it. Odysseus exploits his wish to be *gennaios* as well as his
desire for success and glory. Without the counterbalancing influence of
Philoctetes, he might have become another Odysseus. For a while Philoctetes thinks this is what he is, and damns him as a disgrace to his father, fit
to be cursed along with the Atreidae and Odysseus himself (1284–6).
When these fears are assuaged, he rejoices that Neoptolemus has
turned out to be a true child of Achilles, and not another son of Sisyphus
(1310–12).

Even after Neoptolemus redeems himself by restoring the bow, there
are two reminders of this danger of corruption. First, the awkward
moment when Philoctetes declares that Neoptolemus should on no
account go to Troy to help those who robbed him of the 'prize' of his
father's arms (1363–5). He is alluding to the lying tale which has already
been exposed, but Neoptolemus fails to clear up this final misunderstanding. This omission suggests that Neoptolemus is embarrassed to reveal the
extent of his lies and thus cast a shadow over his burgeoning friendship
with Philoctetes.[33] We are not allowed to forget that this friendship is still
partly based upon a lie. For it was Neoptolemus' original pretence of
Achillean anger at the theft of his 'prize' which seemed to unite them in a
bond of shared enmity (cf. 403 f.)[34] Philoctetes remains unaware of the
truth, but the audience is reminded that Odyssean corruption cannot so
easily be erased, and may have more far-reaching consequences than any
of the characters foresees.

There is a similar undercurrent to the final words of Heracles' speech.
He warns Philoctetes and Neoptolemus that when sacking Troy they
should take special care to show reverence for what concerns the gods, for
Zeus values this above all else (1440–3). These striking lines have been

taken by commentators from the scholiast onward as a veiled allusion to the notorious impiety of Neoptolemus at Troy, in particular his murder of Priam at the altar of Zeus. They thus provide an ominous coda to the theme of moral education.[35] It seems that Achilles' son, whose first instinct was to use force against the helpless Philocetetes, will turn once more from compassion to brutal violence.[36]

Aristotle is not optimistic about the possibility of achieving virtue. Exhortations, he says, are able only to encourage young men who are already of generous spirit, and to render susceptible of virtue the character which is *eugenēs* and truly loves what is *kalos* (*E.N.* 179b 7–9); but such natures are rare, and we should be content if some share in virtue is attained when all conditions are favourable (179b 18–20); these include an appropriate *phusis*, but by itself this is inadequate (103a 13–26); from the very beginning it requires habituation in liking and disliking the right things (179b 20–6; cf. 103b 23–5); only then can reason and argument play an effective role (179b 26–31); practice is still needed in virtuous deeds, which will eventually result in the settled state of character that constitutes true virtue (103a 31–b 25, 105a 17–b 10).

Philoctetes charts the moral progress of a youth endowed with the kind of nature Aristotle requires, one who is motivated by nature to avoid what is shameful (cf. 179b 11 f.). This nature leads him to feel pleasure and pain at the right things: 'The character must somehow pre-exist with an affinity for *aretē*, loving what is *kalos* and feeling discomfort at what is shameful' (179b 29–31)—an apt description of Neoptolemus (cf. especially 902–13). But such a nature remains only a potential. It must be nurtured by benign influences, and confirmed by appropriate behaviour. When the play opens, Neoptolemus is vulnerable to corruption. We see him gradually return to the original promptings of his *phusis* in response to the emotional and moral influence of Philoctetes. This finally results in a purposeful moral choice. It is only through the repeated performance of such actions that the noble *phusis* can realise its full potential and properly earn the epithet *gennaios*.[37]

NOTES

1. On *phusis* see J. W. Beardslee, *The Use of* Φύσις *in Fifth-Century Greek Literature* (Chicago, 1918), especially pp. 22–4 on Sophocles; H. Diller, *NJAB* 2 (1939), 241–57; F. Heinimann, *Nomos und Physis* (Basel, 1965), pp. 89–109; O. Thimme, Φύσις Τρόπος Ἦθος (diss. Göttingen, 1935). The following will be cited by author's name alone: K. Alt, *Hermes* 89 (1961), 141–74; B. M. W. Knox, *The Heroic Temper* (Berkeley, 1964); P. W. Rose, *HSCP* 80 (1976), 49–105. Citations from Sophocles are from Pearson's *OCT* unless otherwise indicated.

2. Many of the numerous references to him are listed by Rose, 97 n. 97 and H. D. F. Kitto, *Form and Meaning in Drama* (London, 1956), p. 114.

3. That Neoptolemus' *phusis* is only a potential is rightly stressed by H. Erbse, *Hermes* 94 (1966), 182, 187.

4. For further examples, mostly from Pindar, see Beardslee, p. 7, Heinimann, pp. 99 f., Thimme, pp. 18–21 (all above, n. 1). Cf. also Theogn. 535–8, Soph. fr. 808 (Radt), Eur. fr. 232, 298, 520 (Nauck²).

5. Cf. also *Hist. An.* 488b 19 f. Knox declares Aristotle's distinction irrelevant to Sophocles (p. 187 n. 18). But while the poet suggests no such verbal contrast (using both adjectives with equal approval), he does exploit the conceptual distinction (cf. *Aj.* 1093–6, *Ant.* 37 f.).

6. On φύω in Sophocles see A. Lesky, *Hermes* 80 (1952), 97 f. It can mean little more than 'be' (so perhaps at 326, 910), but the emphatic usage in the prologue of *Phil.* gives added resonance to later instances which might otherwise seem casual (e.g. 558, 1074, 1244, 1372). Φυ- words in the play are listed by Rose, loc. cit. above, n. 2.

7. Cf. Knox, pp. 122 f.

8. The veracity of this is confirmed by the *Iliad* (see Jebb and Kamerbeek, ad loc.).

9. Cf. Knox, pp. 122, 126. In Neoptolemus' deception speech Odysseus usurps the role of father by calling him 'child' (372) and taking Achilles' arms. Note that in the *Odyssey* Odysseus instructs his real son to lie (W. B. Stanford, *The Ulysses Theme* (Oxford, 1954), p. 262 n. 14).

10. See H. C. Avery, *Hermes* 93 (1965), 285–90. He is called 'man' only twice (910, 1423). See P. Vidal-Naquet, *Mythe et tragédie en Grèce ancienne* (Paris, 1972), p. 172.

11. Cf. M. Nussbaum, *Phil. & Lit.* 1 (1976–7), 33.

12. For his mental pain cf. also 913, 970, 1011 f. and the irony of 671 (on which see R. P. Winnington-Ingram, *Sophocles: An Interpretation* (Cambridge, 1980), p. 286).

13. The text is controversial, but this is the general sense. The passage is also linked with the *phusis* theme by Alt, 170. Cf. *gnomē* in 139, 1467.

14. Note especially βουλεύῃ (1229) and cf. Alt, 166. Νοεῖς (1233) was used of Neoptolemus' earler intentions (889, 918, 921), but this time intention issues in action.

15. Note that children are incapable of *prohairesis* (*E.N.* 111b 8 f.). For a similar sign of adulthood compare Telemachus' rebuke to Penelope (*Od.* 1.345–61). C. P. Gardiner suggests that the hexameters at 839–42 are not simply oracular (the most usual explanation), but indicate Neoptolemus' first assertion of Homeric kingly authority over his men (*The Sophoclean Chorus* (Iowa City, 1987), p. 38).

16. Cf. *E.N.* 151b 34–52a 3; 111b 14 f. *Prohairesis* involves elements of both desire and reason, while its goals are determined by wish (ib. 112a 15 f., 113a 9–12, 139a 31–39b 5).

17. Cf. Rose, 68.

18. Cf. also Odysseus' threats in the name of the army (1241–3, 1250, 1253, 1257 f., 1293 f.).

19. For Socrates see Pl. *Crit.* 48c-d with G. Vlastos, *Topoi* 4 (1985), 6–8.

20. See Knox, p. 123.

21. This parallel is drawn by Knox, p. 136 and others (but see below).

22. Exceptions are his pity for the weeping Patroclus (16.5), which does not issue in action, and 23.534, where out of pity he awards a prize to the *aristos* who has come in last.

23. He responds to Ajax's argument from friendship only to a very limited degree, by dropping his threat to leave Troy altogether. He lets Patroclus join the fight but this is to safeguard his own honour (16.83–90).

24. For Achilles' responsibility see H. Lloyd-Jones, *The Justice of Zeus*² (Berkeley, 1983), pp. 21 f.; R. B. Rutherford, *JHS* 102 (1982), 145 f., 155–7.

25. See Lloyd-Jones (previous note), pp. 17 f.

26. For Achilles as the prototype of the Sophoclean hero see Knox, pp. 51 f.

27. For Philoctetes and renown cf. 249–56 with Alt, 149 f.

28. The superlative is used in the play only of Achilles and Philoctetes (997, 1284; cf. 1313, 1429, also 3). On Achilles as *aristos* see G. Nagy, *The Best of the Achaians* (Baltimore, 1979), pp. 26–35.

29. This interpretation rests on Buttmann's conjecture ὠφελῶν φίλους in 1383. If the mss. ὠφελούμενος is retained, Neoptolemus implies that *ceteris paribus* personal profit is no disgrace. The pursuit of enmity remains subordinate to other priorities.

30. Odysseus' *phusis* is characterized by 'cleverness' (1244) and a craving for 'victory' (1052). Yet he is neither truly wise nor even successful. On his ignobility see my 'The Moral Character of Odysseus in *Philoctetes*', *GRBS* 28 (1987), 307–29.

31. See Rose, 88 f. This possibility is essential to the dramatic tension as well as the ethical implications of the play. This tension is sustained by the fact that Neoptolemus outside this play is best known for his impious violence (see below).

32. The role of these various factors in moral education was a popular topic of discourse in the fifth century, but few would have denied that some element of each is necessary. See W. K. C. Guthrie, *A History of Greek Philosophy* III (Cambridge, 1969), ch. 10.

33. Alternatively, we may imagine that Odysseus really did keep the arms. This is less plausible, but has the interesting consequence that Neoptolemus must radically depart from Achillean standards and sacrifice his 'prize' in order to win renown at Troy.

34. Cf. the scholiast on 59 and Alt, 170 f.

35. See Rose, 102 f.

36. Cf. 998 where Odysseus speaks of sacking Troy as an act of violence.

37. I have presented versions of this paper at Harvard University, the University of Illinois at Urbana-Champagne, and the annual meeting of the Classical Association of the Pacific Northwest (Seattle 1987). I am grateful to those present for their comments, especially Michael Halleran.

HERACLES AND GREEK TRAGEDY[1]

By M. S. SILK

I

Heracles was the greatest and the strangest of all the Greek heroes. A long list of superhuman acts of strength and courage stood to his name, and above all else the famous twelve labours, which began with the killing of the Nemean lion and ended in the capture of the monstrous watchdog Cerberus in Hades. He was a great slayer of monsters, also a great civilizer, founding cities, warm springs, and (as Pindar was fond of reminding his audiences) the Olympic festival.[2] He suffered prodigiously, and he maintained prodigious appetites, for food, drink, and women. He may have had friends, but none close (as, say, Patroclus and Achilles were close), but he did have one implacable and jealous enemy, the goddess Hera. He had two marriages: the first set of wife and children he killed in a fit of madness; the second brought about his own death. He was the son of a mortal woman, Alcmena, and the god Zeus, with Amphitryon as a second, mortal, father; and after his death (by most accounts) he became a god himself and lived on Olympus.[3]

And Heracles is the suffering hero of two surviving Greek tragedies, Sophocles' *Trachiniae* and Euripides' *Heracles*. The *Trachiniae* tells the story of his death at the hands of his devoted second wife, Deianeira. Heracles is on his way home, to Trachis, from one of his many tours abroad. Ahead of him comes a group of captive women. Deianeira, waiting at home, learns that one of the captives is Heracles' latest woman, a princess, Iole. With a mixture of emotions she accepts Iole, but seeks to win her husband back by means of what she thinks is a love-charm, given to her once by the dying centaur Nessus, one of Heracles' many monstrous victims. The 'charm' is in fact a noxious mixture of the centaur's blood and the venom on the arrow that shot him: the gift to Deianeira is his revenge.

Deianeira applies the mixture to a robe, and sends the robe to her husband as a special present. The ointment duly turns into a corrosive acid which brings Heracles to the verge of an agonizing death, as Deianeira soon learns from her son Hyllus. Hyllus had gone in search of his father, and comes back now to denounce his mother as a murderess. Without apology or explanation she kills herself, and Hyllus finds out too late what she had meant to do.

Heracles at last comes back in mortal agony, raging against his wife. When Hyllus succeeds in explaining the truth about the love-charm,

Heracles forgets her and recalls certain oracles once given to him about his death and an eventual 'release from his labours', which he now sees as a euphemism for the same thing; and to Hyllus' distress he binds him to two promises: first, Hyllus is to see that Heracles is burned alive on a pyre; secondly, he is to marry his father's concubine, Iole. Once Hyllus has reluctantly agreed, Heracles greets his imminent departure from this world, 'and all this'—as the closing line of the play assures us—the gods have done: 'all of it is Zeus' (κοὐδὲν τούτων ὅ τι μὴ Ζεύς, 1278).

Euripides' *Heracles* deals with an earlier episode in the hero's life and his first marriage, to Megara at Thebes. Once again Heracles is away, this time on the last of his great labours, the capture of Cerberus in Hades. He returns to Thebes to find his wife and children, along with his father Amphitryon, threatened with death by a tyrant, Lycus. Taking Lycus by surprise, Heracles kills him, but the general acclamation of justice back on earth is suddenly disrupted: Heracles' old enemy, the goddess Hera, chooses this moment of triumph to humble him. She sends Iris, messenger of the gods, with Lyssa, spirit of madness, to drive Heracles mad and, in his mad state, kill the wife and children he has just rescued.

When Heracles regains sanity and discovers his crime, life seems worthless to him. At this moment, his friend Theseus, whom he had helped in Hades and who had heard of the trouble with Lycus, arrives to offer his assistance. Finding Heracles in desperate need, he persuades him to live on, and offers him a new home in Athens. Friendship is the final theme of the play.

Even a bare recital of their plots reveals these to be two strange plays. And the list of strange features in them is substantial, even if we discount mere exoticisms like lurid deaths and Madness herself on stage. In the *Heracles* we have, in the first place, the bizarre rhythm of the play. The opening is a slow suppliant scene in which Megara and Amphitryon wait for death or deliverance; the end is the confrontation, also slow, of Heracles and Theseus. Right in the middle comes all the action: the return of Heracles from the world of death, the melodramatic killing of the tyrant Lycus, the dissonant scene of Madness and Iris, the chilling narrative of the killings of Megara and the children. To achieve this remarkable sequence, Euripides has apparently changed the myth, which put the great labours *after* the mad killings, and indeed made the labours penance and purification for them.[4] This in its own right is a surprising feature of the play.

There is also a surprising Euripidean silence: Heracles is sent mad by Hera, but *why* Hera does this is not made clear, not even—on the surface—comprehensible. Before he is sent mad, furthermore, Heracles himself is curiously unconvincing as a represented character: here too is a feature of the play requiring explanation. (Critics convey their recognition of this phenomenon less by their eagerness to discuss it directly than by a reluctance to raise the question at all; nevertheless, no one who has seen a production of the play could doubt it.) And finally, after all these problems and agonies, the play comes to rest with a long articulation of the theme of friendship. Why this emphasis on friendship? Again, no answer from the play.

Trachiniae is no less strange. Its rhythm, certainly, is as surprising as that of Euripides' play. Both dramas are νόστος plays, whose primary centre of interest is a returning hero and whose primary emotional sequence is the sequence of anticipation and fulfilment.[5] In a νόστος play the returning hero's return is likely to be delayed, as it is in both *Trachiniae* and *Heracles*. But normally, however delayed his return, the returning hero does at least encounter those he is returning to (normally his wife and family). In Aeschylus' *Agamemnon* the returning hero does briefly meet Clytemnestra before she kills him. In *Heracles* the hero meets Megara, before he kills her. But in *Trachiniae*, remarkably, Deianeira and Heracles, though mutually destructive, never meet.

The returning hero of *Trachiniae* is strange too, strangely distant, unlike other Sophoclean heroes. Singled out for suffering as they are, Sophocles' central figures tend to embody a determinate—and determined—isolation from the 'ordinary' characters,[6] but none, not even the mad Ajax or the aged Oedipus, is so remote from family or friends. And associated with this remoteness, there is an extraordinary gulf between our view of Heracles as repellent husband and father, heedless or insensitive to his wife and son, and *their* perception of him as great and glorious. And the gulf is peculiarly obvious, because both Hyllus and Deianeira are peculiarly sympathetic figures themselves: Deianeira, in particular, is by common consent one of the most attractive of all tragic characters. There is, therefore, a huge imbalance of sympathy between our feelings for her and for her great and glorious husband.

But, above all, the end of the play cries out for explanation: Sophocles makes no mention of Heracles' apotheosis.[7] The great hero is dying a revolting death, he blackmails his loyal son into a most distasteful marriage, and 'all of it is Zeus'. On the one hand, this conclusion is disturbingly bleak. On the other, it ignores tradition. Like Euripides in his play, Sophocles has adjusted the saga, in which everything led up to Heracles' ascension to Olympus.[8]

These, we can agree, are two strange tragedies. But stranger, even, than the plays themselves is a remarkable, and widely neglected, fact about them. These tragedies may well be the first two ever composed on the theme of the suffering Heracles: there is in fact no clear sign of any others among the several hundred known tragedies that were produced before the end of the fifth century.[9] And the absence of such tragedies seems yet more remarkable when we observe that in other contemporary dramatic contexts Heracles figures very prominently indeed. He was portrayed with considerable, and increasing, frequency in Attic comedy, as he is in Aristophanes' *Birds* and *Frogs*; he was the single most popular character in Attic satyr-drama, and the satyr-plays known to have featured him include examples by all three of the great tragedians; and he was apparently the mainstay of the Sicilian Epicharmus' mythological burlesques, early in the fifth century, where (as in Attic satyr-drama and as in Aristophanes) we see a grotesque hero whose gross appetites and huge feats of strength provoke laughter, not awe.[10]

In tragedy itself he makes his presence felt, but not as suffering hero: instead, as saviour.[11] This is his role in Euripides' *Alcestis*, although interestingly, in that pro-satyric play,[12] elements of the grotesque satyric Heracles figure too: the hero who rescues Alcestis from the dead also gets drunk first and upsets a household in mourning. The saviour Heracles is attested in the *Alcestis* of Aeschylus' older contemporary, Phrynichus; in the *Prometheus Unbound* of, or ascribed to, Aeschylus himself; in Sophocles' *Athamas*, Euripides' *Auge*, and Critias' *Pirithous*.[13] And a special version of this saviour is Heracles as *deus ex machina*, the divine figure who appears at the end to cut the tragic knot. This is his role in Sophocles' *Philoctetes* and other plays, now lost.[14]

So Heracles is everywhere and everything—except tragic hero. Why should that be? When posed, this question tends to be treated in a perfunctory way and the answers given seem unconvincing and inadequate. For Wilamowitz the complicated and speculative explanation was that Heracles was a Dorian hero, celebrated in Dorian epic, which was lost at an early date and therefore unavailable for the Attic tragedians.[15] However, apart from anything else, Heracles is clearly pan-Hellenic.[16] Jebb's suggestion was that the burlesque Heracles made it difficult to stage the serious Heracles, and that in any case the legends were difficult for tragedy.[17] Recent explanations have concentrated on that second idea: Heracles was all fights against monsters, and these were unsuitable for staging; he was too remote from the world of ideas; his labours, in particular, were 'too lacking in obviously profound content'.[18]

But these explanations overlook precisely that freedom of the tragedians to change or select details of the saga which both our Heracles tragedies exemplify. We need a different kind of explanation, one that concentrates on what the tragedians could *not* change without negating the compelling significance of the Heracles myth itself. Viktor Ehrenberg went part of the way. The trouble with Heracles, he suggested, was that he was a god:

It was usual with the Greeks to make fun of their gods, and Hermes the thief, the sensual and intoxicating Aphrodite, or the voluptuary Dionysus were as old and as real as their severe and sublime counterparts. But no god, however much he might suffer, was ever tragic. . . . Heracles, whether hero or glutton, was always super-human and therefore essentially untragic.[19]

Ehrenberg's is a provocative insight,[20] but incomplete. There is one crucial difference between Heracles, on the one hand, and Hermes, Aphrodite, and Dionysus, on the other. Hermes, Aphrodite, and Diony-sus *were* gods—even if Dionysus, like Heracles, was son of Zeus and a mortal woman. Heracles, however, was not strictly a god, any more than he was strictly a man: he was both and neither. This pecular status of Heracles provides, I suggest, the answer to our question. More than that: my contention is that it provides a coherent explanation *both* for the strange reluctance of the tragedians to portray the suffering Heracles *and* for the strange character of the two Heracles tragedies themselves. The corollary, then, is that we should relate the two plays more closely to each other and to religious ideology than is commonly done.[21]

Within Greek religion, Heracles is unique in his combination of human and divine properties.[22] The Greeks distinguished between sacrifice to a god and sacrifice to a hero. The rituals were different: blood on the altar for one, blood in the pit for the other. The hero-god—$\mathring{\eta}\rho\omega s\ \theta\epsilon\acute{o}s$, as Pindar aptly called him[23]—uniquely received both types of honour.[24] Herodotus tells us that there were in fact Greeks who maintained a double cult of Heracles, with two temples, one for the divine Olympian, the other for the hero.[25] As befitted a hero, he had a human name, deferring to a god (*Hera-cles*), even if, paradoxically, that god was his mortal enemy; he founded the Olympic festival to a god (his father Zeus);[26] he died a human death on Mount Oeta. And yet, like a god, he showed superhuman powers in the cradle, where he strangled the snakes that Hera sent to kill him, and throughout his adult life, notably in such conflicts with death as his wounding of Hades and his capturing of Cerberus, episodes already celebrated in Homer.[27] And then, despite his own death, he had no grave, but instead was transfigured to Olympus to marry eternal youth, Hebe, goddess daughter of Zeus and Hera themselves.[28] The great hero, Heracles $\kappa\alpha\lambda\lambda\acute{\iota}\nu\iota\kappa\sigma s$, differs from other heroes—as Geoffrey Kirk points out—in 'his brutality, his capacity for dishonesty and his voracious appetites';[29] yet, as Ehrenberg's formula serves to remind us, gross vices too are as much divine dispositions as human ones.

Heracles is ambivalent; and despite local variations in myth and cult, it is apparent that, by the classical period, ambivalence is a firmly established part of his persona. Discussing this ambivalence in anthropological terms, Kirk has suggested that the Heracles myths represent a symbolic solution to a fundamental problem of existence, that 'basic opposition' between

Nature and Culture which Lévi-Strauss identified as a central preoccupation underlying traditional mythology.[30] Granted the importance of
Lévi-Strauss and his 'basic opposition', this is, I think, the wrong anthropological model and the wrong opposition, as far as the dynamics of the
Heracles myth are concerned.

Heracles lies on the margins between human and divine; he occupies the
no-man's-land that is also no-god's-land; he is a marginal, transitional or,
better, *interstitial* figure. Following van Gennep, the anthropologist Mary
Douglas defines the powerful significance of the interstitial in traditional
cultures: 'danger lies in transitional states, simply because transition is
neither one state nor the next, it is undefinable. The person who must pass
from one to another is himself in danger and emanates danger to others.'
The unborn child is ambiguous, neither living nor dead: it is, accordingly,
treated by some primitive groups as 'both vulnerable and dangerous'. In
one traditional land-owning society, landless clients have an anomalous
status and so may be credited with special powers, even treated as witches:
'here are people living in the interstices of the power structure, felt to be a
threat to those with better defined status. Since they are credited with
dangerous, uncontrollable powers, an excuse is given for suppressing
them.'[31]

From his birth to his death, Heracles is a clear instance, an extreme
instance, of an interstitial figure: both powerful and vulnerable; viewed
with awe and admiration (as Hyllus, his son, persists in viewing him); also
feared, wherever he goes. He is neither man nor god, so neither man nor
god is ever entirely at peace with him. He is an ideal to dream of and a
horror story to shrink from.[32]

The sense that Heracles is an anomaly of the kind outlined is absent
from much of the literature of early and classical Greece. In many contexts
he is compartmentalized and simplified and his disturbing implications are
played down, as happens when the comic-satyric tradition makes him a
giant buffoon, or again (to take a quite different fifth-century instance)
when sophistic writers like Prodicus and Herodorus turn him into a
prototype of the philosopher.[33]

But there are exceptions. In Homeric epic, Heracles is an extravagant
figure outside the normal heroic sphere. He is an isolated superman who
fights monsters, not a feudal warrior within a social hierarchy who fights
with, and against, others like himself. He took on the gods, Hera and
Hades, in combat; as such, he is alarming (σχέτλιος, ὀβριμοεργός).[34] His life,
as he tells Odysseus in Hades, was a constant paradox: son of Zeus, but
endless pain (Ζηνὸς μὲν πάϊς ἦα Κρονίονος, αὐτὰρ ὀϊζὺν | εἶχον ἀπειρεσίην).[35]
Even in death he is unique, with his self (αὐτός) among the gods on
Olympus and his ghost (εἴδωλον) in Hades; and even this ghost is an
isolated and isolating figure, such that its fellow-shades scatter and shriek

as it approaches.[36] This last passage, and a comparable one in the Hesiodic corpus, may embody different layers of composition, with an earlier description of a mortal Heracles modified in the light of a new conception; for later writers, even so, such passages would serve to sum up Heracles' ambivalence and give it an epic authenticity.[37]

Pindar's treatment of Heracles is noteworthy too. In Pindar, Heracles figures prominently and positively: he is the mighty civilizer, the founder of the Olympiad, a model hero, albeit a very distinctive one.[38] Yet even in Pindar ambivalence comes to the surface. The man who becomes a god, the ἥρως θεός, prompts a disquieting reflection about the 'law' of the world: the νόμος which rules mortal and immortal alike and justifies violent, Heraclean acts.[39] Pindar, again, has much to say about mortals and immortals and their respective territories: human beings have their limits, beyond which, in the name of piety and their own security, they dare not go. And as a recurrent symbol for those limits, he offers the pillars of Heracles, which 'that hero-god set up' as the world's boundary, 'witnesses to the extremes of our voyaging' (ἥρως θεὸς ἃς ἔθηκε ναυτιλίας ἐσχάτας | μάρτυρας).[40] 'Extreme' is the operative word—ἔσχατος—and again and again Pindar uses this word and its derivatives in connection with Heracles,[41] thereby pointing at his special status as precisely as any Greek writer ever did.

However, to allude to, or even to identify, an anomaly, as Pindar does, is considerably less painful than to expose us to its implications with the immediacy that tragic drama involves. The reason why the tragedians avoid Heracles as suffering hero is that a serious treatment of his sufferings means coming to terms with anomalous status, with crossing the limits, with disturbing contradictions. If (to speak in formulae) tragic-suffering man is man's image of his own essential condition, and if god is his projection of what he would, but dare not, aspire to, and is, instead, a helpless prey to, then the enactment of tragic-suffering god-man threatens to involve its audience in an existential inquisition of an uncommonly powerful and painful kind. The pure god, pure hero, pure buffoon, are safe subjects. The suffering Heracles, as a project for tragedy, is exceptionally sensitive material, almost too disturbing, almost taboo. And when tragedy does, eventually, dare to focus on this anomaly, disturbance is conspicuous.

II

The *Trachiniae* is generally dated to the 440s or 430s, the *Heracles* to around 414.[42] The relative chronology these datings imply is not essential to my argument, but I shall assume it for the purposes of discussion.

The *Trachiniae* begins with Deianeira, waiting for Heracles. Her first mention of him is as Zeus' and Alcmena's famous son (19); her first description of him is as fighting the river Achelous, who was her ardent suitor (9 ff., 20 ff.). After the fight, Heracles claimed the frightened woman as his bride, and fear (albeit now, chiefly, fear for him) has remained her companion ever since (27–30). The audience is left to infer the analogy between Heracles and the terrifying monsters he fights. Recent discussions make much of the point: he is a monstrous beast in his behaviour, as in his body code—lionskin, Tarzan club, appetites, and all: he fights monsters because he is one.[43] This is true, so far as it goes. What it conceals is that most of his monstrous opponents belong to the realm of the gods and are often, like Achelous, the great Hellenic river-deity, gods themselves: he fights gods, then, because he is (in part) one too.

As a husband, Deianeira tells us, Heracles is distant: away, always away; forever on the move; not concerned to see the children or to communicate with her in his absence (31–45). Where she is ordinarily dependent on him, on home, on social contact, Heracles is apparently self-sufficient, αὐτάρκης. In the *Politics*, Aristotle notes that the person who through αὐτάρκεια needs no social organization to support him is either to be classed as an animal—or a god.[44] Against Deianeira's nature, then, Heracles' stands out in sharp relief long before his appearance on stage; and we may say of Deianeira what the herald Lichas says of her: being mortal, she is human with human feelings (θνητὴν φρενοῦσαν θνητά, 473). Above all, she feels the human feeling of pity: pity for the captive women, pity for Iole herself, pity still evoked even when she knows who and what Iole is (243, 298 ff., 312 f., 464 ff.).

Heracles pities no-one: not Iole, when he wipes out her city and her family; not Hyllus, when he makes him agree to marry Iole; not Deianeira, when he gathers, grudgingly, that she destroyed him unknowingly; not Lichas the herald, who, in innocence, brought the fatal robe, and Heracles, now certainly in great pain, 'caught him by the foot where the ankle turns in the socket and hurled him at a rock in the sea, beaten by the surf, so that his skull split, and the white brain oozed out of his hair' (779 ff.).

However, there is one occasion when Heracles, now in mortal pain, asks for pity himself. Not yet knowing of Deianeira's suicide and spewing out his fury against her, he commands Hyllus to bring her to him, so that he can give her a tortured death like his own and (with Hyllus looking on) Heracles can judge which parent Hyllus feels more for (1066 ff.). Heracles' inhumanity at this moment is astonishing, yet at the same time we perceive the god-man stripped bare—to man's condition. In this condition he weeps, as never before; he calls out for the pity his despised wife was so good at giving; he acts like a woman himself: 'no spears of battle, no army of giants, no strength of beasts has ever done this to me . . ., but a woman, female, by herself, without a weapon, has destroyed me' (1058–63), 'I sob, I cry like a girl: pity me. No-one ever saw this man like this before. I always took my pain without a sound; now misery finds me out a female' (1070–5). Heracles fights monsters and takes on their monstrousness; faced with a woman, he becomes a woman.[45] There is a curious impression here of a faceless combatant, defined by his particular combats, who takes on the colour of his particular opponents.

In the passage just quoted, Heracles refers to himself as 'this man' (τόνδ' ἄνδρα, 1073)[46] and man reduced to woman (παρθένος, 1071; θῆλυς, 1075), and all because a woman, θῆλυς οὖσα (1062), beat him. That odd expression θῆλυς οὖσα is modelled on, and alludes to, a phrase in the *Iliad* (19.97): Zeus, greatest among men and gods, was once tricked by Hera—'though a female' (θῆλυς ἐοῦσα)—on the day when Alcmena was to give birth to Heracles in Thebes: tricked into denying Heracles the lordship due to him in favour of Eurystheus. The *Iliad* passage comes from the distinctive context of Agamemnon's apology to Achilles and is thus readily called to mind. The effect of the allusion is to counterpoint Heracles' reduction to the status of a mere weak human with an evocation of his hard path, his mighty parentage, and the superhuman powers associated with it that are, nevertheless, still fallible.

There is a definite moment in the play when Heracles stops behaving like a female or a human being of any kind. When he permits Hyllus to tell him why Deianeira sent the robe, what she meant by applying the ointment to it, who supplied her with ointment, his tone suddenly changes. When Hyllus comes out with the word *Nessus* (1141), Heracles senses the relation of events to the old oracle about his fate (1143 ff.). Henceforth he speaks with no more amiability, but with a new authority: he now has access to divine ordinance, to θέσφατα (1150). He continues to refer to himself as 'this man' (1175, 1201), but his perspective is that of a higher being which can look into the future. 'I shall reveal', he says to Hyllus, φανῶ δ' ἐγώ (1164), as Greek gods often talk to men, with 'I' and the simple future.[47] If Hyllus disobeys his instructions about the funeral pyre, Heracles threatens him with a curse from the underworld, like a daemonic Fury, and again employs the authoritative idiom: 'I shall wait for you' (μενῶ σ' ἐγώ, 1201). The curse, of course, is not to come from heaven: Heracles shows no sign of going there.

Hyllus is also to do Heracles 'a small favour' (χάριν βραχεῖαν, 1217) and marry Iole. Hyllus, a man, is shocked at what should not be; but Heracles, like a Dionysus faced with a Pentheus, is concerned about his rights and what *must* be. Hyllus must give him his μοῖρα, his due fate (1239), and again he threatens Hyllus with the gods' curse (1239 f.). Iole is part-cause of the death of both of Hyllus' parents, and to Hyllus the idea of marriage to her is 'impiety' (δυσσεβεῖν, 1245). To Heracles it cannot violate any sacred principle: it is his own pleasure, his τέρψις (1246): the logic is a god's.

What can this cruel play mean? Despite many warnings, we are used to approaching Sophocles through his characters, so that we naturally focus on the contrast here between Heracles and the others, especially Heracles in his distant inhumanity and Deianeira in all her human fallibility, not least her human shifts of mood, to which our sympathies are powerfully attracted. The portrayal of her sequence of feelings about Iole is particularly impressive. We follow it through the first naïve questions—

> Lichas! This one: who is she? She looks special . . .
> One of the royal family?
> Eurytus: did he have a daughter?   (~310–6)[48]—

to her first attempt to come to terms with the truth—

> Love: no-one can fight Love.
> Rules me, rules gods—so why not her?
> . . .
>
>   Whatever they do together,
> No shame in it, no harm to me
> Either. I know the truth—
> What agony is there, now I know the truth?
> He's had his women: none of them
> Have heard me say a word against them.
> Neither will she, even if
> She's lost in love.
> I'm sorry for her . . .   (~441–64)—

and then her reaction against such passive generosity, but a reaction itself of subtle shifts

>   We'll both spin
> Under the same sheet. My reward—share him!
>
> . . .
> I should be angry—but I can't . . .
>   . . . But can
> I share a man: could any woman
> Do it? Look at her: she's in blossom.
> Show me a man, watch his eyes
> Pick the flower. Someone like me,
> Withered: they don't
> Want to know. He'll still be called
> My husband, he'll *be* hers.
>   But angry—
> No, I can't.   (~539–53)

And instead of anger, she makes her fatal plan to win her husband back.

This sympathetic portrayal of Deianeira is naturalistic,[49] but not entirely. On a naturalistic level, it is impossible to gather what she could possibly see in Heracles: can the Heracles she pines for conceivably be the brutal, self-absorbed, yet also featureless phenomenon that we behold? The discrepancy, and equally the featurelessness of Heracles itself, should serve to warn us that something more than character-study ($\dot\eta\theta o\pi o\iota\dot\iota a$) is involved in the contrast between the two figures. The difference between them—indeed between Heracles and most other tragic heroes—is that they belong to different cosmic orders. This is why, in the play, they must never meet: Heracles *cannot* meet his fellow men as such. Heracles and Deianeira communicate only through the death-robe;[50] Heracles and Hyllus only through the threats and commands of one and the total acquiescence of the other.

As a god, Heracles is self-sufficient, $a\dot\upsilon\tau\dot\alpha\rho\kappa\eta s$: hence his distance from the human world of the other characters in the play. As a man, he has a need for relationship with others, which his divinity disrupts and distorts. Gods control men: men are their suffering victims. Accordingly, Heracles in this play is both god the controller (as he controls Iole and Hyllus) and man the suffering victim of a human mistake. Men and gods represent spheres of interest which, in Hegelian fashion, come into conflict, and Heracles, as both, is a Hegelian conflict all in one. He wants something and, as a god, destroys everything that stands in his way; but, as a man, he is vulnerable and so destroys himself as well as Deianeira: they share that, if nothing else.

And what emerges from the conflict? The temptation is to say, 'Heracles *the god*'—at which point the real significance of the strange end of the play comes into view. The apotheosis of Heracles is an established part of the myth, yet Sophocles leaves it unsaid. Heracles' divine aspect, as son of Zeus and slayer of monsters, bulks large in this play, yet Sophocles leaves its natural fulfilment unsaid. At the end of the play, Heracles is dying and, along with his bitter and disillusioned son (1264 ff.), seems confined to the human sphere which the gods, in a separate existence, manipulate and mock: 'all of it is Zeus', though it implies acceptance of tragic reality, is also said in this spirit. The consequence is a poise between expectation and presentation, a conclusion as startling as it is bleak, and a pursuit of painful contradiction to the last.

In his brutality the Sophoclean Heracles embodies a mode of life which, by any human standard, must seem repellent; yet the devotion he inspires in his son and wife, who are the chief victims of his repellent behaviour, seems to place him in some kind of ideal, supra-human plane beyond judgement. The contradiction is fundamental. Situated on the margins between the human and the divine, on the verge of an apotheosis that never comes, Heracles represents *both* those deep, immortal longings which all men feel or repress, and which the Greeks felt to be too dangerous to admit, *and* the huge but human sufferings and dislocations that are felt to go with them. Having chosen to dramatize this disturbing anomaly, Sophocles confronts us with its implications right up to the end.

III

If we take *Heracles* to be later in date than *Trachiniae*, it is tempting to take it as a Euripidean reaction to Sophocles' work. In its representation of Heracles as god and man, *Trachiniae* has a latent schematic quality: Euripides makes the schema more defined. *Trachiniae* embodies a conflict between the god and man in Heracles whose outcome is left open: the comparable conflict in the Euripidean Heracles leads, however painfully, to a resolution. In *Trachiniae* humanity is crushed: in *Heracles* all the movement is towards humanity. The Sophoclean suffering hero is repellent as well as distant: his Euripidean counterpart is honourable and, as the play resolves itself, more and more an identifiable man.

At the beginning of Euripides' play, the suppliants Amphitryon and Megara wait at the altar of Zeus the Saviour. Much of their talk is of Heracles, and they present him to us as the now familiar hero-god, yet also as an unselfish, loving man. He agreed to serve Eurystheus (Amphitryon tells us) in order to help this human father of his, and as a result civilized the world and conquered, or at least set off to conquer, Hades itself (17 ff.). When Heracles at last comes back from this conquest, Megara proclaims him the equal of Zeus the Saviour himself (521 f.); and yet to her he is also a model husband and family man, considerate and even playful with the children (465 ff.), 'most dear' to her in his absence (490), 'most dear' when, against all hope, he does return (514).

When he learns of the danger from Lycus, Heracles plans a revenge of god-like amplitude, which seems to involve a threat to the whole citizen body of Thebes (568 ff.). This response is (in the words of one critic) 'unusually indiscriminate in its ferocity',[51] but actually it is only unusual in human terms. In punishing an offender, Greek gods were always liable to respond like this, even a 'moderate' god like Apollo: one thinks of the devastation he inflicted in retribution for the offences of Agamemnon, for instance, and Coronis.[52] In enunciating his threat, furthermore, Heracles uses phraseology which has the unmistakable violent directness of a god: 'time for me to act: I shall go, I shall annihilate the house':

> ἐγὼ δέ, νῦν γὰρ τῆς ἐμῆς ἔργον χερός,
> πρῶτον μὲν εἶμι καὶ κατασκάψω δόμους.   (565 f.)

The simple threat, the confident cast of thought, and (as with the Sophoclean Heracles) the assertive ἐγώ and future tense combine to evoke the menace of (say) the Aeschylean Furies—

> ἐγὼ δ᾽, ἄγει γὰρ αἷμα μητρῷον, δίκας
> μέτειμι τόνδε φῶτα κἀκκυνηγετῶ—

or the primitive Hesiodic Zeus—

> ἐγὼ ἀντὶ πυρὸς δώσω κακόν—

and Cronus—

> ἐγώ κεν τοῦτό γ᾽ ὑποσχόμενος τελέσαιμι
> ἔργον.[53]

And when Heracles threatens to fill Ismenus with dead bodies and make Dirce's clear water turn to blood—

> νεκρῶν ἅπαντ᾽ Ἰσμηνὸν ἐμπλήσω φόνου
> Δίρκης τε νᾶμα λευκὸν αἱμαχθήσεται   (572 f.)—

he talks like retributive Poseidon in another Euripidean play:

> ταράξω πέλαγος Αἰγαίας ἁλός,
> ἄκται δέ . . .
> πολλῶν θανόντων σώμαθ᾽ ἕξουσιν νεκρῶν.[54]

Yet amidst Heracles' vengeful protestations, human tones are still audible: goodbye, labours! what can be better than fighting for one's family (574 f.)? And our last sight of him before madness intervenes is of an affectionate man philosophizing about men, with his children clinging to him like little boats on tow (ἐφολκίδες),[55] and not a trace of Sophoclean self-sufficiency (631–6). Short as it is, then, this scene that Heracles shares with his human wife and father serves to confirm Megara's talk of *his* ordinary humanity, at least as regards his simple intimacy with the children: that, as he himself remarks, reflects a feeling that unites all men (πάντα τ᾽ ἀνθρώπων ἴσα, 633). And yet—*how* such ordinary traits can possibly be compatible with his huge god-ness is not explained, nor indeed is it explicable. When Homer's huge god, Zeus, feels for his doomed son Sarpedon, he feels with a god's amplitude and grandeur: Sarpedon is close to him; he can save his son or let him die; he must let him die; but he honours him with a rainstorm of blood.[56] The Euripidean Heracles' hugeness is made to coexist with an almost Hellenistic ordinariness: a coexistence as thought-provoking as it is (in point of theatrical character-portrayal) absurd.

Before Heracles' return, his god-heroic aspect was amplified in a magnificent choral ode celebrating his labours (348 ff.). Between his exit and the appearance of Madness and Iris, the revenge is carried out and the tyrant killed; divine justice is perceived as having returned to mankind and another largely choral section reinforces the presentation of Heracles as god-hero in association with this access of divinity (735–814):

$$\dot{\iota}\dot{\omega} \; \delta\dot{\iota}\kappa\alpha \; \kappa\alpha\dot{\iota} \; \theta\epsilon\hat{\omega}\nu \; \pi\alpha\lambda\dot{\iota}\rho\rho\upsilon\varsigma \; \pi\acute{\sigma}\tau\mu\sigma\varsigma. \quad (738 \text{ f.})$$

Heracles seems at once a divine agent of justice and one among its human beneficiaries.

At this point we switch without warning to divine terror. By a chain of command from Hera to Iris and Iris to Lyssa, Heracles is sent mad, and despite an idea once floated by Wilamowitz which has enjoyed some favour,[57] there has been no sign of any insanity in Heracles up to now: the revenge scene, in which Wilamowitz thought he detected the seeds of Heracles' madness, rather, as we see, reveals a god's capacity for action.

Iris and Lyssa appear in person. They are gods, and they refer to Heracles as a man (ἀνήρ, ἄνθρωπος: 825, 835, 846, 849).[58] The opposition between themselves and Heracles is explicitly on this basis. Iris declares that Heracles must pay a penalty—must 'give justice', in Greek idiom—or else 'gods will be nowhere and humanity great':

$$\ddot{\eta} \; \theta\epsilon\sigma\dot{\iota} \; \mu\grave{\epsilon}\nu \; \sigma\dot{\upsilon}\delta\alpha\mu\sigma\hat{\upsilon}$$
$$\tau\grave{\alpha} \; \theta\nu\eta\tau\grave{\alpha} \; \delta' \; \ddot{\epsilon}\sigma\tau\alpha\iota \; \mu\epsilon\gamma\acute{\alpha}\lambda\alpha, \; \mu\grave{\eta} \; \delta\acute{\sigma}\nu\tau\sigma\varsigma \; \delta\acute{\iota}\kappa\eta\nu. \quad (841 \text{ f.})$$

Another lyrical section follows, during which the murders of Megara and the children take place and the chorus and Amphitryon lament. For the time being, Heracles, intermittently so human, is referred to only as 'son of Zeus': ὁ Διὸς ἔκγονος (876), Ζεῦ, τὸ σὸν γένος (887), ὦ Διὸς παῖ (906). In this stress on his divine affiliation, the choral perception of 'disaster from the gods' (θεόθεν ... κακά, 919 f.) serves to associate him with Hera: he is indeed the gods' victim, as before he was their beneficiary; yet he is also, himself, a divine force for evil, as before he was a divine force for good.

For the rest of the play, Heracles is a man. Suddenly the evocations of his divine parentage disappear, or reappear only to be contradicted.[59] In the long messenger-speech that recounts the murders, he is simply 'Heracles' (924, 1004) and 'mortal', 'human' (θνητός): 'I know no mortal man more wretched' (οὐκ οἶδα θνητῶν ὅστις ἀθλιώτερος, 1015). He is a master, a son, a husband, a father, gone mad (952, 965 f., 975 f., 988 f.). When he wakes among the bodies of his loved ones, in ignorance of his breakdown, he reaches out towards his recent exploits in Hades, but only in an effort to make sense of the terrible sight all around him (1101–5). He calls for those dear to him, φίλοι, like an ordinary social being (1106): he shows no pride, only confusion (1091 ff., 1105 ff.)—unlike a hero, let alone a god. Amphitryon treats him as a man. He tells his son what happened, blaming it on Hera and referring to Hera as to a wholly external dimension to which Heracles himself is not related. When Heracles asks who the killer was, Amphitryon's formula for the answer is 'you and your bow and the god who did it' (σὺ καὶ σὰ τόξα καὶ θεῶν ὅς αἴτιος, 1135), which he glosses with the one word μανείς, 'sent mad' (1137). The difference between Heracles sane and Heracles mad is 'the god', divinity, separate from him.

In self-disgust, Heracles thinks of suicide, but is checked by the arrival of Theseus, his relative and friend (συγγενὴς φίλος τε, 1154). Like a man, he is ashamed and hides his face (1159 f.). Amphitryon tells Theseus of the catastrophe and identifies the half-hidden figure as his son, who once fought alongside the gods, σὺν θεοῖσι (1191). Theseus asks: 'what man was born to such unhappiness?' Amphitryon agrees: 'he suffers more than all *other* mortal men' (1196 f.). The whole sequence manifests a distancing of Heracles the suffering man from his divine connections. Theseus' first address to his friend is in terms of friendship (1215). He alludes to Heracles' recent rescue of himself in Hades (1222), but without reference to, or evocation of, any divine status or powers on Heracles' part. When he finally succeeds in rousing his friend, it is by appealing to him as a man enduring heaven's blows (1227 f.), and this polarization is enforced, a moment later, by an ironic variation on a metaphorical *topos*: 'you reach to heaven itself in your wretchedness' (ἅπτῃ κάτωθεν οὐρανοῦ δυσπραξίᾳ, 1240). Heracles' literal distance from the gods is now so marked that he becomes a suitable occasion for the metaphor. He sees himself opposed to the gods against whom men are helpless (1243, 1253), and so, as Theseus says, like an 'ordinary man' (ἐπιτυχόντος ἀνθρώπου, 1248), he proposes to die.

In a long speech to Theseus (1255–1310), Heracles puts under scrutiny his whole life—divine birth, heroic exploits and status, all the labours and the madness that went with them—and from a human perspective rejects its meaning. That life was, and always had been, ἀβίωτος, no life at all (1257). There was a continuity of excess, he senses, between his super-human labours and the mad killings, which he sums up by designating the killings as his 'last labour' (1279); and now he turns his back on it all. Other people, in scorn, may call him 'son of Zeus' (1289), and Zeus, 'whoever Zeus is', may indeed have begotten him (1263) (and the liturgical formula, ὅστις ὁ Ζεύς, serves as another confirmation of his distance from heaven), but Amphitryon is his real father now (1265). Human relationship, φιλία, is what he craves (1281–4). Even as the first man of Greece, he stands opposed to heaven (1303–10); and the opposition is reiterated by Theseus a little later (1320 f.). Theseus tempts him back to life with an offer of φιλία and a new home in Athens, where Heracles will be honoured in stone memorials and sacrifices after his death (1323–35). The honour is a hero's honour and presupposes Heracles' heroic past, but what is stressed is his death, stressed by a double formula: 'when you die, when you go to Hades' (1331). Euripides, therefore, does what Sophocles had never done, and negates Heracles' apotheosis altogether.

Heracles' second long speech (1340–93), notoriously disjointed, begins with a much-discussed proclamation of the self-sufficiency of the gods:[60] a *real* god 'lacks nothing' (δεῖται ... οὐδενός, 1345 f.). Its relevant significance is that Heracles is, and can only be, proclaiming such a conviction as a far from self-sufficient man: it is a man's pious idealism, not a god's inside knowledge, that informs these words. Heracles accepts Theseus' offer, recalling his labours, but in tears, like a man (1356). He is just another of Hera's victims—Megara, children, himself (νεκρούς τε κἀμέ), all human victims on a par together (1392 f.). The final moments of the play show him as all-too-human, still in tears (1394), too distraught to move (1395), praying for some escape from his pain (1397), led by his friend's hand, as if by his own son (1398–1401). No longer the famous Heracles of the labours (1410, 1414), behaving like a woman (1412), humbled by his fate (1417), he follows his friend like a little boat on tow (ἐφολκίδες, 1424)—therefore (as we recall his own earlier image for his children, 631) like a child himself. In this moment, as in the whole of the last part of the play, Heracles is presented as a man who thinks and feels as a man; and he appeals directly to, and engages, human feelings. He does so by courtesy of Theseus, whose arrival (supposedly motivated by loyalty to Heracles and rumours about Lycus, 1163–71) is hardly less arbitrary than that of any *deus ex machina*. Theseus, let us say, is a *homo ex machina*, whose *humanitas*, literal and spiritual, presents Heracles at last with the perspective from which to dismiss and disown his divine patrimony.

If the obvious 'problem' in *Trachiniae* is the invisible apotheosis, the equivalent in *Heracles* is the unexplained madness. There are two questions here. First, in the madness scene, Iris speaks of Heracles' 'punishment': he must 'give justice' (842); but *for what* should he 'give justice' and be punished? Secondly, what is the status of Madness, Lyssa, herself? To take the second question first: Lyssa, on the face of it, is an external, independent deity, presented as such by her staging alongside Iris. Unlike Iris, though, Lyssa is not an established deity. She is a personification—not invented by Euripides,[61] but still a personification—and what she personifies can be taken to be Heracles' madness as easily as madness *tout court*. There was, indeed, another myth about a manic killing by Heracles (the victim then was Linus, his music-teacher): an audience would find no difficulty in taking this madness as Heracles' own.[62]

More to the point, the way Euripides represents the character Lyssa itself invites the audience to start thinking along these lines. The dialogue between Iris and Lyssa is, by any standard, extraordinary. Iris calls for Lyssa to send the hero mad; yet Lyssa, Madness herself, demurs, is embarrassed, points to Heracles' virtues and achievements, sees no reason for punishing him at all (843 ff.). Her words, furthermore, suggest an identification with him. She hesitates, she seeks to protect him, she refers to him as φίλος (846) (and there was an old proverb that a φίλος is a second self).[63] Her response is calculated to evoke a parallel image of Heracles striving to fight off the madness in himself. And when she agrees to do her job, the identification is verbalized more pointedly still. She will cast her being onto the house and 'do the killing first, and he, the killer, will not know' (ἀποκτείνασα πρῶτον· ὁ δὲ κανὼν οὐκ εἴσεται, 865). The phraseology looks back to the traditional Greek conception of double determination for inexplicable events,[64] but in a way that sums up the intimate relationship between Heracles and herself. He is the killer and she is the killer, because she is both independent of him and an aspect of him. The staging makes her external; the words tend to suggest her internality; she is, therefore, both, even more clearly than other destructive deities of the psyche, like Dionysus in *Bacchae*.[65]

But it is not—to restate the point—that Heracles was 'mad all the time'. There is no psychological continuity between Heracles in his madness and Heracles before the madness:[66] there is, rather, a metaphysical continuity between Heracles *per se* and the divine realm, of which madness (as Greek ideology tended to affirm) was one part.[67] When Heracles, in Theseus' presence, rejects his divinity in recoiling from his madness, he is himself tacitly affirming their affinity.

And for what is Heracles punished? We all know Hera is jealous: her jealousy is assumed in the play.[68] But jealous of what? There was a traditional motive that Hera, as consort of Zeus, was jealous of his bastard son, but this reason is both too general and too remote from the play itself to be persuasive, and it is certainly nowhere mentioned in the text. The nearest thing to an answer in the play is those words by Iris on the punishment: if Heracles does not pay the penalty, 'gods will be nowhere and humanity great' (841 f.). This is hardly an answer itself, but if we are to put a gloss on it, we might say: the cosmic order will be upset, Heracles is a threat to it, not because he is a man, nor indeed because he is a god, but because he is anomalous and neither.[69] What Euripides does is leave the question open in favour of the new emphasis on friendship, and therefore on Heracles' humanity, which dominates the rest of the play. However, that emphasis itself, perhaps, provides confirmation that our gloss is to the point.

Heracles ends the play as a credible man: wretched, special, but credible. He begins it as a wholly incredible combination of man and god. The god-man whose whole life, virtually, has been spent on the super-human plane, who can come back from the kingdom of death and behave like a good family man who has been kept late at the office, represents a quite fantastic aggregation of attributes. Euripides' play is not and never becomes a psychological study in the sense that (say) *Bacchae* is. What matters is Heracles' status, as it matters in *Trachiniae* (for all the many differences between the two plays); but Euripides solves the problem of Heracles' status by first presenting him as a psychological impossibility and thereby creating a need for credibility which is satisfied by exploding all his anomalousness out of him in a monstrous aggressive explosion.

That explosion—the madness—is presented as an arbitrary explosion such as gods create, but also as a necessary explosion, necessary in metaphysical terms as well as necessary on the level of character. The combination of god and man is unstable and must be blown apart to permit a new, simpler and comprehensible stability, whereby Heracles becomes a suffering man in whom we can believe and to whom we can relate. The cost of the explosion is very great. Much is destroyed: not only Megara and the children and Heracles' life in Thebes, but his status as a god. Hera and the gods are arbitrary and inexplicable. The pious, wretched figure who leaves the stage leaning on a friend is a representative of lucid humanity with no god left in him.

More schematic, then, than Sophocles' play, *Heracles* dramatizes a conflict between the god and the man in Heracles, and ends by clearly destroying one element, the god, and isolating the other, the man. The whole shape of the play is calculated to throw the god-man opposition into relief. What Sophocles does through the antithetical presentation of Heracles and Deianeira, Euripides does through the violent concentration of action in the middle of the drama and especially the juxtaposition of Heracles the saviour-god and Heracles the manic killer: lucid humanity is isolated, however painfully, at the end, rejecting a divine potentiality, rejecting a capacity for madness, rejecting both as intolerably arbitrary manifestations of a cosmos which, in desperation, it invests with pious hopes.

The logic of Euripides' drama is dependent on his inversion of events in the myth. *Inter alia*, by abandoning the sequence of madness followed by labours, he avoids any suggestion that Heracles can be redeemed by a saviour-god's exercise of his superhuman powers. Only the human values of friendship (it seems) can provide that redemption; and this representation of friendship as a Heraclean resource is itself a departure from mythic tradition of the most radical kind.

So, unlike Sophocles, Euripides resolves the great paradox. But as in Sophocles the progress towards a resolution involves a violent collision of spheres which cannot peacefully coexist. And as in Sophocles the god-man Heracles cannot meet his 'fellow'-men, even his beloved family, without posing a threat to them and destroying them.

IV

My argument is that the distinctive features of the two plays derive from their special common feature, the hero Heracles. As a dangerously disturbing hero, he is avoided by the tragedians. Comedy values disturbance; other genres can simplify it; but not tragedy. When the tragedians do dramatize the sufferings of Heracles, he produces disruptions at various levels. His presence dislocates the overall structure. On the level of character, it produces a huge imbalance of sympathy in *Trachiniae* and a credibility gap, violently filled, in *Heracles*. Besides this, it generates a number of otherwise inexplicable features, of which the coming of the madness in *Heracles* and the missing apotheosis in *Trachiniae* are the most obvious. The suffering Heracles embodies too much in the way of ideals and taboos to do anything less.

'The purpose of myth', according to Lévi-Strauss, 'is to provide a logical model capable of overcoming a contradiction.'[70] The Heracles myth, on the contrary, is all contradiction itself, contradiction which the tragedians explore at some cost to the tragic norms and to our emotions.[71]

NOTES

1. The original basis of this article was a paper read in 1984 to the Classical Association at University College, Cardiff, and to audiences at the universities of Wrocław and Kraków in Poland, and subsequently published in revised form in *G & R* 32 (1985). I am grateful to members of all those audiences for their thoughts, and also to Geoffrey Arnott for comments on the first published version. In its newly revised form, the article includes a number of modifications, several stimulated by these responses, others by ordinary reconsideration, others again by work published since the article was first written. For further discussion of some of the issues raised and references to secondary literature beyond items cited in the notes, see Jens-Uwe Schmidt, 'Die Götter-Wirklichkeit oder menschliche Erfindung? Überlegungen zum Herakles-Drama des Euripides', *Theologie und Glaube* 77 (1987), 443–59; J. D. Mikalson, 'Zeus the Father and Heracles the Son in Tragedy', *TAPA* 116 (1986), 89–98; H. F. Johansen, 'Heracles in Sophocles' *Trachiniae*', *C & M* 37 (1986), 47–61 (with some pertinent thoughts on Heracles as 'hero').

2. *Ol.* 2.3, 3.11 ff., 6.68 ff., 10.43 ff.; *Nem.* 10.32 f., 11.27.

3. On the incongruities in Heracles' persona, see the concise discussion by G. S. Kirk, *The Nature of Greek Myths* (Harmondsworth, 1974), pp. 176 ff.

4. See the cautious summary of the evidence by G. W. Bond, *Euripides, Heracles* (Oxford, 1981), pp. xxviii–xxx, and W. E. Higgins, 'Deciphering Time in the *Herakles* of Euripides', *QUCC* 47 (1984), 89–109.

5. νόστος plays: see O. Taplin, *The Stagecraft of Aeschylus* (Oxford, 1977), pp. 124 f.

6. See B. M. W. Knox, *The Heroic Temper: Studies in Sophoclean Tragedy* (Berkeley and Los Angeles, 1964).

7. The thoughtful discussion by P. E. Easterling, *Sophocles, Trachiniae* (Cambridge, 1982), pp. 8–11, 16–18, argues, in effect, that the original audience might have read the apotheosis in. The point is rather that Sophocles (without negating the apotheosis) gives them no encouragement to do so: see further above, pp. 125–7 and Mikalson (above n. 1), 92. An interesting alternative interpretation is offered by R. L. Kane, 'The Structure of Sophocles' *Trachiniae*', *Phoenix* 42 (1988), 208–11.

8. And, it may be, the burning of Heracles alive was a ritual act belonging to that ascension: see Karl Reinhardt, *Sophocles* (Eng. tr., Oxford, 1979), pp. 62 f., and Easterling (above n. 7), pp. 17 f.

9. On Zielinski's guess that Aeschylus' *Heracleidae* covered the ground of *Trachiniae*, see H. Lloyd-Jones, appendix to the Loeb *Aeschylus* (London and Cambridge, 1957), II. pp. 588 f. There are no visual remains that suggest tragic representations earlier than an illustration of *Trachiniae*, for which see A. D. Trendall and T. B. L. Webster, *Illustrations of Greek Drama* (London, 1971), III.2.11. Heracles is presumed to have been a main figure in Ion's *Eurytidae* (*TGF* I.99 f. Snell), whose contents (as well as date) are a matter for conjecture, but there is no reason to suppose that this Heracles was a suffering Heracles. It has been suggested, however, that Ion's *Alcmene*, *Eurytidae*, and satyric *Omphale* formed three parts of a connected Heraclean tetralogy, of which the unattested play was a genuine suffering-Heracles tragedy, conceivably on the lines of *Trachiniae*. But these speculations (for which see Schmid-Stählin, *Gesch. Gr. Lit.* (Munich, 1934), I.2. pp. 88 and 517, A. von Blumenthal, *Ion von Chios* (Stuttgart, 1939), p. 33) are not evidence.

10. See the convenient summary in G. K. Galinsky, *The Herakles Theme* (Oxford, 1972), pp. 81–100. Attested satyr-plays include Aeschylus' *Kerykes*, Sophocles' *Heracles at Taenarus*, and Euripides' *Syleus*.

11. By ignoring this distinction, Schmid-Stählin (I.2. p. 88) and others give a misleading picture of Heracles as a tragic character. A recent example: Bernard Knox, *Word and Action* (Baltimore, 1979), p. 9.

12. See A. M. Dale, *Euripides' Alcestis* (Oxford, 1954), pp. xviii ff.

13. *Alcestis, TGF* I. 73 Snell: the play is generally presumed to have been a tragedy, but could have been a satyr-play: cf. Dale (above n. 12), p. xiii. *Prometheus Unbound*: M. Griffith, *Aeschylus, Prometheus Bound* (Cambridge, 1983), pp. 285 ff.; *Athamas*: A. C. Pearson, *The Fragments of Sophocles* (Cambridge, 1917), I. pp. 1ff.; *Auge*: T. B. L. Webster, *The Tragedies of Euripides* (London, 1967), pp. 238 ff.; *Pirithous*: A. Lesky, *Die tragische Dichtung der Hellenen*³ (Göttingen, 1972), p. 525.

14. Such as Astydamas' *Antigone*: see G. Xanthakis-Karamanos, *Studies in Fourth-Century Tragedy* (Athens, 1980), pp. 49 f.

15. U. von Wilamowitz-Moellendorff, *Euripides, Herakles* II² (Berlin, 1895), pp. 69 ff.

16. As his presence in Homeric and Hesiodic heroic mythology obviously shows (see the survey in Galinsky (above n. 10), pp. 9–22) and as the cult evidence confirms (on which see L. R. Farnell, *Greek Hero Cults and Ideas of Immortality* (Oxford, 1921), pp. 103ff.). See also Bond (above n. 4) on *Heracles* 1254.

17. R. C. Jebb, *Sophocles, The Plays and Fragments*, Part V (*The Trachiniae*) (Cambridge, 1892), pp. xxi f.

18. So P. J. Conradie, *Herakles in die Griekse Tragedie* (Utrecht, 1958), p. 134; Galinsky (above n. 10), p. 41; Kirk (above n. 3), p. 203.

19. *Aspects of the Ancient World* ('Tragic Heracles') (Oxford, 1946), p. 146.

20. Which raises fascinating questions about the origin of tragedy. If we believe, as many scholars do, that tragedy developed from the worship of Dionysus and originally dealt with the sufferings of Dionysus, we must take Ehrenberg's pronouncement as an argument that early tragedy was not 'essentially' tragic. Aristotle, at least, would have agreed, albeit on different grounds (*Po.* 1449a 19–24).

21. In reaching this conclusion, I have profited from the discussion by Ehrenberg (above n. 19), pp. 144 ff., and from various remarks by A. P. Burnett in *Catastrophe Survived* (Oxford, 1971), pp. 157 ff. ('The Madness of Heracles'), much as I would have to disagree with both interpretations in other respects.

22. And quite distinct even from those other heroes with two fathers, one human and one divine, like the Dioscuri and Theseus.

23. *Nem.* 3.22.

24. Summarized by Kirk (above n. 3), pp. 176 f; see further Farnell (above n. 16), pp. 95 ff., 155 ff.

25. Hdt. 2.44.

26. Pi. *Ol.* 6.68 ff., 10.43 ff.

27. Pi. *Nem.* 1.35 ff.; *Il.* 5.395 ff. and 8.367 f.

28. First recorded in *Od.* 11.601ff. (on which see above, pp. 121–2).

29. G. S. Kirk, *Myth: Its Meanings and Functions in Ancient and Other Cultures* (Cambridge, 1970), p. 177. Heracles' gross features are summarized by Galinsky (above n. 10), pp. 16 f., 81 ff.

30. Kirk (above n. 3), p. 85 (cf. ibid. pp. 206 ff.).

31. *Purity and Danger*[2] (London, 1969), pp. 96, 95, 104. See, further, Douglas, *Implicit Meanings* (London, 1975), ch. 17 ('Self-evidence'); on the concept of 'interstitial status' and its application to classical antiquity, W. M. Beard, *JRS* 70 (1980), 19 ff.; and for a partial parallel to Heracles' own situation in ancient religious practice, rather than myth, S. R. F. Price, *JRS* 70 (1980), 28 ff.

32. Like Faust, up to a point; and it may or may not be relevant that the Faust who breaks the bounds of ordinary mortality is also a grotesque folk-hero. Contrast the type represented by Euripides' Medea: essentially human, but endowed with some superhuman capability which makes her sinister and alien in the human sphere.

33. See Galinsky (above n. 10), pp. 56, 101 ff.

34. *Il.* 5.403. The Homeric Heracles is surveyed by Galinsky (above n. 10), pp. 9 ff.

35. *Od.* 11.620 ff.

36. *Od.* 11.601 ff.

37. Hes. fr. 25.25 ff. Both passages were suspected by the Alexandrians (see the *OCT* apparatus ad. locc.), but must be fairly early: cf. Easterling (above n. 7), p. 17 n. 29.

38. See Galinsky (above n. 10), p. 29 ff.

39. *Isthm.* 3/4.71b ff., *Nem.* 3.22; fr. 169.1 ff. Fr. 169 is notoriously difficult to interpret: see the summary in G. Kirkwood, *Selections from Pindar* (Chico, 1982), pp. 347 f.

40. *Nem.* 3.20 ff.; cf. *Ol.* 3.43 ff. and *Isthm.* 3/4.29 f.

41. See M. S. Silk, *Interaction in Poetic Imagery* (Cambridge, 1974), pp. 35 (with n. 5) and 137; in the light of the present discussion, the remark on p. 35 that Pindar's association between Heracles and ἐσχατ- is 'wholly personal' is somewhat misleading.

42. See Easterling (above n. 7), pp. 19 ff., and Bond (above n. 4), pp. xxx ff.

43. See especially Charles Segal, *Tragedy and Civilization: An Interpretation of Sophocles* (Cambridge, Mass., 1981), ch. 4, an interpretation dependent on the 'beast–man–god' series assumed by French structuralists to underlie much Greek mythologizing: see e.g. M. Detienne, 'Between Beasts and Gods' in *Myth, Religion and Society*, ed. R. L. Gordon (Cambridge and Paris, 1981), pp. 215 ff.

44. *Pol.* 1253a 27 ff., a passage rightly adduced by C. M. Bowra, *Sophoclean Tragedy* (Oxford, 1944), pp. 136. Menander's all-too-human Cnemon wrongly *thought* he was αὐτάρκης (*Dysc.* 714), while Herodotus' Solon pertinently reminded Croesus that man cannot be αὐτάρκης because his fate is in the hands of God (Hdt. 1.32.8–33).

45. He has also been in servitude to a woman, Omphale (70), and been conquered by desire for another, Iole (489), thanks to the power of the goddess Aphrodite (497): cf. R. P. Winnington-Ingram, *Sophocles: An Interpretation* (Cambridge, 1980), pp. 85 f.

46. Similarly in 1175 and 1201 (also spoken by Heracles) and 1018 and 1113 (spoken by the Old Man and the choregus).

47. See the passages cited above, pp. 127–8 with n. 53.

48. This and the following set of Deianeira 'translations' (my own) represent a condensed version, whose verse idiom is aimed at conveying her moods and whole being with more immediacy and even accuracy (cf. n. 49 below) than a close translation can hope to. The lines originally formed part of a composite English-Greek verse drama called *Heracles* based on portions of *Trachiniae*, *Heracles*, *Alcestis*, and *Frogs*, which was devised for the King's College London Greek Play Tour of North America in 1983.

49. Hence the propriety of 'natural' modern English here.

50. Cf. Segal (above n. 43), p. 94.

51. Burnett (above n. 21), p. 165.

52. See *Il.* 1.8 ff.; Pi. *Pyth.* 3.25–37.

53. Aesch. *Eum.* 230 f.; Hes. *Op.* 57, *Theog.* 170 f. Similarly (ἐγώ + future): *Il.* 15.260 f. (Apollo), 21.334 f. (Hera), 24. 462 (Hermes); *Od.* 1.88 (Athene); Aesch. *Eum.* 232 (Apollo), 735 (Athene); Soph. *Aj.* 69 f. (Athene); Eur. *Hipp.* 1420–2 (Artemis), *Her.* 871 (Lyssa: cf. n. 58 below). An unnoticed usage? Others, of course, *can* speak of themselves as ἐγώ in the future tense, e.g., Homeric heroes (as *Il.* 12.368, *Od.* 1.214) and celebratory poets (as *H. Cer.* 495, Alcm. 29

Page, Pi. *Pyth.* 4. 67), but gods are peculiarly likely to do so, because 'it is almost a definition of divinity that its will must be done' (J. Gregory, 'Euripides' *Herakles*', *YCS* 25 (1977), 258).

54. *Tro.* 88 ff.

55. The word ἐφολκίς is sometimes used with more specific reference to *lifeboats* (I owe the thought to Geoffrey Arnott), a use which could add a significant resonance to the image here. However, the evidence (such as Ach. Tat. 3.3–4) is very late, and there is no means of confirming the ascription of the sense to ἐφολκίς in the classical period.

56. *Il.* 16.431–61: 'close' is φίλτατον (433).

57. Proposed by Wilamowitz (above n. 15), pp. 128 f., but subsequently abandoned, *Deutsche Literatur-Zeitung* (1926), 853.

58. Like Heracles himself, Lyssa uses the gods' idiom, ἐγώ + future (above n. 53). However, there is no perceptible echo here, as there is in the instance noted in n. 67 below (and as there are between some of *Iris*' words and earlier moments in the play: see W. G. Arnott, *MPL* 3 (1978), 12 f.).

59. Disappear: apart from a single despairing question by the choregus (1087f., ὦ Ζεῦ, τί παῖδ' ἤχθηρας ὧδ' ὑπερκότως τὸν σόν ...;). Contradicted: 1263–5, 1289 (on which see above, p. 130).

60. See Bond (above n. 4) on 1341–6.

61. We first meet her as goddess—and *dramatis persona*—in Aeschylus' lost Ξάντριαι (fr. 169 Radt).

62. For Heracles' killing of Linus, see Gow on Theocrit. *Id.* 24.105.

63. Arist. *Eth. Nic.* 1166a 31f.: ἔστι γὰρ ὁ φίλος ἄλλος αὐτός (likewise 1170b 6 f.).

64. See E. R. Dodds, *The Greeks and the Irrational* (Berkeley, 1951), ch. 1, and cf. *Her.* 1135 (with Bond, ad loc.) and the general position taken by W. Desch, 'Der Herakles des Euripides und die Götter', *Philologus* 130 (1986), 8–23.

65. Cf. Bennett Simon, *Mind and Madness in Ancient Greece* (Ithaca, 1978), p. 136. K. H. Lee, 'The Iris–Lyssa Scene in Euripides' *Heracles*', *Antichthon* 16 (1982), 50 f. offers a pertinent summary of divergent views on the question of Lyssa's status, but (as it seems to me) makes little headway with the question itself.

66. Compare and contrast Ehrenberg (above n. 19), p. 159.

67. Cf., e.g., the daemonic language spoken by the mad Ajax (Soph. *Aj.* 243 f.), the inspired direction possessed by Oedipus in a state of λύσσα (Soph. *O.T.* 1258), the popular beliefs attacked by the Hippocratic Περὶ Ἱερῆς Νούσου, and Plato's belief in μανία θείᾳ δόσει διδομένη (*Phdr.* 244a). It is noteworthy that the language of Heracles' revenge-speech (above, pp. 127–8) is echoed by Lyssa: καὶ κατασκάψω δόμους (Heracles, 566) ∼ καὶ καταρρήξω μέλαθρα καὶ δόμους ἐπεμβαλῶ (Lyssa, 864).

68. See Bond (above n. 4), pp. xxiv ff.

69. Cf. Burnett (above n. 21), p. 179. Bond (on 841 f.) misses much of the point by considering, and duly rejecting, the Aunt Sallyish proposition that 'Heracles has become too great and has committed ὕβρις, for which he will now be punished'. It is not anything that Heracles has *become* that matters, and ὕβρις (which is committed only by men) is not relevant. No more convincing is the conclusion of K. H. Lee (above n. 65), p 51–3: 'we are invited to measure our own notions of δίκη and of what deserves punishment against those of the gods' (p. 53). Here ambivalence between human and divine has been transferred, inconsequentially, from Heracles' person to audience reactions.

70. 'The Structural Study of Myth' in *Structural Anthropology* (London, 1968), p. 206.

71. At a tangent to this conclusion, I note with pleasure the following formulation: 'The [Lévi-Straussian] assumption that the opposition is prior, the mediation [= the 'model capable of overcoming a contradiction'] the necessary response, is ... questionable.... [In most cases, if not all,] the so-called mediating term should be seen as logically prior to the opposition constructed around it. ... I would suggest that Greek myth could be approached not as a system intended to mediate opposition ... but rather as a series of attempts to separate out oppositions from the features of problematic terms in order to "place" them' (from an unpublished paper by Helen King, read to the Warburg Institute, London, 1983: 'The Dynamics of Category: An Approach to the Generation of Greek Thought-Patterns').

EURIPIDES AND THE UNEXPECTED

By W. GEOFFREY ARNOTT

I should like to begin like a preacher in his pulpit, by citing two texts. In a lecture given at Harvard University in 1950 on the subject of 'Poetry and Drama' T. S. Eliot said: 'I tried to keep in mind that in a play, from time to time, something should happen; that the audience should be kept in the constant expectation that something is going to happen; and that when it does happen, it should be different, but not too different, from what the audience had been led to expect.'[1] My second text comes from the paper that has most effectively influenced my own ideas on the subject of Euripides' clever exploitation of the unexpected in his plays: R. P. Winnington-Ingram's 'Euripides: *Poietes Sophos*', published in the second volume of *Arethusa*. Winnington-Ingram ends his paper with these words: 'It makes me wonder whether, in the words of Oscar Wilde, Euripides was not capable of resisting everything except temptation—the temptation to be clever.'[2]

These two texts define my theme. Like most great writers, Euripides transmuted the influences which he absorbed from his own time and environment into his own idiosyncratic visions. His creative life belonged almost entirely to the second half of the fifth century B.C., almost entirely to the dramatic festivals of one city, Athens. Then and there the sophists were preaching scepticism about religion and morality, and using all the tricks of rhetoric to do so. Euripides was fascinated by the sophists. His own mind operated at their intellectual level. Yet Euripides was not himself a sophist, but a dramatist working in and often against the conventions of contemporary Attic tragedy. His verbal cleverness partly reflects the sophistic emphasis on rhetoric, but partly also Euripides' own intellectual preoccupation with precise analysis of motives and ideas. In the techniques of drama he was an experimentalist who exploited tradition-al forms and methods in order to secure new and sometimes paradoxical effects. Books and articles abound on this aspect of Euripides, and many more doubtless will be written. The subject is so fat that it can be compressed within the girdle of a single paper only by a process of triple selectivity.[3] First, I limit my present investigation to a very few types of Euripidean experiment with the unexpected: games with familiar dramatic conventions, for instance, and the deliberate employment of red herrings. Secondly, my illustrations for each point of technique are highly selective; they can be easily supplemented from other scenes and other plays. Thirdly, for convenience of reference the illustrations are generally confined to a small sample of Euripides' plays, four in all: the *Electra*,

Helen, *Medea*, and *Orestes*. They range in date from 431 B.C. (when the *Medea* was produced) to 408 B.C. (the date of the *Orestes*, produced two years before Euripides' death). Their atmospheres include high tragedy, melodrama, even tragicomedy. Euripides exploited the unexpected at all stages of his career in all sorts of play, even if the most startling effects and the most outrageous experiments are found in some of the less tragic tragedies he wrote in the last fifteen years of his life.

I start by looking at some of the ways in which Euripides exploits the dramatic conventions of his time. Winnington-Ingram's paper has already investigated some of the games that Euripides is prepared to play with those dramatic conventions which regulate space and time. In Greek tragedy chorus and actors are spatially separated; the actors belong to the long, narrow stage, while the chorus occupy the circular dancing-floor of the orchestra in front of it. Again, the sequence of alternating choral songs and dramatic scenes is pointed by conventional formulas such as the one by which the arrival on stage of a new but often expected character is announced. The audiences who went to see Euripides' plays were soaked in such conventions; they were in the habit of seeing 13 new tragedies every year at the two major Athenian festivals alone. It is easy to see how Euripides could exploit his audience's expectation that a particular convention, a particular formula would be handled in the time-honoured way. Winnington-Ingram aptly draws attention to the unusual announcement of the messenger's arrival in the *Electra*.[4] Orestes and Pylades had left at the end of the preceding scene in order to assassinate Aegisthus, and the chorus had sung their choral ode which by convention occupied the time that would have been required for that planned act of murder. At the beginning of the new scene (747) convention required the arrival of a messenger who would give an exciting eyewitness account of the murder, an arrival which would be prefaced by a few lines announcing that the chorus-leader or one of the characters had spotted the messenger's approach. But here Euripides does not quite follow the convention; instead, he plays with it by opening his new scene with a frustrating little exchange between Electra and the chorus-leader in pessimistic terms; Electra thinks the plan has misfired and she talks of suicide. The exchange closes with Electra saying 'We are beaten, *for* where are the messengers?'; here that single word 'for' implies the tragic convention that royal murders are immediately followed by messenger speeches about them. 'Where are the messengers?', and the chorus-leader replies 'They'll be here'. Sure enough, the next line is spoken by the messenger who has apparently crept up on them unawares and unannounced.

Euripides may seem here to be exploiting convention a trifle cynically,[5] but there are parallels to the 'Where are the messengers?' ploy which are equally novel but altogether lacking in cynicism. In the *Helen*, produced a

few years after his *Electra*, Euripides rejects the traditional legend of the
dissolute Helen and resurrects in its place the clever but much less familiar
fantasy that Stesichorus had introduced into literature nearly two centuries before. In Euripides' play the real Helen neither yielded to Paris nor
went to Troy, but was whisked off to Egypt by the gods for chaste asylum.
Paris, Menelaus, and the rest were compelled to fight and suffer at Troy
for a phantom Helen which the gods had substituted for the real woman.
Egypt, however, is not quite a chastity belt for its beautiful new resident,
although when the play begins it is seventeen years since she was parted
from her dear Menelaus and Helen's legendary beauty cannot now have
been quite what it was. Theoclymenus, king of Egypt, has fallen in love
with her. To escape his suit Helen takes sanctuary at the tomb of
Theoclymenus' father on stage. She has just learnt that Menelaus is still
alive and now very near at hand, after being shipwrecked with a few of his
companions. She turns to musing, and apostrophizes her absent husband
with these words (540): 'Woe is me, when will you be here?' If Euripides
had wanted simply to repeat his *Electra* ploy here, he would have allowed
Menelaus to enter the stage at this precise moment. In fact he goes two
better than that. Menelaus does pop up at this second, but not through one
of the normal stage entrances. He springs up like a Jack-in-the-box from
behind that very tomb on which Helen is taking sanctuary. Menelaus had
made his initial entry on to an empty stage in the previous scene while
Helen was in the palace, and had then concealed himself behind the tomb.
Secondly, with consummate irony Euripides prevents Helen from recognizing her husband at first. The shipwrecked Menelaus is dressed only in a
piece of sail-cloth. He resembles a barbarian thug, not a Greek king.
Helen's first words after her musing appeal for the reappearance of her
husband are a surprised 'Oh, who's *that*?', and she assumes that this oddly
dressed person must be one of the king's slaves, planted there to spy on
her.

A further variation of this 'Where are the messengers?' device is found
in the *Orestes*, which Euripides produced four years after the *Helen*. It is
an error to consider the *Orestes* as a sequel to the *Electra* and *Helen*, even
though it portrays the situation of Orestes and Electra just after the
murders of Aegisthus and Clytemnestra and on the morning after Helen
and Menelaus have at last arrived back from their wanderings. Early in the
Orestes we meet Hermione, Helen's innocent daughter, dispatched by her
mother with offerings for Clytemnestra's grave. Then, towards the play's
grim climax, nervously we await her return. Orestes and Electra have now
been sentenced to death by the people of Argos, and together with Pylades
they are planning to murder Helen and kidnap Hermione as hostage. The
plot is set up, and Orestes asks (1211), 'When will Hermione be here at the
palace?' Electra replies, 'Look, I think she's near the house—the time just

fits!' Both tragic convention and Euripides' previous exploitations of it would lead an audience to expect Hermione's arrival at this precise moment. In fact Euripides here deliberately frustrates these expectations. What immediately ensues is totally different. First, the plotters sound a ghastly echo of the *Choephoroi* by invoking the ghost of Agamemnon, and then Orestes and Pylades go off into the palace to murder Helen. Now Electra is alone with the chorus. They engage in a lyric duet which switches from the subject of Hermione's imminent arrival to the projected off-stage murder of Helen. In order to build up suspense, Euripides delays the expected two climaxes by alternating between the themes of Hermione's arrival and Helen's murder. First the audience concentrates fearfully on the imminent arrival of Hermione; then they switch attention to Helen's murder; back again then to Hermione; back once more to Helen. And just when the audience is now wholly involved in Helen's murder, to the accompaniment of Helen's off-stage shrieks 'I'm murdered' (1296) and 'Menelaus, I'm dying' (1301), just as Electra shouts maniacally 'Murder, butcher, slaughter her' (1302 f.), just as we all wait for final confirmation of the news of Helen's death at the climax of her agony, Euripides takes the opportunity to make his final switch. The chorus-leader interrupts 'Quiet, quiet. I heard a sound on the foot-path by the palace' (1311 f.), and Hermione innocently arrives. This device of leading his audience towards a climax and then stopping short for a diversion elsewhere is very typical of Euripides.

Enough of this 'Where are the messengers?' ploy. It is time to turn to the chorus. Here another group of scenes clearly shows how Euripides first exploits, then breaks the convention of the spatial separation of chorus and actors in Greek tragedy. Actors kept to the stage, the chorus kept to the orchestra in front of it. In the *Hippolytus* and *Electra* Euripides plays with this convention without actually breaking it. The *Hippolytus* passage was fruitfully discussed by Winnington-Ingram.[6] While Hippolytus thunders his disgust against the nurse off stage, Phaedra stands on stage with her ear to the door, recoiling with horror before the abuse she overhears. 'We are lost,' she says to the chorus (575 f.), 'stand by the door here, and listen to the tumult that falls on the house!' The chorus-leader replies to Phaedra, '*You* stand by the door, it's up to *you* to tell *us* what happens in the palace.' Euripides knows, and his audience knows, that tragic choruses do not troop up on to the stage, and the dramatist here exploits this tragic convention cleverly—or is it outrageously? It depends on one's criteria of what is dramatically appropriate.

A similar trick is played years later in Euripides' *Electra*, near the beginning of that play. Electra is on stage, in front of the modest farmhouse to which she has been relegated upon her marriage, and the chorus are where we expect them to be, in the orchestra. Suddenly Orestes and

Pylades rise up before them from their hiding-place, and frighten the life out of Electra and chorus alike. Electra suggests flight (218 f.): 'Run, you take the path and I'll go into the house, to escape these criminals!' The implication is that Electra should disappear into her house, and the chorus escape through the *parodos* arches that lead from the orchestra. But tragic choruses do not leave the orchestra during the course of a play without a conventionally dramatic reason, such as that of indicating a change of scene. Escaping from strange young men is not a conventionally dramatic reason; here again Euripides seems deliberately to be playing with convention.[7]

In the *Electra* Euripides only teases; Electra panics, but the chorus in fact remain in the orchestra. For the next logical step after teasing we must look at the *Helen*, whose novelty so shocked and delighted the audience on its first production. The scene in question is the one that directly precedes Menelaus' entrance as a half-clothed castaway. Helen has just heard a false report of Menelaus' death, and the chorus-leader advises her to go off into the palace and consult Theonoe, the clairvoyant sister of the Egyptian king. 'Go into the house' says the chorus-leader (317), and by the brocards of dramatic precedent an audience will expect Helen to depart alone for her consultation at the end of the scene, leaving the chorus either to sing a choral ode or to welcome the next character. What does happen is totally unexpected. The chorus-leader appends to her 'Go inside the house' something quite remarkable: 'I volunteer to go inside the house with you and join you in your consultation of the lady' (327 f.). Helen agrees. At the end of a short lyric dialogue between Helen and the chorus, the chorus mount the stage and go off into the palace either with or just before Helen.[8] Euripides has broken the rules of convention, and no doubt he enjoyed doing so.[9] But on this occasion there is a great deal more to it than clever gamesmanship. The device has an important dramatic purpose. Menelaus can now enter for the next scene on to a completely empty stage and hide himself behind the tomb without being seen by any character on the stage or by the chorus in the orchestra.[10]

So far my illustrations share a common factor: they all exploit the conventions of Greek tragedy. I now turn to a new group, in which Euripides exploits the unexpected very differently, by scattering false clues in such a way that the audience is deluded into incorrect forecasts or false assessments of a situation. The Euripidean red herring is a fish of many varieties, some simple, some complex. A simple variety turns up in the messenger speech of the *Electra*. It exploits an important fact of which not all critics are accurately aware. A quotation will illustrate this fact. In the century after Euripides' death the comic poet Antiphanes complained that the tragedian had an unfair advantage (fr. 191 Kock, Edmonds):

O, Tragedy's a lucky sort of Art;
The house will know the plot before you start.
You've only to remind it. 'Oedipus'
You say, and all's out—father Laïus,
Mother Jocasta, daughters these, sons those,
His sin, his coming punishment . . .
We comic writers have more urgent needs;
All's to invent: new names, new previous deeds,
New situations, new solutions, new
Starts.[11]

This criticism contains a grain of truth and a grain of falsehood. When the audience were informed of the title of the tragedy they were going to see, they would be able to predict fairly often the relationships of the leading characters and also some of the salient incidents in the myth that concerned them. In a play about Clytemnestra, Aegisthus, Orestes, and Electra, for instance, the audience would know that the first two were killed by the last two. About some plots, however, the audience would be very imperfectly informed in advance, either because the dramatist had invented much of the story himself (as with Euripides' *Orestes*), or because he had filled in the details of a relatively unfamiliar myth (as in the case of the *Helen*). Even the most familiar stories might have their details varied significantly in different tragedies. Take, for example, Orestes' murder of Aegisthus. In Aeschylus' *Oresteia* Aegisthus is murdered with a minimum of fuss off stage in the palace, as a necessary but subordinate preliminary to the matricide. In Sophocles' *Electra* Clytemnestra is killed first, and the play ends immediately before the murder of Aegisthus, with murderer and victim departing inside together. And what about Euripides' *Electra*? Here Euripides plays with the limitations of his audience's knowledge. They know that Aegisthus is going to die, but not how or when. The messenger speech reveals just how cleverly Euripides exploits this incomplete knowledge. Directly after his unusual entry, which has been discussed earlier in this paper,[12] this messenger begins by announcing the one fact that all the audience were able to predict: Orestes is victor, and Aegisthus lies on the ground (762 ff.). But how did he die? The messenger explains. Euripides meanwhile lays a trail of red herrings, or, to be more precise, a trail of possible murder weapons. Orestes and Pylades had waylaid Aegisthus while he, with a few attendants, was sacrificing a bullock in a country garden. Aegisthus invited Orestes and Pylades to take part in the sacrifice, and they agreed. The red herrings begin to swim. We hear first that Aegisthus' servants lay aside their weapons (798) in order to help the king with his sacrifice. They are now unarmed; one obstacle to Aegisthus' murder is thereby removed. The audience must wonder whether Orestes will take his cue from the grounding of these weapons and kill Aegisthus immediately. No: it is a false clue, and the climax is delayed a little. Next, Aegisthus takes a straight knife from the sacrificial basket (810 f.), kills the bullock with it, and then offers the knife to Orestes (817), suggesting that his guest should show his skill by flaying and dismembering the carcase. Orestes takes the knife (819); the audience is again expectant; surely Orestes will now use the knife to kill Aegisthus? Expectations are again frustrated; Orestes puts the knife to its proper purpose, of flaying and cutting up the bullock. In fact a further dozen lines pass before Orestes asks for a cleaver to split the bullock's breastbone (836 f.), and then? Surely the murder now? No, not quite yet; 'Let me split the breastbone,' says Orestes, and taking the cleaver he smashes ... —I wonder whether here too Euripides deliberately selected and placed his words in order to make their reference ambiguous?[13] Does Orestes *smash* Aegisthus? The audience may have been expecting a designation of the king to follow the word 'smashes' as its object, but if so, their expectations are again cheated. Orestes simply smashes the breast-bone. The murder of Aegisthus follows three lines later, finally achieved after three false clues.

The reason why Euripides lays this false trail in his *Electra* is not hard to seek. By making his audience wonder at each mention of a weapon whether this is going to be the climactic moment of murder, he sets everybody on tenterhooks and builds up tension. For a further and more brilliant exploitation of this technique—more brilliant because its creation of suspense is linked to a precisely calculated expository purpose—we must turn once again to the *Orestes* and to the way in which this play handles the fate of Helen.[14]

Helen had returned to Argos on the previous evening, slinking into the royal palace under cover of darkness. Orestes, Electra, and Pylades determine to kill her as an act of desperate vengeance. After Pylades has expounded his plan (1105 ff.) he and Orestes go off into the palace to commit the murder. The audience is now fully prepared for Helen's death off stage in the palace. Meanwhile Electra and the chorus sing a lyric duet. Electra is listening at the palace door. She can hear no sound: have the murderers' swords been blunted by Helen's beauty (1287)? Then from inside the palace the cry of the victim is heard: 'Help me, Pelasgian Argos, I'm being foully murdered' (1296). Five lines later Helen repeats her off-stage shriek: 'Menelaus, I'm dying' (1301). In 408 B.C., when the play was first presented, an audience was well accustomed to such off-stage cries at the irreversible moment of death. The children in Euripides' *Medea*, for example, had so cried out twenty years before; more recently Clytemnestra had done so in his *Electra*. And yet the audience must have been surprised here by Pylades' plan and by Helen's death screams, for Helen was never so murdered in the other versions of the myth that the audience could have been expected to know. What is Euripides up to?

The audience waits for an explanation, for confirmation that the murder has really occurred. At this point Euripides dazzles his audience by substituting for the expected messenger speech an eccentric monody by a Phrygian slave. This particular instance of the unexpected has been much discussed, and neither the choice of character nor the form of his narrative concerns me here. The barbarian slave was an eyewitness of the events in the palace. Orestes and Pylades sat before Helen's chair and begged her for life. Helen was engaged in the dutiful housewife's chore of spinning. Orestes asked her to step down to the hearth with him. She followed him unsuspectingly. Pylades hustled away all her slaves and locked them out. The two men now drew their swords, and (1460 ff.)

> Like wild boars in the hills they stood,
> Faced her and said 'You're going to die, to die.
> Your murderer is your own damnable husband
> Who betrayed his brother's son, left him to die
> Here in Argos.' And Helen screamed, she screamed
> And with her white arms she beat her breast,
> Struck her poor head, and ran,
> Ran in her golden sandals.
> Orestes came forward, grasped her hair,
> Forced her head back over her left shoulder.
> He was going to thrust his black sword in her throat . . .[15]

The slave's monody fixes those previously heard off-stage cries precisely in their context, and it has now reached the very moment of the death blow. But at this climactic moment the chorus-leader intervenes, asking about those slaves of Helen that Pylades had hustled away, and the Phrygian slave pauses to tell what had happened to them. Once again Euripides has brought Helen to the moment of death and then deliberately switched our attention elsewhere just before the *coup de grâce*. Why is he playing this game, which film and television serial-writers have since trivialized, of ending sections of his play with the audience still in suspense?

The Phrygian slave returns to the story of Helen eighteen lines later (1490 ff.), with words that are designedly ambiguous:

> Poor Hermione arrived at the palace
> At the point when the mother who bore her
> Sank to the ground to die . . .

The word here translated 'at the point' is the preposition ἐπί, and it is followed by the dative φόνῳ (i.e. 'the killing'). With this case ἐπί may mean either 'on the point of' or 'directly after'. There can be no doubt that Euripides has chosen it here deliberately for its ambiguity. For a brief while longer he wishes to be evasive. Then at last, after his trail of misleading clues, he reveals the solution to his little mystery.[16] The murderers have been diverted by the arrival of Hermione, leaving Helen either dead or about to die. They seize Hermione, and (1493 ff.)

> Then once more
> They turned to butcher Helen. But she
> Disappeared out of the room,
> Right out of the palace, O Zeus and Earth,
> O Light and Night, whether by magic
> Or some thieving trick of the gods.

As in the messenger speech of the *Electra*, Euripides has repeatedly teased his audience with delusory anticipations of the climax; but here there is another dimension to his exploitation of the unexpected. The audience had been cheated into believing that Euripides, in his apparent intention of killing Helen off, was rejecting the more familiar versions of the myth, which apotheosized Helen instead of giving her a merely human end. Here the red herrings not only make the story more exciting, they also enable the poet to delay his climax and to make the solution more surprising of a very unconventional plot.

In these examples from the *Electra* and *Orestes*, the red herrings, unlike good Victorian children, were heard but not seen. Euripides, however, did not confine his exploitation of misleading clues only to the narrative part of his tragedies. He liked to throw audiences visually off the track as well. His method was a clever one, although our ignorance of many aspects of ancient play production prevents an accurate assessment of its visual effectiveness. The final scene of the *Medea* provides an excellent example of the technique, as N. E. Collinge observed in a perceptive little paper.[17] Medea's magic has killed Jason's new bride and the bride's father. Medea herself has disappeared into the palace to murder her two young children. Jason now enters. He knows his bride is dead, but he hopes still to rescue his children and punish Medea. After learning from the chorus-leader that his children too are lying dead inside the palace (1309, 1313), he immediately gives his orders (1314 ff.):

> As quickly as you can unlock the doors, men,
> Undo the fastenings. I wish to see this double evil,
> My children dead, and her—her I shall repay.

The audience's visual attention is now wholly directed on those palace doors at the back of the stage, and I dare say that the play's first producer ensured that the men unlocking the doors did all they could to mislead the audience into thinking that the imminent spectacle of horror would be revealed through those opened doors, just as similar spectacles had been in so many earlier tragedies. But while the audience's eyes are glued on the doors, Medea appears far above them, probably on the flat roof of the stage-building that represented the palace. She rides triumphantly in the chariot of the Sun, holding the corpses of her children in her arms, totally out of reach now of the puny mortals below:

> Why do you batter and unbar these gates,
> Searching for the corpses and me the murderess?

These first words of hers (1317 f.) are clearly intended to raise the audience's eyes from their false target to the true one.[18] It is a powerful stroke of theatre, justified by the contents of the scene it introduces.

Euripides repeated this stroke successfully in the *Orestes* twenty years later, when memories of its original impact would have faded enough for its effective re-exploitation. But the repeat, as often in Euripides, brings in exciting new features. The final scene of the *Orestes* opens in a way remarkably parallel to its counterpart in the *Medea*.[19] Orestes, Pylades, and Electra have retired into the palace, and a rumour about Helen's murder has reached Menelaus. He enters the stage like Jason before him, and again the attention of the audience is directed at the palace doors on the back wall of the stage, as Menelaus orders them to be opened (1561 ff.):

> Let the doors be opened. Men, I command you,
> Push wide the gates. Let us at least
> Rescue my daughter from the hands of the killers,
> And recover my poor wife's body. In revenge
> I'll kill with my own hands the murderers of my wife.

And as the bolts of the doors creak and clatter, with the eyes of the audience riveted on the expected tableau that will be revealed (they think) when the doors are open, once again a voice is heard from the roof (1567 ff.):

> You there, don't lay a finger on that door, you, I say,
> Menelaus, with your towering, insolent threats,
> Or else I'll tear apart the ancient cornices
> And smash your head with this coping-stone . . .

The speaker is Orestes, and on the roof with him are Electra, Pylades, and the hostage Hermione. Hermione has a sword at her throat, and the murderers carry flaming torches for firing the palace. The spectacle is as impressively horrific as its counterpart in the *Medea*, and the device of directing the audience's eyes initially in the wrong direction is identical. But this *Orestes* scene has one major surprise yet in store. There is first an angry conversation between Orestes and Menelaus, in which Orestes lays down impossible conditions for the release of his hostage. As the exchange closes, with Orestes already telling Pylades and Electra to fire the palace, Apollo suddenly appears as *deus ex machina* in order to resolve the

impasse. It is not relevant to my present purpose to debate the acceptabil-
ity of Apollo's controversial settlement of the dramatic problems, but only
to point out that Apollo has Helen there with him in process of apotheosis,
and that in the original production the god would have been swung out on
a crane above the heads of the figures on the roof, thus creating a triple-
decker effect which in its time would have been novel and spectacular.

It would be very easy to extend this list of examples of the techniques
that Euripides uses in order to exploit the unexpected, and this could be
done without any departure from my brief, which limits the illustrations
basically to four selected plays. For example, the *Medea* provides at least
three further, and very different, exploitations by Euripides of surprise,
suspense, and the unexpected. Medea's first entry in this play is preceded
by a lively account of her distraught, unstable state, and by blood-curdling
off-stage laments in which Medea threatens suicide and the murder of her
children, her husband, and his new bride. Yet when Medea eventually
appears on stage she is entirely in control of herself and delivers a tautly
argued, rational speech. Then later, after Medea has announced her
decision to murder her children, she calls them out on stage (894), where
they remain for a time; then they go off, then come back again, and then go
off for the last time all in the space of some 200 lines after Medea had first
called them out. As Sir Denys Page has noted in his commentary on the
play, 'these frequent departures of the children are of very powerful
dramatic effect: we know that at any moment now they will be leaving the
stage for the last time; each time they leave we think "this is the last time;
we shall not see them alive again"': and our suspense is renewed with each
return to the stage.'[20] The third exploitation of the unexpected contains a
delightful irony. It comes at the end of the messenger speech, after the
deaths of Jason's bride and of Creon her father have been described with a
delicate, lurid vividness. I quote this messenger's closing words (1224 ff.):

> Our human life I've always thought a shadow,
> Nor do I fear to say that those who seem
> Wise among men and careful about words—
> They really are the biggest fools of all.
> For of mortal men there's none that is happy (εὐδαίμων);
> When wealth flows in, one man might be perhaps
> Luckier (εὐτυχέστερος) than his neighbour, but happy (εὐδαίμων)? No.

Messengers in Greek tragedy are notoriously prone to moralize at the ends
of their speeches, but none other so delightfully as this. After pouring
scorn on those fools who care too much about words, he goes on to draw
a nice verbal distinction between εὐδαιμονία (internal happiness) and
εὐτυχία (external good fortune): a perfect example of the type of quibb-
ling he has just now so scornfully labelled. Could any messenger speech

end in a way so unexpected, or so ironically parodic of the dramatic convention that Euripides himself so often follows?

But I have no intention of tailing off this paper with a dull, disorderly collection of briefly sketched examples. That way lies mental indigestion. Better to close with one final illustration different in kind from all the previous ones, although of course it contains its unmistakable Euripidean flavour. It comes from a scene of the *Helen* which has always delighted audiences and critics alike. Helen has tried in vain to persuade Menelaus that she is the genuine Helen, and that the creature just shipwrecked along with Menelaus was only a phantom. At this point one of Menelaus' shipwrecked companions[21] enters (597) with the news that the phantom Helen has disappeared into thin air. Menelaus now realizes who the real Helen is, and the scene ends with a lyrical duet of reunion between Helen and Menelaus. The shipwrecked companion, however, makes no effort to leave the stage, either during or after the reunited pair's duet, although his primary dramatic purpose—that of reporting the disappearance of the phantom Helen—is now achieved. Why does he linger? The audience must have wondered what new trick Euripides had up his sleeve. At the end of the lyrical duet, the shipwrecked companion comes forward, and after a brief conversation with Menelaus he takes the centre of the stage to deliver a long, rambling speech which does nothing to advance the plot. He maunders on like another Polonius, with thoughts about the gods, the relation of hard work to fortune, the past experiences of Menelaus and Helen, Helen's reputation, the wedding long ago, and the qualities desirable in a good slave. This speech, as A. M. Dale's commentary on the play well notes, has 'a degree of artlessness deliberately intended to characterize the speaker'.[22] Menelaus puts up politely and good-humouredly with the shipwrecked companion's ramblings, and orders him to carry the news of the real Helen's discovery back to the rest of Menelaus' shipwrecked crew. The amusing little interlude appears now to be over, and we look forward impatiently to the next developments in the plot. 'It shall be done, my lord,' says the shipwrecked companion (744), and we are ready for him to leave. But no: he still lingers on stage, and now he launches into an attack on prophets and prophecies, which may have had a certain relevance to the story and to the Athenian situation in the aftermath of the Sicilian failure, but here—! With an audience growing more and more impatient for this windbag to depart and for the plot to get moving again, what could be more inappropriate? Has Euripides miscalculated? I do not think he has. By retaining this Polonius a little while longer, he is leading up to a diverting theatrical stroke which is made possible only by the audience's increasing impatience over the garrulity of a minor character. At the end of his speech about prophets and prophecies the shipwrecked companion finally departs, wafted on his way by a polite

comment from the chorus-leader. Helen now comes forward and begins
with a very business-like 'Well then' ($\epsilon \tilde{\iota} \epsilon \nu$), thus suggesting to the audience
that they may now look forward with relief to speedy developments in the
action. But what really happens? This is the speech of Helen's, inaugur-
ated by its business-like 'Well then' (761 ff.):

> Well then: so far, so good. But, my poor husband,
> How did you escape from Troy? There's no advantage
> In learning this, but when you're close to someone,
> You long to hear even about his sorrows.

Euripides was always ready for a game with his audience. He usually knew
just how far he could tease them. Here he must have calculated that when
they heard this last speech of Helen's, designed so obviously to introduce a
brilliant but oh! so long narrative by Menelaus about all his adventures
these last seven years as he tried in vain to sail home from Troy, being
buffeted here, there, and everywhere except on to his native Peloponnese,
his audience would have had enough. They would be likely to rebel. No
red herring was ever dangled more infuriatingly. Menelaus' reply (765 ff.)
deserves full quotation:

> Your single question asks me so very much.
> Why must I tell you of the Aegean disasters,
> The Euboean beacons of Nauplius, and Crete,
> The Libyan towns I came to, the crags of Perseus?
> If I sated you with stories, I'd be as pained
> In the telling as I was in the suffering.
> That would be double agony.

To this Helen responds in words that the whole audience must have
echoed (772), 'Your answer was far better than my question.' And as the
plot now does begin to move forward very quickly, we shall leave it there,
for Euripides' present game is over.

And so is this paper, in which I have tried to illustrate some of the ways
in which a serious dramatist can use his skill to lighter ends. By teasing his
audience, by laying false clues, by exploiting the conventions of tragedy,
Euripides panders partly to his own cleverness, but partly to the
audience's need to be exploited, partially misled, and surprised. It would
be folly to claim that such devices are Euripides' most important memorials, or that they are likely to please everyone. 'Be clear,' said the god
Dionysus to Euripides near the end of Aristophanes' *Frogs* (1445), 'and
not so clever.' Nevertheless, in its exploitation of the unexpected, Euripides' cleverness solves some purely dramatic problems and thereby has
its own justification, as I hope my readers will agree. And even if they do
not altogether agree, at least Euripides, unlike Mrs. Luna in Henry
James's novel,[23] did have the courage of his own frivolity.[24]

NOTES

1. The Theodore Spencer Memorial Lecture of 21 November 1950 (London, 1951), p. 32. In the first act of Tom Stoppard's play *Rosencrantz and Guildenstern Are Dead* Guildenstern puts the point more ironically: 'What a fine persecution—to be kept intrigued without ever quite being enlightened.'

2. 2 (1969), 142.

3. This limitation of scope, together with the organization of my material that it involves, has certain inevitable consequences, which have given rise to demurrers on the part of some Euripidean scholars with whom I have had the privilege of discussing this paper: particularly Professor Richard Kannicht, to whose generously detailed comment my final draft owes a great deal. The central objection is this: that by presenting my ideas in the way that I do, I deliberately turn my back on a question of central importance: the question, to whom are the developments in each particular scene that I discuss a surprise? To the audience primarily, or only to the characters on stage at the time, or to characters and audience together? That this distinction is always relevant and occasionally of crucial importance, I make no attempt to deny; but if my paper had been focused on that question, it would have been a different paper, and several points of a different kind would have been at least blurred, if not entirely removed from the field of vision.

4. Op. cit., 131 f.

5. A trifle cynically, and yet at the same time (as Kannicht does well to remind me) with a precisely calculated dramatic intention. Electra's suicide threat in the brief preamble to the messenger scene (755) picks up the similar threats that she expressed at the end of the previous episode (686 ff., 695 ff.), and thus emphasizes the depressive side of her hysterical character at a moment of nervously tense uncertainty.

6. Op. cit., 131. Cf. also Méridier's and Barrett's annotations ad loc., and Peter Arnott (not to be confused with the author of this paper), *Greek Scenic Conventions* (Oxford, 1962), pp. 36 f.

7. In Sophocles' *Philoctetes*, which was produced some years after Euripides' *Electra*, the older dramatist plays with dramatic convention in a way curiously parallel to that of Euripides here. Philoctetes asks the chorus to withdraw (1177), the chorus agree to do so (1180), but then Philoctetes changes his mind (1182) and the chorus remain on stage. Here clearly Sophocles plays his game with the conventions of tragedy in a situation of high dramatic quality, in order to illuminate one effect of pain on a heroic character.

8. There is some doubt over the precise moment of the chorus's exit; cf. the commentaries of Dale on 374 and Kannicht on 385.

9. It would have been an attractive bonus to the argument if I had been able to claim that this was the first time that a tragic chorus had made so dramatic an exit on to the stage and off by the palace's central door in the middle of a play, but such a suggestion would be injudicious: too many fifth-century tragedies have passed into total oblivion. Admittedly, there are only four or five other known instances of a tragic chorus leaving its post in the orchestra in the middle of a play. At Aesch. *Eum.* 231, Soph. *Aj.* 814, Eur. *Alc.* 743, and *Rhes.* 565, the chorus leaves the orchestra and then later return through the *parodoi*, so never stepping on the stage. Eur. *Phaethon*, fr. 781 Nauck² = 245 ff. Diggle, is more puzzling. It is often alleged that here either the main chorus itself or a secondary chorus is ordered into the palace during the play by Merops (cf. P.Decharme, *Euripide et l'esprit de son théâtre*, pp. 424 ff.; W.Ritchie, *The Authenticity of the Rhesus of Euripides*, pp. 118 ff.), but recently powerful voices have been raised against that interpretation (cf. Diggle's edition of *Phaethon*, p. 150 n.2).

10. Cf. Kannicht's edition of the play, ii. 10 f.

11. This translation is basically Edmonds's.

12. Pp. 50 f.

13. The Greek runs λαβὼν δὲ κόπτει ... When the actor paused on this verb at the penthemimeral caesura, the audience could not immediately have known whether an object such as νῶτον Αἰγίσθου was likely to follow it or not.

14. Cf. B. Gredley, *GRBS* 9 (1968), 415 ff., especially his comment: 'It would seem that Euripides has deliberately created a false impression of Helen's murder, and suspended its refutation for over a hundred verses in order to make the news of her disappearance the more unexpected and effective.'

15. The author of this paper must acknowledge responsibility for this and other pieces of translation from the *Orestes*. Elsewhere the generally excellent versions of the Chicago *Complete Greek Tragedies* are used, except where a more literal rendering of a phrase or sentence is required in order to convey Euripides' purpose more exactly.

16. Unfortunately, Euripides' deliberate effect has been marred by later interpolators. After the Phrygian slave has finally and clearly announced the mysterious disappearance of Helen, he is confronted *in the text as we now have it* by Orestes, and a dialogue of muddled opacity follows in which Helen is referred to as dead (1512 f., 1534, 1536), disappeared (1555 f.: 'an idle rumour'), dead again (1566, 1579), and disappeared again (1580 ff.), without any apparent dramatic point for the twitching and switching. Muddle is removed and point restored by the deletion of 1503–36 as a later interpolation, as Gredley's paper (loc. cit. n. 14 above) convincingly argues; cf. M. D. Reeve, *GRBS* 13 (1972), 263 f.

17. *CPh* 57 (1962), 170–2.

18. Cf. K. Reinhardt, *Tradition und Geist* (Göttingen, 1960), p. 237.

19. Cf. especially H. Strohm, *Euripides: Interpretationen zur dramatischen Form (Zetemata,* xv: Munich, 1957), pp. 126 f.; N. C. Hourmouziades, *Production and Imagination in Euripides* (Athens, 1965), pp. 30 and 168; and T. B. L. Webster, 'Euripides: Traditionalist and Innovator', in *The Poetic Tradition* (edited by D. C. Allan and H. T. Rowell: Baltimore, 1968), pp. 29 and 32.

20. In his note on 894, where Page wrongly assumes an extra exit (1053) and an extra return (1069) of the children. Contrast his note on 1053.

21. He is not a 'messenger', despite what the manuscripts say; see Kannicht's commentary, ad loc., and (more briefly) Dale, ad loc., and Gredley, 410 n. 2. Kannicht's commentary discusses this scene in lively and illuminating detail, but his general interpretation of it differs substantially from mine.

22. Dale's commentary, on 711 ff.

23. *The Bostonians*, ch. 19.

24. This paper has benefited greatly from the positive criticism of several scholars: particularly A. D. Fitton-Brown, R. Kannicht, and M. D. Reeve. My debt to them is gratefully acknowledged.

ADDENDUM

On the alleged spatial separation of chorus and actors (pp. 139—42), contrast the remarks of O. Taplin, *Greek Tragedy in Action* (London, 1978), pp. 11 and 183 n. 3. On the sequence of Medea's (1) emotionally distraught laments, (2) calmly rational arguments (p. 148), see D. J. Conacher, *Maia* 24 (1972), 199–203. Cf. also Arnott, *Mus. Phil. Lond.* 3 (1978), 1–24; *Antichthon* 16 (1982), 35–43 (along with R. Hamilton's riposte, *AJP* 108 (1987), 585–99); *Antichthon* 17 (1983), 13–28.

FORMAL DEBATES IN EURIPIDES' DRAMA[1]

By C. COLLARD

The prime dramatic character of Greek tragedy is agonistic. Its myths for the most part show men struggling toward some goal, in conflict with one another, or against some force of circumstance or destiny, which is often personified in a god. Tragedy is at the same time a dramatic form restricted severely by theatrical conditions. The number of its speaking actors is held to three. It avoids the staging of any physical action like an assault or battle, let alone catastrophe, or death—for whatever reasons of narrative tradition, aesthetic convention, or simple impracticability. Despite certain ritual or symbolic aids to representation such as music, dance, and gesture, it is in consequence a drama of extreme, sometimes exclusive, verbal concentration. Exposition, development, climax, resolution, action and reaction—all movement occurs in the narrow room of at most three stage persons at any one time debating to confirm or change their attitudes or intentions—often, with a single character so placed debating within himself, in monologue or soliloquy, or in relief or opposition to another voice. My subject here is this last *mise-en-scène*: the deliberate working up of the ordinary exchange between characters into the opposition of one character to one or two others in a formal debate.

Jacqueline Duchemin has claimed[2] that tragedy's agonistic character— and particularly its formal debates—are in part its natural inheritance from a long popular or pastoral tradition of dramatic poetry—a primitive mimetic poetry, she means, of alternating or amoibaic form, which represents two contrasted characters or interests. She notes that debates as an established dramatic form, the *agon* of tragedy, appear first in Sophocles and Euripides (that is, in the surviving plays, the earliest of which, the *Ajax*, is generally put at *c*.450 B.C.); but they are absent from Aeschylus. Earlier, she had drawn attention to two other literary forms strongly reliant on the formal opposition of characters or forces. One of these, comedy, developed its idiosyncratic *agon* well before the formal debate became established in tragedy; Duchemin's other analogy, the historians' use of contrast as mode in dramatic narrative or reported argument, is less cogent from the point of synchronism, but indicative in a general way of her truth. The spoken word, and especially the reported argument, is as natural to Greek historiography as it is to Greek poetry, let alone poetic drama, when we consider the chief place of oral epic in time and influence in the Greek literary tradition. Duchemin therefore sees Aeschylus' use of alternating and pointed dialogue, especially stichomythia, as the linear ancestor of the more stylized exchanges in Sophocles and Euripides; she suggests that, while the sudden appearance of formal debates in Sophocles and Euripides around 450 is chiefly through the influence of contemporary developments in sophistic argument and rhetorical technique, it is certainly not due entirely to the sophists or rhetors. Rather, tragedy owes much to the sophists, but may itself have influenced them, from the time of its own sudden growth in Aeschylus' lifetime; it may actually have provided some kind of model for their agonistic discourses or ἀντιλογίαι.

I begin with these general remarks because, despite warnings by sensitive critics,[3] there is still an instinctive temptation to isolate Euripides' formal debates from their dramatic setting. The temptation stems from their often rigidly antithetical and symmetrical appearance in the printed text; I doubt whether these symmetries are quite so immediate to a theatre audience, but an audience is as likely as a reader to pick up the measured matching of arguments within the debates; and Euripides sometimes gives the impression of presenting and matching debating points for their own sake. Older critics of Euripides told us that our instinct is right, and that the poet is guilty of self-indulgent digression for the sake of rhetorical display, at the cost of dramatic continuity and relevance. Besides, Euripides' formal debates tend to compare badly with those of Sophocles. In this poet the debates are less rigid in structure; they are more naturally accommodated to episodic development; they are always more circumstantial in their argumentation; there is a sense of firm dramatic control as well as harmony of style.[4] Yet debates in Sophocles are often not less evidently 'formal' than in Euripides; at the end of *Ajax*, for example, Menelaus forbids Teucer to bury his brother, in a long rhesis (1052–90); Teucer replies in kind (1093–1117), but then debate gives way to angry argument; the episode ends without resolution, and after a stasimon the final episode (1223 ff.) begins with another formal exchange between Teucer and Agamemnon, running on into the reconciliation worked by the selfless broker Odysseus. There is no stiffness, no lack of circumstance, no feeling of abstraction about these debates, in this earliest surviving play of Sophocles as in the last, the *Oedipus at Colonus*: here, in the long central episode (720–1043), formal exchanges, in rhesis and dialogue, first between Creon and Oedipus, second between Theseus, Creon, and Oedipus, surround a central passage of vigorous action as Creon abducts Antigone and Ismene and then threatens Oedipus—but Sophocles gives the whole episode fluent variety. Form never dominates. Unitary structures, 'blocks' of action or matter, are avoided, for the long speeches are kept at differing lengths and dialogue never settles into stichomythia; there is constant shift in focus and mood, in the pace of argument as well as of action, fitting the busy movement of the characters onto, from, and across the stage.

What is 'formality', then, that it marks off one scene from another, distinguishing organized debate from ordinary exchange? The easier and less satisfactory distinction is purely according to form, less satisfactory because it subjects to taxonomy something not originally specific. Nor can taxonomic description be rigid: formal debates are too various and loose in structure, despite frequent responsion or symmetry between their various elements in position, length, or even content.[5] The only constant features are long 'set' speeches from each of, or all the antagonists—for sometimes there are three, not two, participants—but the length, structure, and style of these speeches are very flexible. Other elements vary even more, and may indeed be altogether absent, so that, at the barest, two opposing speeches stand almost on their own, with little introduction, or consequence, dramatic or thematic. These other elements are, first, animated dialogue, stichomythic or irregular in form, sometimes very long, preceding or following the two main speeches, or, very rarely, between them; second, shorter single speeches by the participants, usually at the end of the debate; and last, brief interventions by the chorus, normally two lines in length, to mark important divisions in the whole structure—that is, they punctuate the debate at the end of the long set speeches, where they tend to have a flatly neutral or sententious character.

The further definition of 'formality' relates to content and style. It is something more, however, than the concentration of the long speeches, or the whole debate, on a single issue toward which the parties have opposite views or intentions. We might describe many dialogue scenes in those terms, most of all those in which one character makes a long appeal to another and receives acceptance or rejection in reasoned terms, quite often in a long reply. It is rather that an issue, or the problems inherent in a crisis, become the subject of a debate through their explicit proposition by one of the participants, in Euripides sometimes through a positive challenge to argument. Indeed, Euripides commonly signals a formal debate with such words as ἀγών, ἀγωνίζεσθαι, ἄμιλλα λόγων. Such headlines, or combative premisses, mark out Euripides' formal debates most obviously from those of Sophocles; and they show his more deliberate recourse to the modes, even formulas, of forensic debate or sophistic argument. So, for example, Tyndareus reviles Orestes for the matricide:

> What argument could there be about wisdom with Orestes here? If what is good and what is not good are clear to all, was ever man more fool than he, who did not look for justice nor had resort to Greece's common law? (*Or.* 491–5).[6]

Such headlines often draw responses which accept the ground of argument marked out by the opponent, as Orestes takes up this attack by Tyndareus:

Old man, I truly fear to speak against you when I am likely to outrage you. I know, for killing my mother I am impure, but under another head, pure, in that I have avenged my father (*Or.* 544–7).

Even to define formal debates risks isolating them still further in criticism from their dramatic setting. Their success as scenes depends very much on the skill of their introduction to the stage, in the incident from which they spring, and in the harmony of their theme with the main direction of the plot, in terms of the motives or feelings they expose. They can reveal the grounds of disagreement or hostility, present or past (for they are often necessarily retrospective, like the arguments of Theseus and Hippolytus (*Hipp.* 902–1089), or, in *Electra* (998–1146), between Clytemnestra and Electra). In leading to conflict subsequently dramatized or reported by a messenger, we might expect them to occur either at the start of a play or at a critical turn of the action; indeed, most do occur before the climax. Or they may expose the history of a conflict already fought to its end, and so have no outcome except to deepen enmity or confirm hatred, as in the debate between Hecuba and Polymestor at the end of *Hecuba* (1129–1292). Or they may, exceptionally, end in agreement, rather than continuing or exacerbated hostility: so the final scene of *Heracles* in which Theseus argues the hero into enduring life, in continued proof of his ἀρετή (1214–1404: see below). Or they may have a more subtle function, as the debate between Admetus and Pheres in *Alcestis* (614–740) serves to reveal Admetus' helpless and angry disillusion after his wife's death. Or, in this same dramatic intention, they may tend to dispose the audience's sympathies towards one or other of the disputants. Here, it is worth noting that the 'winner' of a debate, where victory in it means success for a policy, or 'moral victor', whose just or sympathetic case is rewarded by victory in a subsequent conflict—the 'winner' normally speaks second, and there is no come-back for the first speaker in a reasoned speech of rebuttal, only retaliation with abuse in fast and often colloquial stichomythia.[7]

The starkest debate, least 'natural' in effect, will be one between two characters which pre-empts the dramatic room of a whole episode, thrust abruptly on an audience. The only surviving debate which risks this impression is that in the early *Alcestis* (614–740). Indeed, Euripides moves steadily throughout his work away from two-character debates cast rigidly in block-form towards the greater freedom of three-person scenes incorporating debates, rather than debates simply among three participants.[8] Conflicts most of the debates remain, usually without resolution, and they still most often precede the climax, but there is a refinement in their quality. They tend to show more of the internal constitution of the debaters, in a way consistent with their general role in the action (and this we might expect when we recognize the dovetailing of the debates into episodes): they circumstantiate inflexibility of attitudes, usually in one only of the debaters. The recognition of this more precise but subtle function is due to Strohm,[9] whose book was published before the nature and mode of characterization in Greek tragedy received its newest discussion.

In the early plays, Euripides frequently presents the issues of 'suppliant' drama in a formal debate,[10] which resembles a trial, either of the suppliant or of his persecutor, sometimes of both together. Trial-scenes are as common in the late plays, where the expansion from two to three characters increases variety and flexibility, in stage-movement of the parties, their disposition and sympathies but also in emotional range. Scenes in which one of two debaters is judge, perhaps even also prosecutor, of the other, are strong but simple drama; it is enough to think again, and only, of Theseus and Hippolytus (*Hipp.* 902–1089). There is at once greater richness, however, in scenes where two debaters plead before a third person who judges them, like Eurystheus' herald and Iolaus before Demophon at the start of *Heraclidae* (111–287), Helen arguing for her life against Hecuba before Menelaus in *Troades* (860–1059)—or where the third party waits helplessly on the outcome of a debate in which one of the debaters has power of decision, like Andromache the beneficiary of Peleus' worsting Menelaus (*And.* 547–765), or in *Phoenissae* (435–637: see below), Jocasta the victim of Polynices' and Eteocles' sterile confrontation. Trial-scenes inevitably are formal debates and feel most successful as drama, for they accommodate convincingly the strongest single external influence on the tragic *agon* as a whole, the law-court *plaidoyer*. The Athenian audience no doubt responded as readily as we to courtroom drama, because of its immediacy to our own experience and our easy identification with the emotions of the stage-persons—and because the formalities of forensic debate by their very familiarity seem less obtrusive, less interruptive of the illusion of tragic myth. That is something of a paradox, but it relates to the further problem of apparently incongruous intellectual content of these debates which I touch below. In trial-debates the speeches are shot through, exactly as they were in the law-courts of contemporary Athens, with all manner of emotional colour and narrative, or special pleading; and they are carefully organized with calculated switches from attack to defence, pre-emptions of the opponent's argument, appeals to probability, sententious or self-righteous recourse to moral truths.[11] The imagination of transfer from δικαστήριον to σκηνή is completed by the accompanying dialogue, carefully phased, where it precedes the long speeches, in its range from methodical question and answer to sudden accelerations in pace as a crack in the defence is widened, or, after the main speeches, impassioned charge and rebuttal, recrimination, hostility and defiance, which are the regular stuff to end formal debates, gain theatricality from the forensic ambience.

If in trial-scenes the mere illusion conspires with the formality, perhaps even artificiality, of some debates, in other places Euripides seems to yield to extraneous pressures in allowing the long speeches to develop a momentum of their own, as a character pursues an argument for its own sake and not that of the basic issue. Sometimes there is damage to the consistency of these persons' ἤθη καὶ διάνοια, but A. M. Dale wisely told us how to take such excursions as Euripides' own instinctive response to the 'rhetoric of his dramatic situation'.[12] We need to recognize there the poet's intellectual personality breaking poetic convention in an unprecedented way. This greater immediacy, like the whole illusion of the trial-scene, stands with the rhetorical cast Euripides gives not only most speeches in formal debates, but many other long speeches in scenes of quite differing temper (it helps create the impression that there are many more formal contrasts of argument than there actually are). So the easy yielding of any speech to technical analysis, or to taxonomic description with rhetorical labels, must not *de suo* induce its further misappreciation on grounds of irrelevant or digressive content as one governed entirely by its own ends, self-contained and self-indulgent.

The rest of this paper illustrates very selectively the development in Euripides' use of debates between his early and late plays, in the general ways I have described. Some other aspects of debates are left to implicit example.

First three early plays, in which Euripides sets an agonistic scene, or formal debate, at their very end, in order to show a conflict or hatred which lasts beyond the action the whole play has resolved: *Medea*, *Heraclidae*, *Hecuba*. Medea, her cruel vengeance taken, escaping on the μηχανή in her magic chariot, calls down in triumph to the helpless and embittered Jason (*Med.* 1317 ff.). She rejects his accusation of the children's murder, defiantly refusing him their burial. There are short rheseis, of unequal length, and fierce stichomythia (1323–88), then a final curiously dissonant exchange, in anapaests, half-abusive, half-pathetic; familiar idioms of lamenting parents help the play to its end on a note of tragedy (1389–1414).

This agonistic setting for the final display of Medea's fury is comparable with the end of *Heraclidae*, which shows Alcmena cruelly insistent on the death of captive Eurystheus in vengeance for his persecution of Heracles and the family (*Hcld.* 928 ff.).[13] While Alcmena is clearly the prosecutor (and judge), and Eurystheus the defendant, yet the premiss of her attack is contested before Eurystheus speaks. Euripides brings out the repellent vindictiveness of Alcmena by showing her ride down the moral objection that she flouts the law (of Athens, where they now are), which forbids the execution of captives. Such an objection cannot come from the equally immoral Eurystheus, so that it is raised by a third party, hesitantly by one of Alcmena's own side and, not less significantly, by a servant. Nor is it raised in a rhesis, only in a dialogue between the servant and Alcmena (961–74),[14] which divides her speech of accusation (941–60) from Eurystheus' speech in defence (983–1017). Form is adapted to accommodate the priority in dramatic logic. Or, Euripides' conception of the scene required separation of two issues both meriting exposition by formal contrast, the general problem of rights over captives and Eurystheus' particular excuse to Alcmena of being made the agent of Hera's cruelty. So Euripides wrote one loosely agonistic scene, from which the formality of plaintiff and defendant still comes strongly out.[15] That Eurystheus picks up the servant's moral objection, at the end of his speech, in his ambiguous appeal for a life which he admits is justly forfeit (1009 ff.), is in character with his special pleading. It does not lessen the impact of this extraordinary conflict: the former victim is now callous in revenge, the former persecutor now helplessly protests—just as the end of *Medea* reverses the sympathies the play's whole course has fostered. How could Jason merit such vengeance? Is justice truly justice in the hands of Alcmena?

Like Medea, like Alcmena, Hecuba too is extreme in vengeance. The end of the play, it has to be admitted, is weak in dramatic logic. It is hard to know whether Euripides uses the trial-scene (*Hc.* 1129 ff.) to help out this weakness theatrically, or the debate is his chief purpose. The treacherous Polymestor has been lured into the women's tent by Hecuba, with Agamemnon's acquiescence, and blinded; and his sons have been killed. Polymestor returns to the stage, stumbling about in a frenzy of pain, crying his fury in a broken dochmiac song, groping for Hecuba (1056–1107). The noise brings Agamemnon, who is aghast at Hecuba's vengeance, but prevents Polymestor falling on her. 'Stop,' says Agamemnon, 'put away your savagery and speak, that I may listen to you and her in turn and decide the justice of your suffering' (1129–31).

This headline to the ensuing *agon* is not a little forced, because when Hecuba got Agamemnon's complicity in luring Polymestor to the tent, she gave him a long explanation (760–802) how she sent her son Polydorus for safety to live with Polymestor, together with much gold; and how the discovery of Polydorus' body points to Polymestor as traitor, thief, and murderer. Now, Polymestor, as the unsympathetic defendant, speaks first, and a remarkable speech it is: a specious narrative of how he killed the Trojan Polydorus to prevent an enemy of Agamemnon growing strong behind his back, and then an account, *misericordiae causa*, of the horrible vengeance Hecuba took on him inside the tent (1132–82). In its richly evocative language this is more a messenger-speech than a law-court defence, but Hecuba rebuts it with a conventionally methodical demolition of Polymestor's case (1187–1237).

Agamemnon's role as judge in this trial is artificial: he has already conceded Hecuba the justice of her revenge. Besides, this is no ordinary trial, a debate *post factum*, but one in which both opponents have done murder and injured the other, in which they argue their cases after both have acted in them. Agamemnon thus serves only dramatic realism, in a simple way, compounding the illusion of a stage trial which upholds the justice and immunity of Hecuba, and she is vindicated when Agamemnon banishes Polymestor, the formal act which ends the play. Without Agamemnon we would have a scene like the end of *Medea* or *Heraclidae*, when unquenchable hatred crushes its now pathetic victim. Hecuba and Polymestor come out from Agamemnon's verdict only for a bitter stichomythia (1252–79) in which Hecuba's triumph is turned to ashes when Polymestor prophesies her transformation into a dog and her daughter Cassandra's death from Clytemnestra. Euripides' penchant for aetiology (Hecuba's death and transfiguration at the headland Cynossema: 1271–3) invades even stichomythia here, its function a weak corroboration of the plot's veracity; but it also provides in its harsh meaning for Hecuba Polymestor's only satisfaction for his punishment at her hands. Once again, as in *Medea* and *Heraclidae*, it brings a readjustment of sympathies in the play's last words; it makes us re-examine the extremity of Hecuba's vengeance.

The *Heracles* too, from Euripides' 'middle' period, has a final debate (1214–1404), but one which achieves harmony rather than confirms estrangement. This outcome is implicit from the start in the long-standing friendship of the disputants, Heracles and Theseus. The *agon* between the two is a contest of will; Theseus forces Heracles to resist the suicide that tempts him as punishment for, and escape from, the shame of having killed his children: he must be true to his ἀρετή, must live to surmount dishonour. This is a long scene in which the formality of debate is skilfully concealed. There are four long speeches, two shorter ones by Theseus each preceding a longer one by Heracles, but the central pair are the important ones; and Theseus as 'winner' speaks, as usual, second. Formal variety matches shifting emphasis in theme. Theseus' first speech (1214–28), with its charge to Heracles to brace up, is not answered at once: a stichomythic dialogue (1229–54), in which Theseus presses home this encouragement, avoids the immediate formal opposition of rhesis to rhesis. Heracles' first speech (1255–1310) half takes up Theseus' charge, half moves to new argument; Theseus' second speech (1313–39) has the same form: its first half insists again on Heracles' holding firm, its second half anticipates his concession with its promise of Athenian reward.

Similarly again in Heracles' last speech (1340–93), his concession, the formal conclusion of the debate, gives way to pathetic farewells to his father, wife, and dead children. The whole scene thus gets a natural forward movement, avoiding rigidity and 'block-form' for the debate.

In this fluent handling of a debate the *Heracles* has the accomplished style of a late play. The first debate in *Hecuba* (216–443), even earlier than *Heracles*, is also of interest to the greater variety the form enjoys in later Euripides. In a lyric scene Hecuba and Polyxena together lament the daughter's imminent sacrifice to Achilles' ghost (154–215): so two of the participants to the debate, whose sympathies are close and who form one side of it, are shown together before the entry of the third, Odysseus, to fetch the girl (216 ff.). Argument between Hecuba and Odysseus for the girl's life begins at once, but cannot affect what is determined. The victim Polyxena listens in silence, then accepts. Further, the unsympathetic party speaks second here, for good dramatic reasons: the tragedy of the helpless victim is emphasized.

Thus the scene in *Hecuba*, in which a debate is easily incorporated; the episode runs out on one of Euripides' favourite motifs, the voluntary death of a sacrificial heroine. Look now at the strikingly similar course of a scene in *Phoenissae*, which shows perfected technique (435–637).[16] It too has a lyric prelude, in which Jocasta welcomes Polynices on his return to Thebes. She sings a monody (301–54) which conveys passionately an aged mother's yearning for her estranged sons' reunion in happiness. A dialogue between Polynices and Jocasta (357–434) introduces the debate, associating these two participants and building sympathy for Polynices as the wronged exile. His final words to Jocasta are the headline to the debate proper: 'it lies with you, mother, to resolve these wrongs, reconciling kin to amity, and to end the suffering for me, yourself, and the whole city' (435–7).[17]

Three lines from the chorus announce Eteocles' entry, and twice repeat the key-word 'reconciliation'. Eteocles' first words give the debate a familiar start: 'Mother, I am here; it is a favour to you that I have come. What must I do? Let someone start the talking' (446–7). Briefly, Jocasta enjoins the brothers to drop their hostility and to present and receive each other's arguments fairly: 'Let some god be judge and reconcile the wrong', she ends (467–8). Thus, dexterously, Euripides withdraws the third participant, indeed the promoter of the debate, from the position of judge into that of witness and, finally, victim. The brothers argue: Polynices the simple justice of his case, to be restored to Thebes where Eteocles broke their agreement (469–96); Eteocles his greed for sovereignty once enjoyed, unashamedly (499–525). Now Jocasta adds a long plea for reconciliation in which she matches the arguments of her two sons (528–85). Helpless victim Jocasta may be, but Euripides uses her as an independently strong voice in the debate—in the way an audience might react. A clever speech, this: it satisfies the internal logic of the debate proper, answering the general questions it raises; but it also suits the dramatic and ethical needs of the scene. Jocasta has brought the brothers into debate: her speech shows the possible accommodation of their mutual stubbornness and in that throws up the tragedy of what follows. For at once Eteocles rejects further argument (588–93); and the closing dialogue, in the deliberately faster rhythm of tetrameters (594 ff.), typically inflames incompatible stances into implacable enmity. This is well-chosen variation in tempo, matching διάνοια, but the quality of the scene goes beyond careful development and pace. Jocasta lays bare Polynices' motives before the debate proper begins; his antagonist, Eteocles, enters only at the start, for he needs no preparation: he is not an exile seeking reparation and his motives are otherwise straightforward. Euripides purposely builds this sudden and vivid conflict of two quite differing personalities, their contrast starker because Eteocles has a rugged selfishness; so it exposes Jocasta's helplessness more cruelly.

Groupings of three participants similar to that in *Phoenissae*, where the sympathy of two is matched against the inflexibility of the third, are found also in *Bacchae* (170–369) and the *Aulic Iphigenia* (1098–1275). In *Bacchae* the overtones are more resonant than in *Phoenissae*, the sense of theatre more telling. After the parodos evoking the power of Dionysus, the aged Cadmus and Tiresias affirm their worship of the god in an uneven but natural sequence of short speeches and dialogue (170–214). Then Pentheus enters to deliver a tirade against the Lydian stranger (215–62), blind in his prejudice as he is stage-blind to the old men in their Dionysiac livery. A sure dramatic imagination conceived this argument, in which antagonisms of conviction and submission, of wisdom and arrogance, have countervailing and ironic theatrical contrasts between physical weakness and strength, age and youth. There is no dialogue in the debate, no stichomythic widening of the gulf argument cannot bridge: after the long, responding speeches of Pentheus and Tiresias come irregular shorter rheseis from both sides when Pentheus, isolated by his inflexibility, can retreat only to harsher threats.[18]

The debate in the *Aulic Iphigenia* similarly fills an episode but is even more tersely expressive. Clytemnestra has found out Agamemnon's intention to sacrifice Iphigenia; with her weeping daughter she comes out to confront Agamemnon with his deception (1098 ff.). Iphigenia listens silently to their exchange, as irregular in form as the emotions it depicts. Then Clytemnestra launches into a long repudiation of the sacrifice (1146–1208). The rhesis of Iphigenia follows, supplicating Agamemnon for her life (1211–52); this is a pleading speech, but it deploys pathos, evoking situations of filial love and its return, methodically, like arguments. Both these speeches are set off by distichs from the chorus, but not Agamemnon's reply, for that closes the episode (1255–75). Its brevity too is the measure of the scene's success. Agamemnon admits his misery, but also his inability to resist the pressure from both gods and Greeks to punish Troy. The shortness of his answer and the speed of his exit mark his discomfort; and there is no final angry stichomythia to the debate to weaken the impact. The scene leaves an impression of naturalness, therefore—nothing too rigid in the opposition of arguments, though they have been presented and countered in formal style, for these have been subjective and emotional pleas to which surrender or defiance are equally impossible.

Helen shows the same grouping of three participants but in a situation of much lighter charge (857 ff.). Helen and Menelaus plead together, each in long speeches (894–943, 947–95),[19] for the help of Theonoe in escaping her brother Theoclymenus. Theonoe is thus in the role of judge. But the debate is remarkable in two ways. It has extraordinary compactness and symmetry: it begins and ends with a rhesis by Theonoe, its arbiter, and these two speeches (865–93, 998–1029) enclose the two by the appellants, there being no other dialogue. Further, it lacks all hostility, even contrast in argument, for the appellants make common cause for the judge's favour. It is significant here that of the three plays usually classed together as romantic melodramas or intrigues, *Ion*, the *Tauric Iphigenia*, and *Helen*, only *Helen* has this fully formal debate: that in *Ion* (517–675) is very loose in structure, and the *Iphigenia* has only an 'embryonic' *agon* (674–722).[20] There are no conflicts or explicit animosities between characters in these plays which lend themselves to exposition in the usual way of formal debates. If Euripides does intend contrast with debate-form in *Helen*, and does not simply stage the scene for its own effect or to emphasize formally the crisis, the contrast is subsidiary and ethical: it lies in the differing tones of Helen, who mixes supplication with the claims of right, and of Menelaus, who rests his case straightly and sturdily on right alone.[21]

The very long second episode of the *Orestes* (348–806) is the most subtly contrived of all scenes incorporating a formal debate, and makes the best conclusion to this paper. The chorus sing of the misery and madness in Agamemnon's family. Menelaus enters on his return from Troy (348); he is aware of Agamemnon's and Clytemnestra's death—and of Orestes' condition. Orestes at once engages him in dialogue, entreating his protection against death by public vote for the matricide (380–455). Menelaus' reply is prevented by the entry of Tyndareus, whose joy at greeting him is cut short by finding him in Orestes' company (456–80). A very brief dialogue (481–91) headlines the debate which now follows between Tyndareus and Orestes: the prize is the sympathy of Menelaus, who relapses into the role of third party, or silent judge; he must decide whether to honour his obligations to Orestes as his nephew, or to respect his father-in-law Tyndareus' disgust for Orestes. In this introductory dialogue Menelaus protests to Tyndareus that it is the Greek way always to honour kinship; Tyndareus retorts that it is also the Greek way not to put oneself above the law, as Orestes has done. Then Menelaus: 'Wise men reject slavish servitude to necessity.' Tyndareus: 'Well, you go on in that belief; it's not going to be mine.' Menelaus: 'Your anger is as little wise as old age generally.' Tyndareus: 'What argument could there be about wisdom with Orestes here?'[22] This is the extraordinary start to the debate about wisdom, σοφίας ἀγών, between Tyndareus and Orestes: Menelaus, initially sympathetic to his nephew, has prompted its theme, but takes no part in it; and when it is done he comes out with his sympathy for Orestes almost destroyed.

For Tyndareus' long rhesis (491–541) develops naturally from the relation between wisdom, or sense, and law, into an attack on Orestes' lawlessness, which he invites Menelaus not to condone; and Tyndareus strengthens the honesty of his case by admitting the lawlessness of his own two daughters, Helen and Clytemnestra. Orestes' answer (544–604) protests the rightness of his matricide, putting down a lawless woman (and he hits at Tyndareus on Tyndareus' own admissions); and Orestes blames Apollo's command, who now deserts him.

Tyndareus and Orestes argue, without concession. After their speeches, there is no exacerbation, only a stiffly angry rejection of Orestes' plea by Tyndareus; he will go to the assembly, he says, to incite its condemnation of Orestes to death. With Tyndareus' second and briefer speech (607–29), the debate proper ends. Orestes turns to renew his case to Menelaus, but finds him reflecting, in doubt where he earlier defended Orestes to Tyndareus. So Orestes pleads again (640–79), formally marking out his case, claiming a return for Menelaus' debt to Agamemnon in the Trojan war, and for Menelaus' duty to the family. Menelaus' reply (682–715) is subjective and evasive, half promising help, half expressing helplessness: this is no considered reply, no argued rejection. He goes out immediately, much as Agamemnon runs from Clytemnestra and Iphigenia (*I.A.* 1275).

Now Orestes is deserted, his friend Pylades comes in, still within this one episode, to give it a logical climax in a mood of despair and yet hopeful excitement (725–806): two old friends, alone again, find for Orestes a new strength: he resolves to confront the assembly while it deliberates his execution, and defend himself before it.

The cleverness of this scene is its richly convincing dramatic sequence, the introduction and interplay of three persons in a variation upon a straightforward debate with three participants. The power of decision over Orestes' life lies with Menelaus, who veers from instinctive sympathy, from actual defence of Orestes, to desertion—but the moment, the process of this change is artfully concealed by the place and order of the forces: for the set debate is between Tyndareus and Orestes, and Menelaus responds only with doubt. The same artful disposition of formal elements makes his final speech appear none the less as the delayed judgement in the debate. Menelaus and Orestes begin the episode in dialogue; Tyndareus arrives and Menelaus listens to his σοφίας ἀγών with Orestes; then Orestes and Menelaus confront one another again. This in a sequence of rigid dialogue, formal debate comprising two rheseis, then two rheseis again—but while Orestes' second rhesis, to Menelaus, is formal in method, agonistic in tone, Menelaus' final speech is not a rebuttal of argument but a natural confession of helplessness. So Euripides avoids a stiffly abrupt end to the debate, working a smooth transition to the episode's climax between Pylades and Orestes. This is his mastery of form.

NOTES

1. A paper read to the Liverpool Branch of the Classical Association in March 1974. I have condensed the main text but added the notes.

2. *Dioniso* 43 (1969), 247–75, a supplement to her analytical study *L'ΑΓΩΝ dans la tragédie grecque* (Paris, 1945[1], 1968[2]), esp. pp. 11–37.

3. Since F. Tietze's important corrective to older views of Euripidean rhetoric (*Die euripideischen Reden und ihre Bedeutung*, Breslau, 1933), I would name: A. M. Dale, *Euripides: Alcestis* (Oxford, 1954), pp. xxvii–xxix (cf. *Collected Papers*, Cambridge, 1969, pp. 151 f., 274 f.); W. Clemen, *English Tragedy before Shakespeare* (London, 1961), pp. 45–7 (original German edition, Heidelberg, 1955); H. Strohm, *Euripides: Interpretationen zur dramatischen Form* (München, 1957), pp. 3–49 (the richest and most sympathetic study of the *agon*, to which this paper is more widely in great debt than the particular acknowledgements may suggest); T. C. W. Stinton, *Euripides and the Judgement of Paris* (London, 1965), p. 38 f. For other literature on the Euripidean formal debate see: E. R. Schwinge, *Die Verwendung der Stichomythie bei Euripides* (Heidelberg, 1968), p. 33 n. 1 ('symmetry'); A. Lesky, *Die tragische Dichtung der Hellenen*[3] (Göttingen, 1972), p. 507 n. 4 (dissertations), and my *Euripides: Supplices* (Groningen, 1975), commentary on lines 87–262: C (general).

4. Debates in Sophocles, perhaps for these very qualities, have had little separate discussion, but see T. B. L. Webster, *An Introduction to Sophocles*[2] (London, 1969), pp. 148–55, and A. A. Long, *Language and Thought in Sophocles* (London, 1968), pp. 155–60; both note other literature.

5. It was the major achievement of Tietze (n. 3 above) and Duchemin (n. 2 above) to insist on the irregularity, rather than the regularity, of formal debates.

6. 491 πρὸς τόνδε σοφίας τίς ἂν ἀγὼν ἥκοι πέρι; Porson: πρὸς τόνδ' ἀγών τις σοφίας ἥκει πέρι. codd. Dramatic context and the logic of the argument (cf. below, p. 164) bar Bothe's ἀσοφίας and it must be struck from Murray's *OCT*.

7. On the order of speakers in formal debates see A. C. Schlesinger, *CPh* 32 (1937), 69 f., and, e.g., A. M. Dale's commentary on *Alc.* 697.

8. Strohm (n. 3 above), pp. 44 f.

9. Strohm, pp. 46 f.

10. Strohm, pp. 16 ff.; cf. J. Gould, *JHS* 93 (1973), 89 n. 76, etc.

11. For these technical devices see Duchemin, *L'ΑΓΩΝ* (n. 2 above), pp. 167–216.

12. For the reference see n. 3 above.

13. The interpretation of this scene is made hard by major textual uncertainty: see G. Zuntz, *The Political Plays of Euripides*[2] (Manchester, 1963), pp. 125 ff., and *CQ* 41 (1947), 48 ff.

14. For the distribution of 961–74 between Alcmena and her servant (Barnes, Tyrwhitt) see Zuntz, *Political Plays*, loc. cit.

15. Cf. Duchemin, *L'ΑΓΩΝ*, pp. 76 and 121.

16. For the affinities cf. Duchemin, *L'ΑΓΩΝ*, p. 122.

17. 438–42 are an interpolation: E. Fraenkel, *Zu den Phoinissen des Euripides* (SB Bayer. Akad. Phil.-hist. Kl. 1963/1), pp. 25 f.

18. The sensitive appreciation of the episode by R. P. Winnington-Ingram, *Euripides and Dionysus* (Cambridge, 1948), pp. 40–58, recognizes the real but deftly concealed formality of argument; for the long speeches see pp. 45–53.

19. For the structure of these two speeches, and of the episode as a whole, see W. Ludwig, *Saphenia* (Tübingen, 1954), pp. 43–50 and 100–4.

20. See Duchemin, *L'ΑΓΩΝ*, pp. 76–8 and 121.

21. Cf. Duchemin, *L'ΑΓΩΝ*, pp. 118; Ludwig (n. 19 above), pp. 48 ff.; Lesky (n. 3 above), pp. 419 f.

22. Cf. n. 6 above.

ADDENDUM

The text of 1975 has not been changed, apart from a few small corrections to references; to have rewritten it would have been false to its original conception as a lecture (see n. 1).

The paper has generally been cited with approval, but not everything has gone unquestioned. I would, I think, now concede something to criticism on two points: (1) that I have applied the term 'formal debate' rather too widely, by including scenes which have many, but not all, of the compositional elements typifying the *agon* as narrowly defined at pp. 155 and 158 of the paper (see in particular M. Lloyd, *The Agon in Euripides* (Oxford, 1992); my now more circumspect approach may be seen in the discussion of *Hecuba* 216–443 (p. 161 of this paper) in my *Hecuba* (Warminster, 1991), ad loc.); and (2) that I have sometimes used inappropriate criteria of rhetorical relevance or texture, e.g. at p. 154 (see in particular M. Heath, *The Poetics of Greek Tragedy* (London, 1987), pp. 130–7, whose own position is given by, e.g., p. 131, 'rhetorical ethos is a matter of assuming in a given speech the *persona* which best suits and supports the thought there expressed'; and S. Goldhill, *Reading Greek Tragedy* (Cambridge, 1986), pp. 230 ff.). I might defend myself against those criticisms by observing that my intention in the paper was to evaluate the 'formal debate' as a dramatic form in its totality—something recognized by D. J. Conacher, 'Rhetoric and Relevance in Euripidean Drama', *AJP* 102 (1981), 3–25, who (esp. at 18–25) has very useful supplementary remarks on the *agon*; to his generally wider treatment of rhetoric in drama should be added especially R. Buxton, *Persuasion in Greek Tragedy* (Cambridge, 1982), with (pp. 162 ff.) remarks on the *agon*; and on Euripides, B. M. W. Knox in *Cambridge History of Classical Literature*, I. *Greek Literature* (1985), pp. 327–30.

Two details:

n.6: the text of *Or.* 491 continues to exercise editors. Bothe is followed by C. W. Willink, *Orestes* (Oxford, 1986), who dismisses Porson as involving 'too much alteration' and 'inferior'. M. L. West, *Orestes* (Warminster, 1987) changes to πρὸς τόνδ' ἀγών τις τοῦ σοφοῦ γ' ἥκει πέρι, like Porson giving the *agon* the positive headline ('wisdom') which I am sure it must have.

n.17: *Pho.* 438–42 are retained as authentic by both E. Craik, *Phoenissae* (Warminster, 1988) and D. Mastronarde, *Phoenissae* (Leipzig, 1988).

EURIPIDES' *ALCESTIS*

By MICHAEL LLOYD

Alcestis not only contains an unusual mixture of serious and comic elements, but the plot itself seems to be pulling in two quite different directions. There is a happy ending in that Alcestis is restored to Admetus, and Admetus contributes to this by his hospitality to Heracles. But much of the play seems to deal with failure: Alcestis is shown to have more to lose by her death than other characters in Euripides who sacrifice themselves, and her sacrifice does not even seem to succeed, in that the life which it gains for Admetus comes to seem worse than death to him. Admetus himself has been criticized for having accepted the sacrifice in the first place, for being concerned with his own suffering rather than feeling genuine grief for Alcestis, and for offering inappropriate hospitality to Heracles.

Interpretations of the play have tended to emphasize one aspect of it at the expense of the other, and even those which recognize both its happy and its unhappy elements have had difficulty in explaining the relationship between them. One popular view is that Admetus comes to realize only after Alcestis' death that he should not have allowed her to die for him, and that he is rewarded by having her returned to him for his increasingly sincere sorrow and perhaps also for his hospitality to Heracles.[1] But it is not clear that Admetus' sorrow is any less sincere at the beginning than it is later, and he does not at any stage conclude that he ought not to have accepted the sacrifice, a question never properly discussed in the play. Heracles would have rescued Alcestis whether or not Admetus had felt sincere sorrow for her death: he is prompted only by Admetus' hospitality, and it is not clear how this virtue could be thought to balance out his alleged selfishness in accepting the sacrifice. 'As a husband he is perhaps not up to the standard, but then what a host!' was Verrall's scornful summary of this kind of interpretation.[2]

Verrall himself thought that the play makes more sense if it is taken as a comprehensive condemnation of Admetus, and this view was taken up by Kurt von Fritz in an influential article.[3] Von Fritz argued that we must be critical of Admetus from the start because we know that he has accepted the sacrifice, so that his lamentation can at no stage be taken seriously. He never realizes that he should not have accepted the sacrifice, but remains egotistically obsessed with his own suffering. Even his hospitality to Heracles is not to his credit: Admetus is concerned only for his reputation, he betrays Alcestis by offering hospitality so soon after her death, and Heracles would have rescued her anyway if Admetus had only told him what was the matter. The main point of the Heracles scenes, von Fritz thinks, is to show the difficulties Admetus has got himself into by accepting the sacrifice. In general, von Fritz argues that Euripides has undermined the moral presuppositions of the myth by showing what is really involved in a man's accepting the sacrifice of someone else's life to save his own. The happy ending is an ironic reversion to the atmosphere of the myth and, like that of *Orestes*, it is not to be taken seriously. Other scholars have followed von Fritz in emphasizing Euripides' realistic treatment of a somewhat naïve myth, but have argued that the point of this is less to condemn Admetus than to demonstrate the tragic way in which he cannot realistically profit from the sacrifice.[4]

Thus von Fritz and his followers have found consistency in *Alcestis*, but only at a high price: the happy ending, in particular, is a stumbling block, and the virtue of Admetus' hospitality, of which Heracles himself is clearly aware, cannot be explained away so easily. Anne Burnett has gone to the opposite extreme, emphasizing the happy ending but glossing over some of the unhappy elements of the plot.[5]

One of the most important features of Euripides' treatment of the story is that Alcestis' offer to sacrifice herself, and Admetus' acceptance of that offer, are not represented in the actual play but took place at some indeterminate time before the beginning of the action. *Alcestis* is not the only play by Euripides to begin with some crucial event or decision already in the past. In *Medea*, for example, Jason has already left Medea and married Glauce when the play begins, while at the beginning of *Hippolytus* Hippolytus has already angered Aphrodite and she announces her determination to punish him in the prologue (*Hi.* 21 f.). She has already afflicted Phaedra with love for him when the play begins, just as Dionysus has already driven the women of Thebes mad at the beginning of *Bacchae*. Several plays (*Heraclidae, Andromache, Supplices, Heracles, Helen*) begin with a suppliant tableau, a vivid way of representing a state of affairs that has already built up to a crisis.

In many of these plays, including *Alcestis*, crucial events from the past are, as it were, re-enacted in the play itself. Thus, in Medea's first scene with Jason (*Med.* 465 ff.), the points made by both characters are those which would naturally have been made when Jason was thinking of leaving Medea in the first place. Orestes re-enacts his decision to kill Clytemnestra in his speech in the *agon* with Tyndareus (*Or.* 544 ff.), and in the *agon* of *Phoenissae* Eteocles and Polyneices re-enact the dispute that led to the present crisis (*Pho.* 465 ff.). In *Alcestis*, the scene in which Admetus agrees to the requests made by Alcestis in return for her sacrifice (*Alc.* 280 ff.) might more naturally have taken place when she first offered to die, and his scene with Pheres (629 ff.) re-enacts what might have been said when the question of Pheres dying for him arose in the first place.

It would not, in fact, have been difficult for Euripides to arrange the play in such a way that it actually showed Pheres' original refusal to die and Alcestis' offer to do so. It is thus all the more significant that he has not done this, but begins the play with these events already in the past. The reason, I would suggest, is that Euripides concentrates on what is to happen given that the sacrifice has already been made and accepted, just as in the other plays the emphasis is on the resolution of the crises that have built up before they begin. He suppresses the question of whether Admetus should have accepted the sacrifice at all (in the *agon* it is Pheres' refusal to die, not Admetus', that is re-enacted), a question that could not have been avoided if that acceptance had been shown in the play itself. Similarly, there is less emphasis on Alcestis' heroic decision to die, a kind of decision which Euripides often represented in his plays, and more emphasis on what she has to lose by dying. Some scholars have thought that the point of this, especially as Euripides has introduced a gap between Alcestis' offer and the day of her death,[6] is that her attitude to the sacrifice has changed: perhaps she regrets, as a wife and mother, the offer that she made as a bride and her death appears as a melancholy duty, the reasons for which are less compelling than they had been.[7] But, although it is true that Alcestis seems less enthusiastic than Euripides' other self-sacrificing characters, there is no evidence that her attitude has changed.

The account of her last moments is in three sections: the maidservant's speech (152–98), the lyric dialogue between Alcestis and Admetus (244–72), and their speeches with the ensuing stichomythia (280–392). The maidservant's speech describes Alcestis' farewell to her household and, while revealing her feelings for Admetus indirectly,[8] it serves primarily to show the richness of the life that she has sacrificed. In this she differs from the other characters in Euripides who sacrifice themselves, but argue that life would in any case have been worse than death for them: Macaria (*Heraclidae*), Polyxena (*Hecuba*), Evadne (*Supplices*), Menoecus (*Phoenissae*), Iphigenia (*I.A.*). But Alcestis also differs from them in that she will eventually be restored to life, and the life which she regains will only have any content if we see at the beginning of the play what she has to lose. The happy ending would be rather ironic if Alcestis had gone to her death with the relish of some of the other characters and then had to live again. Thus, while Euripides normally shows his self-sacrificing characters at the moment of making their choice, when the reasons in favour of death are uppermost in their minds, he shows Alcestis on the point of death, when she naturally thinks of what she has to lose.

When Alcestis and Admetus first appear on stage together at line 244, Alcestis addresses the elements and the bridal chamber before vividly experiencing her death and bidding farewell to her children, but she says nothing to Admetus and does not even seem to be aware of his presence. Admetus himself has been accused of a failure to communicate: he has been thought lacking in genuine emotion, and more concerned for his own grief than for Alcestis.[9] But the emotional impact of the present scene is due precisely to Alcestis' being too preoccupied with her impending death to take any notice of Admetus; while Admetus, however hard he might try, cannot literally share her experience or do anything to alleviate her suffering. His language is emotional enough: ὦ τάλαινα (250), οἴμοι (258), ὦ δύσδαιμον (259), οἰκτράν (264), οἴμοι (273), and he repeatedly associates their suffering (246, 258, 265). But he cannot suffer for her, or even communicate with her. This is not due to his insensitivity or to any coldness towards him on the part of Alcestis: Euripides is not interested in touching farewells, but with the inevitable estrangement from the living of those on the point of death. Alcestis shows her fear of death more clearly than other heroines,[10] but we do not usually see them in the process of dying: Antigone shows similar fear (S. *Ant.* 806 ff.), but still would not retract the decision that led to her death.

Alcestis now delivers a speech (280–325)[11] in which she reminds Admetus what he owes her and enjoins him not to remarry. This speech is quite different in purpose from the speeches by other self-sacrificing characters (e.g. *Hcld.* 500–34, *Pho.* 991–1018, *I.A.* 1368–1401) in which they explain their decision to die. They are all trying to persuade others that it is right that they should die, and thus concentrate on the purposes of their sacrifices, while Alcestis has already had her sacrifice accepted and thus has no further need to go into the reasons for it. The purpose of her speech is to make Admetus promise to look after the children, and she thus stresses how much she has sacrificed and how much he owes her.

Alcestis points out that she could have remarried and lived in royal prosperity (282–6),[12] just as Macaria says that she has sacrificed her prospects of marriage for the safety of her brothers and sisters (*Hcld.* 579–83). But Macaria (*Hcld.* 591f.), like Iphigenia (*I.A.* 1398f.), speaks of the good achieved by her sacrifice as a substitute for marriage and children, while Alcestis says nothing of what makes her sacrifice worthwhile. Alcestis also differs from the other heroines in thinking of the enjoyable life that she could have led: Macaria (*Hcld.* 516–27) and Menoecus (*Pho.* 1003–5) contemplate the reproaches that they would deservedly incur if they refused to die, Polyxena would have endured a life of slavery (*Hec.* 359–66; cf. *Tro.* 634–83), Evadne does not want to live without Capaneus (*Su.* 1004–8).[13]

For Burnett, Alcestis is typical in that 'she expects a profit for those who will survive . . ., in that children who would else have been orphans (288) are yet to have both a mother and a father (377)'.[14] And again, 'she has bought a prolongation of her husband's life but she does not see this as a mere extension of the physical processes of Admetus' flesh. It is Admetus as husband and father, master of a hearth, lord of a household and ruler of a land that she would preserve.'[15] Grube goes further: it is the children's safety that she dies to ensure, and for some time yet they will need protection of a kind that Admetus can give and she cannot.[16] But the children will be just as much orphans for her death as they would have been for his (165, 276, 297, 397), and Alcestis is always said to be dying for her husband rather than dying for them (18, 155, 180, 282, 284, 462, 620, 1002).[17] The emphasis is always on what she has to lose, rather than on the purpose of her sacrifice, but this does not mean that she is disillusioned: Euripides shows her death rather than her offer to die so that she might appropriately lament what she has sacrificed, and the point of this is to make clear the richness of the life to which she will eventually be restored.

Admetus has been much criticized, both for having accepted the sacrifice and for lamenting Alcestis' death when he himself has profited from it.[18] It is, however, remarkable that, in the earlier part of the play, Alcestis' death is treated largely as a normal death. This suggests that Admetus' laments are appropriate, and that these laments are not undercut by irony can be shown by an examination of the general treatment of death in the play.

The ineluctability of death is one of the most prominent themes in *Alcestis*, and it is for this reason that the play had a great influence on epitaphs and consolation literature generally.[19] In the second strophe of the parodos (112–21) the chorus reflects on death: 'Neither oracles nor burnt offerings can avail now, not even the most distant oracles, only sought on grand occasions or in desperate need—those of Apollo in Patara or of Zeus Ammon (Amen-Ra) at the oasis of Siva' (Dale's paraphrase). Only Asclepius could have brought Alcestis back but he is dead himself, struck down by the thunderbolt of Zeus (127 f.).[20] The chorus later prays to Apollo to help now as he helped in the past (220–5), but they now know that Alcestis is alive and Apollo is invoked as the god of healing: he is not asked to infringe the boundary between life and death, nor is it supposed that he could do so. He has indeed made possible the substitution of Alcestis for Admetus but, as he says in the prologue (43–6), this does not involve actually cheating death. The servant remarks that Admetus, in begging Alcestis not to die, is τἀμήχανα ζητῶν (202 f.), Admetus himself says that he would have needed the power of Orpheus to bring her back (357–62),[21] and the chorus wishes that it had a similar power (455–9). Heracles' advice to the servant (773 ff.) is based on the belief that we only live once, and should therefore make the most of the life that we do have. These ideas are summed up by the chorus in an impressive ode (962 ff.): nothing is more powerful than Necessity, it cannot be overcome by prayers, sacrifice, or by any Orphic or Asclepian lore, and even the edicts of Zeus must be in harmony with it. They tell Admetus to endure because he will not bring back the dead by weeping (985 f.): even the children of gods must die.[22]

Thus *Alcestis* contains many statements of the ineluctability of death, more indeed than any other tragedy, and several of these statements are framed in the specific terms 'only Orpheus or Asclepius could bring people back from the dead'. But *Alcestis* is also the one play in which someone actually is brought back from the dead, and Heracles appears with Alcestis immediately after the powerful and explicit ode on Necessity. Furthermore, we are reminded of earlier statements about death even after Alcestis has been rescued: Heracles' wish that he could have brought Alcestis back (1072–4) recalls similar wishes by Admetus (357–62) and the chorus (455–7), and Admetus' reply that it is not possible to bring back the dead (1076) recalls the chorus' advice to him (985f.).[23]

What, then, are we to make of these repeated statements about death? Those that are made before Alcestis' rescue cannot be undercut by our knowledge that Alcestis will, after all, be rescued:[24] this would destroy much fine poetry which is indeed true of the world as we know it. Kullmann has argued, followed by Gregory, that Necessity is shown to be best for men by Admetus' failure to derive any real profit from overcoming it. As Gregory puts it, Euripides 'constructs *Alcestis* around a suspension in the normal operations of death, the better to demonstrate the advantages of the usual arrangement'.[25] This may be true, but it does not solve the present problem: the normal operation of death is not said to be best for men, it is said to be ineluctable. For von Fritz it is the happy ending that is not to be taken seriously, but Alcestis' restoration to life cannot be dismissed simply because it is unrealistic: it is on exactly the same level of probability as her ability to save Admetus in the first place, which is the presupposition of the whole play.

Surely the point is that Euripides must treat death as final if the story is to have any force, and he does this by using the language normally associated with death right up to the moment when Alcestis is restored to Admetus. Her return to life would make no impact if it were not presented as a wholly unusual and unexpected event. We thus have a model for understanding Admetus' expressions of grief: if Euripides is prepared to treat Alcestis' death as normal by emphasizing the finality of death even at the cost of some inconsistency, then there is no reason why it should be surprising for Admetus to act as he would in the event of a normal bereavement. We are to some extent encouraged to forget both what preceded Alcestis' death and what will happen after it, and the dramatic advantages of this should be obvious.

The chorus is sympathetic throughout, and always speaks as if Admetus has suffered a normal bereavement (e.g. 144,[26] 221, 226), so that there is nothing odd about his expressing his own suffering (246 f., 258 f., 264 f.). It has been argued that it is bizarre for Admetus to connect Alcestis' death with his own (278 f.), and even to say that her farewell to life is worse than death to him (274), when he has after all accepted the sacrifice for his own benefit. But the chorus has sung that he has suffered enough to make him hang himself (227–9), and even that his bereavement shows that marriage brings more grief than joy (238–43; cf. 411–15, 878–88). The chorus even consoles him by telling him that everyone has to die (418 f.), which may seem an odd thing to say to Admetus,[27] but which is entirely consistent with the way in which Alcestis' death is presented for most of the play. Admetus' reaction is surely appropriate given that Alcestis' death is already inevitable when the play begins: he would be intolerable if he accepted her death complacently, as Pheres does (cf. 614–28), and planned to live happily ever after as in the naïve folktale.

The same applies to Admetus' appeals to Alcestis not to leave him. Burnett compares Admetus to the dissuader in the standard sacrifice action who 'bewails his own fate since he must lose a loved one, complaining that he is destroyed and begging the victim not to abandon him'.[28] In this he resembles Iolaus (*Hcld.* 539 ff.), Hecuba (*Hec.* 382 ff.), and Clytemnestra (*I.A.* 1459 ff.). But the dissuader does not elsewhere benefit from the sacrifice himself, and Knox thinks that the audience must 'sense the jarring incongruity of Admetus' appeals to his wife not to die . . . the one person who cannot possibly beg Alcestis not to abandon him and beg to be buried with her is her husband Admetus'.[29] But Admetus everywhere uses the standard language of lament: how else is he to react?[30]

Admetus' laments have not only been criticized for being inappropriate but also for being insincere. I have already mentioned some criticisms of his contribution to the lyric scene with Alcestis (244–72), and his reply to Alcestis' speech (328–68) has been condemned as frigid and tasteless. Grube, for example, writes that he 'racks his imagination for extravagant images to convince Alcestis',[31] and contrasts his manner here with his more sincere sorrow later in the play. Admetus' speech is indeed elaborate, but the point is that he is shown to make renunciations similar to those of Alcestis in a speech of similar length: his promise not to remarry (328–35), a natural response by a bereaved husband (cf. *Hi.* 858–61), echoes Alcestis' sacrifice of the possibility of a second husband (282–6);[32] his promise to hate his parents (336–42) recalls her criticism of them (290–8);[33] and his promise to give up festivity (343–7) means that he, like Alcestis (286), renounces an enjoyable life. The rest of Admetus' speech shows how much his happiness depends on her: he will preserve contact with her by means of an image,[34] and in dreams (348–56); he would have liked to descend to Hades to bring her back (357–62); he looks forward to being reunited with her in death (363–8).

Admetus' speech is thus an appropriate expression of grief, but is nevertheless paradoxical: the whole point of Alcestis' sacrifice was that he could, within limits, live a normal life and not have to make the renunciations that she has made. But far from planning to profit from the sacrifice he mimics it himself, and we see as the play progresses that the life that he has gained is intolerable to him. The climax of his recognition of this is the ἄρτι μανθάνω speech (935–61) in which he explains lucidly why Alcestis is better off dead than he himself is alive. Two points about this speech should be noted. Firstly, Admetus' grief is no more sincere or deeply felt here than it has been previously: as I have argued, his grief has been real enough from the beginning. Secondly, the dramatic emphasis is not on any recognition by Admetus that he ought not to have accepted the sacrifice in the first place, but on his unhappiness given that he has done so.[35] In real life, of course, this would imply that he ought not to have accepted the sacrifice and that his present unhappiness could have been avoided. But in Euripides' play the emphasis can be placed on how Admetus is to react given that he has accepted the sacrifice, without the question being raised of why he did so in the first place. Admetus' suffering is thus expressed, not in terms of guilt, but in terms of the immediate problem that there is nowhere for him to go now (cf. the similar dilemmas at *Her.* 1258 ff., *Med.* 475 ff., *Pho.* 1595 ff., Soph. *Aj.* 457 ff.): inside his house is intolerable because Alcestis' bed and throne are empty and the children and servants lament (944–50; cf. Iphis' lament about the emptiness of his house at *Su.* 1094 ff.); outside he would have to endure the sight of other women and the criticism of the ill-disposed (950–60).

Admetus' unhappiness, culminating in this speech, has usually been taken to show that the sacrifice is a failure or that he ought never to have accepted it. But, given the situation with which the play begins, he can react in one of two ways: he could have lived happily ever after as in the folk-tale, or he can be desolated as he is in the play. And surely he behaves as he ought to behave, and it is to his credit that he laments. This would be true even if Alcestis were not going to be restored to him, but is especially so given that she is: he can no more be reconciled to losing her than she can be to dying if the ending is to be truly happy.

But there would not have been a happy ending at all if Admetus had not given hospitality to Heracles, and in his scenes with Heracles he is subjected to a different kind of test.[36] When he presses hospitality on Heracles he shows that, for all his grief, he has not forgotten his public obligations; and in the final scene he shows that he is not prepared to betray Alcestis by taking a new wife, even at Heracles' insistence. Admetus has sometimes been criticized for giving hospitality to Heracles,[37] but it is clear that his difficulties are due only to his refined moral sensibilities: he could have enjoyed himself with Heracles and treated this as part of the good life which Alcestis died to give him, or he could have turned Heracles away without more ado and given himself over to lamentation. But the first of these courses of action would have betrayed Alcestis, and the second would have compromised his reputation for hospitality[38] and meant that Alcestis would not be rescued. Admetus does exactly the right thing by admitting Heracles but not joining in the festivity himself. His hospitality is questioned by the chorus (551 f., 561 f.), but their objections serve only to prompt Admetus' convincing defence of what he has done (553–60, 563–7): he has the last word in this exchange with the chorus,[39] and the ensuing ode (569–615) shows that they recognize the merits of his treatment of Heracles.[40] The chorus compares his reception of Heracles with the good treatment of Apollo (καὶ νῦν, 597) which brought him prosperity (τοιγάρ, 588; cf. 9 f.) and the chance to escape death, and this suggests that they regard his hospitality as a virtuous action from which he might be expected to profit.[41]

When Heracles discovers the truth he is at first shocked (816, 822), but at 833 f. his shock turns into the determination to save Alcestis that he expresses in his speech (837–60). The way in which this happens suggests that it is precisely shock and gratitude that motivate him, and we are not encouraged to consider what Heracles would have done if Admetus had simply told him what was the matter in the first place. His praise of Admetus echoes that of the chorus in the ode: he twice describes Admetus as γενναῖος (857, 860) which recalls the chorus' reference to τὸ εὐγενές (600), just as αἰδεσθείς (857) recalls αἰδῶ (601). He thus agrees with the chorus' verdict, and guarantees that the ode is to be taken seriously. He also implicitly corrects the servant's criticisms: the servant had said that he was too hospitable (809) while Heracles praises his exceptional hospitality (858); and the servant thought Admetus' αἰδώς excessive or misplaced (823) while Heracles praises it (857).

The gratitude that Heracles expresses here must be remembered in the final scene when he reproaches Admetus for having deceived him (1008–18) and gets his revenge by playing a trick of his own: doubtless Heracles has been embarrassed, but it would be absurd to deny that this embarrassment is outweighed by his gratitude. The emphasis in this scene is on Heracles' trick, and this demands that that he adopt a distant and reproachful air; it would also be tiresomely repetitious for him to state his gratitude yet again. Admetus naturally apologizes now that his deception seems to have failed (1037 f.), but he still believes that he did the right thing at the time (1039–41).

Heracles' trick is a neat reversal of Admetus' deception: Admetus had pretended that another woman, not Alcestis, had died, while Heracles presses Alcestis on him, pretending that she is a mere prize woman; Admetus reminds Heracles that he has other Pheraean friends with whom the woman can be deposited (1042–8), while previously he had refused to let Heracles stay with these same friends (539); earlier it was Admetus who observed that lamentation does nothing to bring back the dead (541, 553–9), while now he rejects similar advice from Heracles (1091); the palace that seemed large enough to accommodate the revelling Heracles (546–50) now has no room for the unknown woman (1051–61). It is Admetus' merit to recognize the difference between the two situations: the presence of a woman is an intrusion in a way that the presence of a friend is not, and it is more important to give hospitality to a friend than to run a hotel for his prize women. Furthermore, Admetus can reasonably expect Heracles to be considerate now that he knows the truth.

Heracles begins by asking Admetus merely to look after the woman, but after a time he suggests that Admetus take her as a new wife (1087). There is a serious point here: Admetus promised Alcestis that he would not remarry, and the children were both witnesses and pledge of this promise (371–6); the chorus has said that he would be hated both by themselves and by the children if he broke that promise (464 f.). Clearly the final scene of the play is in some sense a test of Admetus' ability to keep his promise, and some scholars have argued that he fails.[42] What happens is rather ambiguous. Admetus stoutly resists the pressure that Heracles puts on him for some time (1088–1106), but eventually he grudgingly gives way (1108) and tells the servants to take the woman inside (1110). But Heracles is not satisfied with this (1111), and also refuses to take her in himself (1113); he insists on giving her to Admetus himself and Admetus is forced, much against his will, to accept her (1118) before he discovers who she really is. The last lines of the play are given over to rejoicing that Alcestis is alive, and no comment is made on whether Admetus has passed or failed the test of fidelity. There would be no problem if Heracles had made some comment, or if Admetus had either refused to accept the woman at all or had been shown explicitly yielding to temptation as Pentheus is (*Ba.* 811ff.). It is more likely that the emphasis is on Admetus' failure of Heracles' test in that he shows that he can no more resist pressure from a friend than Heracles himself could, while he is shown to succeed in Alcestis' test, in that he expresses the utmost reluctance to admit the unknown woman, and clearly does not take her as a second wife. Heracles' revenge in fact depends on the assumption that Admetus is faithful, because he would not otherwise have been embarrassed by his pressure to accept the woman.

The tension between the happy and unhappy elements of the play can thus be resolved if it is interpreted in terms of the development of the action from the initial situation. The play can be seen as an examination of how a man who has already accepted the sacrifice of his wife's life to save his own is to behave, and my conclusion is that Admetus behaves correctly throughout the play. He does not plan to live happily ever after, and he would be intolerable if he did so, and he rightly repudiates complacency like that of Pheres. But neither does he lose all sense of what he has to live for, as we see when he continues to give his characteristic hospitality. He is presented with a series of problems in the play, but the dramatic emphasis is on his successful negotiation of them and not on how he incurred such problems in the first place, and this is why Euripides does not show his acceptance of the sacrifice in the play itself. In particular, the apparently unhappy elements of the plot, Alcestis' death scene and Admetus' despair, are, in the context of the whole play, as positive as the rest: in her death scene we see the richness of the life that Alcestis has sacrificed, but she will also be restored to it; it is right that Admetus should be unhappy, and this also shows what he has lost and will regain.

NOTES

1. Thus, e.g., U. von Wilamowitz-Moellendorff, *Griechische Tragödien*, vol. 3 (Berlin, 1906), pp. 65–97; G. M. A. Grube, *The Drama of Euripides* (London, 1941), pp. 129–46; D. M. Jones, 'Euripides' Alcestis', *CR* 62 (1948), 50–5. Robert Browning's *Balaustion's Adventure* is a version of the play incorporating comment and interpretation from a similar point of view to that of the scholars mentioned above.

2. A. W. Verrall, *Euripides the Rationalist* (Cambridge, 1895), p. 30.

3. K. von Fritz, 'Euripides' Alkestis und ihre moderne Nachahmer und Kritiker', *A und A* 5 (1956), 27–60 = *Antike und moderne Tragödie* (Berlin, 1962), pp. 256–321. A somewhat similar view is taken by W. D. Smith, 'The Ironic Structure in *Alcestis*', *Phoenix* 14 (1960), 127–45.

4. e.g. A. Lesky, 'Der angeklagte Admet', *Maske und Kothurn* 10 (1964), 203–16 = *Gesammelte Schriften* (Berne, 1966), pp. 281–94, partly retracting the interpretation of the play offered in his fundamental study *Alkestis, der Mythus und das Drama* (Leipzig, 1925); H. Rohdich, *Die euripideische Tragödie* (Heidelberg, 1968); W. Kullmann, 'Zum Sinngehalt der euripideischen Alkestis', *A und A* 13 (1967), 127–49; J. Gregory, 'Euripides' Alcestis', *Hermes* 107 (1979), 259–70.

5. A. P. Burnett, *Catastrophe Survived* (Oxford, 1971), ch. 2.

6. Cf. A. M. Dale, *Euripides, Alcestis* (Oxford, 1954), p. xvi.

7. Thus Wilamowitz, op. cit., p. 87; von Fritz, op. cit., p. 302; Kullmann, op. cit., 139. Such views are criticized by Dale, op. cit., pp. xvi–xvii.

8. K. Reinhardt, *Sophocles* (tr. Harvey & Harvey, Oxford, 1979), p. 246 writes, 'it would be impossible to put this moving farewell to her bed and an equally moving farewell to her husband side by side in the same passage'. A. M. Dale, *Collected Papers* (Cambridge, 1969), pp. 146 f. argues that Alcestis' feelings for her husband are implicit in the story, and do not need to be stated directly. A different view is taken by E.-R. Schwinge, *Die Stellung der Trachinierinnen im Werk des Sophokles* (Göttingen, 1962), pp. 42–69.

9. S. A. Barlow, *The Imagery of Euripides* (London, 1971), pp. 56 f. writes that Admetus is 'wrapped up in his own platitudes and concern for his own grief'.

10. Thus, e.g., von Fritz, op. cit., p. 304, Schwinge, op. cit., p. 48, J. Schmitt, *Freiwillige Opfertod bei Euripides* (Giessen, 1921), p. 74.

11. On the relation between song and speech in such tragic episodes see Dale on *Alc.* 280 ff., W. Schadewaldt, *Monolog und Selbstgespräch* (Berlin, 1926), p. 143, L. H. G. Greenwood, *Aspects of Euripidean Tragedy* (Cambridge, 1953), pp. 131–9, J. Gould, *PCPS* n.s. 24 (1978), 51.

12. Alcestis adapts a common theme: other heroines lament that they will never marry while Alcestis, already married, speaks of the delights of a second marriage.

13. Alcestis' οὐκ ἠθέλησα ζῆν ἀποσπασθεῖσά σου (287) means 'I decided not to live ...', not 'I could not bear to live ...': what she says here is a reason why Admetus should be grateful (she continues οὐδ' ἐφεισάμην ἥβης, 288 f.). Cf. Dale on 284–9, and LSJ s.v. ἐθέλω for the difference between ἐθέλω and βούλομαι. Schwinge, *Glotta* 48 (1970), 36–9 argues that because Alcestis uses the aorist ἠθέλησα her attitude has now changed. He is rightly criticized by A. Rivier, *MH* 29 (1972), 135 f.

14. Burnett, op. cit., p. 26.

15. Burnett, op. cit., p. 34.

16. Grube, op. cit., pp. 129 f.

17. S. Trenkner, *The Greek Novella in the Classical Period* (Cambridge, 1958), pp. 69 f. points out that in stories of this kind it is only when there are no children to continue the γένος that it is essential that the wife should die: by showing that Admetus has already had children Euripides emphasizes that it is for him personally that Alcestis dies.

18. e.g. von Fritz, op. cit., pp. 264 f., Lesky, op. cit., p. 282.

19. Cf. R. Lattimore, *Themes in Greek and Roman Epitaphs* (Urbana, 1942), p. 46.

20. Asclepius was actually punished for bringing people back from the dead, but no mention is made of this either here or at 3 f. when Apollo refers to his death.

21. In early versions of the story Orpheus was successful in bringing back Eurydice: cf. C. M. Bowra, 'Orpheus and Eurydice', *CQ* 2 (1952), 113–26 = *On Greek Margins* (Oxford, 1970), pp. 213–32.

22. For this consolatory motif see Menander Rhetor 3.413–14.

23. A distinction between Thanatos and Hades is implied at 871, but this distinction is not consistently maintained. Heracles is prepared to rescue Alcestis from the Underworld itself if he fails to defeat Thanatos at the tomb (850–4). See Dale on 24–6, 871.

24. R. Hamilton, *AJP* 99 (1978), 293–301 argues that we are not encouraged to expect that Alcestis will be rescued at all: equal emphasis is put on Apollo and Thanatos in the prologue, and Thanatos does not believe Apollo's prediction that Alcestis will be rescued.

25. Gregory, op. cit., 261.

26. In line 144 the chorus comments on what Admetus has lost, and the maidservant replies οὔπω τόδ' οἶδε δεσπότης, πρὶν ἂν πάθῃ. Dale observes, 'the servant's allegiance is less divided', but it was a commonplace of Greek thought that one cannot fully understand suffering without actually experiencing it: cf. *Alc.* 1078, *Her.* 1249; Soph. *Trach.* 142 f., 446 f., *O.C.* 562–8. The maidservant does not mean that Admetus' understanding of his loss is less than it ought to be but that, inevitably, he will only know what he has lost when Alcestis has actually died. She later (201–3) describes his sorrow without criticism.

27. Thus, e.g., T. G. Rosenmeyer, *The Masks of Tragedy* (New York, 1963), p. 219.

28. Burnett, op. cit., p. 27; cf. Schmitt, op. cit., pp. 73 f.

29. B. M. W. Knox, *Word and Action* (Baltimore, 1979), p. 334.

30. Admetus even begs Alcestis not to betray him (προδοῦναι) by dying (202, 250, 275), which may seem odd, especially as Alcestis died because she did not want to betray him (180). But this is the standard language of lament, and Theseus, who is responsible for Hippolytus' death, begs him not to die in similar terms (*Hi.* 1456). Cf. A. Rivier, 'Sur un motif de l'Alceste d'Euripide', *Actas del III Congreso Espanol de Estudios Clasicos* (Madrid, 1968), pp. 286–95; M. Alexiou, *The Ritual Lament in Greek Tradition* (Cambridge, 1974), pp. 163 f., 176, 182–4, and Index II s.v. 'reproach'.

31. Grube, op. cit., p. 136.

32. Admetus renounces a νύμφη Θεσσαλίς (331), while Alcestis has given up the chance to marry ἄνδρα ... Θεσσαλῶν ὃν ἤθελον (285). Cf. Burnett, op. cit., pp. 35 f.

33. Admetus' parents are also criticized by the chorus (466–70) and by Heracles (516). Greek parents normally dreaded that their children should predecease them, an inversion of the natural order (cf. Lattimore, op. cit., section 49). Elsewhere in Euripides, Hecuba (*Hec.* 382–8) and Andromache (*An.* 408–20) are prepared to die to save their children, while Iolaus is prepared to die to save Heracles' children (*Hcld.* 453–5). At *Her.* 322–5 Amphitryon asks to be killed before Heracles' children so that he will not have to see them die.

34. This does not show that Admetus is a pervert: cf. Burnett, op. cit., p. 36, Trenkner, op. cit., p. 69.

35. Thus Dale, op. cit., p. xxv.

36. The Heracles scenes are carefully interwoven with less happy scenes, giving effective contrasts of mood. The play is roughly symmetrical, with the Pheres scene at the centre, surrounded by two Heracles scenes (476–567, 747–860), which are themselves framed by two sections of lament for Alcestis (393–475, 861–1005); the play begins and ends with sections in which Alcestis is alive (1–392, 1006–1163). That the Pheres scene is central structurally does not mean that it is central to the meaning of the play, as von Fritz, op. cit., p. 307, believes: the Aegeus scene is not the most important in *Medea*. Other views of the structure of *Alcestis* are taken by H. Strohm, *Euripides* (Munich, 1957), pp. 166–8 and V. Castellani, *AJP* 100 (1979), 487–96.

37. D. W. Lucas, *The Alcestis of Euripides* (London, 1951), p. 6 writes of 'a tasteless and ostentatious act of hospitality'. Cf. Verrall, op. cit., pp. 30–2, von Fritz, op. cit., p. 59.

38. Admetus has been criticized for being concerned with his reputation, e.g., by G. K. Galinsky, *The Herakles Theme* (Oxford, 1972), pp. 67–71, but this is to misunderstand that Greek expressions of the form 'I am afraid of being called X' often imply 'I am afraid of deserving to be called X'. Cf. K. J. Dover, *Greek Popular Morality* (Oxford, 1974), pp. 226–9.

39. Cf. O. Taplin, *The Stagecraft of Aeschylus* (Oxford, 1977), pp. 205, 309 f. on the effect of a character having the last word.

40. This ode has always been a stumbling block for those determined to criticize Admetus' hospitality: see Verrall, op. cit., p. 35.

41. This is a version of the common story in which someone gives hospitality to a god or hero and profits as a result: cf. A. P. Burnett, *CP* 65 (1970), 15 ff.

42. e.g. E.-R. Schwinge, *Die Verwendung der Stichomythie in den Dramen des Euripides* (Heidelberg, 1968), p. 109; von Fritz, op. cit., pp. 262 f.; Verrall, op. cit., p. 69.

ADDENDUM

Apart from one or two minor corrections, this article appears here as it was first printed in 1985. Since then two articles on *Alcestis* have appeared which should be mentioned here: R. G. A. Buxton, 'Euripides' *Alkestis*: Five Aspects of an Interpretation', in *Papers given at a Colloquium on Greek Drama in Honour of R. P. Winnington-Ingram*, ed. L. Rodley (London, 1987); and M. Dyson, 'Alcestis' Children and the Character of Admetus', *JHS* 108 (1988), 13–23. Dyson (p. 19 n. 11) rightly criticizes my inadequate treatment of the Pheres scene, and I deal more fully with this part of the play in my book *The Agon in Euripides* (Oxford, 1992).

DOMESTIC DISHARMONY IN EURIPIDES' *ANDROMACHE*

By IAN C. STOREY

To the Memory of Norma P. Miller

The *Andromache* of Euripides has not had a good press. Sandwiched between more immediately attractive plays such as *Medea* and *Hippolytus* and the more controversial dramas such as *Electra* and *Heracles*, it has for the most part languished in obscurity with the other less appealing plays of the 420s (e.g. *Heraclidae*, *Hecuba*). More than one critic has been overtly hostile, and what interest has been shown has tended to focus on its odd tripartite structure, the elegiacs unique to tragedy in Andromache's lament (103–16),[1] the possibility of its production other than at Athens (*Σ ad* v. 445, evidence of a most doubtful kind),[2] and the two well-known anti-Spartan diatribes (445–63, 595–604).

The structure in three movements (1–765, 766–1046, 1047–288) and the lack of a central character (Andromache after all exits with Peleus at 765, with two major scenes still to be played) have left the critics puzzled as to Euripides' intentions with this play.[3] The negative assessments of earlier critics (e.g. Lucas—'the play falls feebly and mysteriously to pieces')[4] have yielded to a wide variety of interpretations. Some have adopted a naïve patriotic approach, relating to Athens, the war, and her interests in the North West (Robertson, Goossens). Garyza found the central theme of the play to be love and the relationship between women; for him Hermione is as much the centre of attention as Andromache. Erbse, on the other hand, regards Andromache as central; her superior ethical standards dominate the play, and she reappears at the end with Peleus as a silent symbol of *arete*. This reappearance of Andromache as *kophon prosopon* has been recently supported by Golder; the arguments against her appearance in this scene with Peleus are in my opinion convincing.[5] For Boulter and for Lee the tragedy is an exploration of *sophrosyne* and *to sophron*, concepts crucial to the extant *Hippolytus*. Stevens regards Andromache as an early sketch for *Trojan Women*; Troy and the War are an *arche kakon*, bringing 'bitter consequences for victors and vanquished alike'. Kamerbeek considers the play to be about Andromache principally; it is 'une expérimentation ... de tragédie d'intrigue'. Burnett includes this drama among her 'catastrophes survived'; for her the divine order is benevolent, reinforcing the nobility of Andromache and Peleus. Friedrich, on the other hand, finds a pessimistic theology; the play is a savage attack on Apollo. Kitto, who with Garyza was instrumental in rescuing *Andromache* from earlier hostile criticism, considers the work to be 'not incidentally, but fundamentally, a violent attack on the Spartan mind ... in particular on three Spartan qualities, arrogance, treachery, and ruthlessness'. Conacher and Webster both find the unity in the tripartite structure to be the repeated motif of abandonment, despair, and deliverance for Andromache, Hermione, and Peleus (Webster), or for Troy, Sparta, and Phthia—a Tale, as it were, of Three Cities (Conacher). Finally, in a neo-Verrallian extravaganza, Vellacott advances a bizarre interpretation consisting of a pessimistic view of war and of women, the centrality of the absent Neoptolemus, and an incredible view of Menelaus as Machiavelli.

My purpose in this paper is to call attention to a theme which has not yet received due attention, whose variations and restatements provide a 'subtext' to the main action. This is the theme of 'domestic disharmony' or 'domestic dislocation', in which the tragedian explores the motif of the *oikos* (or *domos*) disjointed. Let us begin with the first five lines:

> O land of Asia! O city of Thebes,
> whence with a golden hoard of dowry
> I came to the royal hearth of Priam,
> given to be Hector's wife and mother of his sons,
> in time past I was Andromache, envied by all.

The scene created is the procession and arrival of the bride from her father's to her husband's home, her marriage with her husband, and the bearing of his children, hallmarks of the perfect union. Yet in the succeeding lines we see her new home destroyed, her husband killed, and her son murdered (8–11); her *oikos* has been violently disrupted. As many as eight such disruptions can be found in the play, as Euripides shows us how disharmony rules the relationships of this play. The key words to watch for in *Andromache* are *domos*, *oikos*, *gamos*, *lechos*, *posis*, and the rare, but significant, *nympheumata*. Of these *oikos* is found more often in *Andromache* than in any other extant play; *lechos* is widely used in only three plays (*Medea*, *Andr.*, *Helen*); of the eight instances of *nympheumata* in extant Euripides, four occur in this play. These domestic terms (plus two further words which I shall add later) are the words of significance for this drama, the counterparts of *sophron* in *Hippolytus*, of *peitho* in *Hecuba*, or of *neos* in *Suppliant Women*.

I do not propose to subject the play to a running commentary on the use of these key words, but I should point out certain sections of the tragedy where these word-clusters are expecially prominent and where the text will repay a close reading: the prologue (1–116)—crucial for the first statement of these themes—Hermione and Andromache (147–231), Andromache and Menelaus (384–463), the second stasimon (464–94),

Peleus to Menelaus (590–640), Hermione and Orestes (920–1008)—a scene rich in these key words—Thetis' epilogue (1231–80).

The first *exemplum* of this theme is the marriage of Hector and Andromache, established in the opening lines as the ideal and standard against which all other relationships are measured. Even in death Andromache's devotion to her husband is repeatedly made clear (97, 108, and 222–5, a rather bizarre passage in which Andromache asserts that she nursed Hector's bastards 'so as to do nothing to hurt you'). The word *posis* in her mouth always refers to Hector, never to the son of Achilles. The bloody death of Hector is recalled on at least four occasions (7–8, 97, 108, 399–400), and Andromache is still called 'wife of Hector' (656, 908, 960). Characters in this play are more frequently called by their relationship than by their actual name (e.g., Hermione as 'the Spartan' or 'daughter of Menelaus', Thetis as 'daughter of Nereus', etc.). The domestic relationship is as important as one's actual identity. Thus the marriage of Andromache and Hector is established as an ideal, disrupted by the events of war.

The second relationship, that between Andromache and Neoptolemus, is the replacement of harmony by force. Eleven lines apart (4, 15) the same word, *dotheisa*, is used to describe Andromache given in marriage and given as spoil of war. The disharmony of their relationship is stressed throughout. Andromache is from a proud city in Asia, Neoptolemus of 'an island race' (14). She is a slave woman living with a free man (12; cf. 64, 90, 155, 434), and above all she is living with the man whose father murdered her husband (171–2, 403: 'I am a bride to Hector's murderers'). Her unwillingness is stressed (36, 390: 'I slept with my master by force'). The critics differ on the extent of Andromache's affection for Neoptolemus, but Kovacs is surely wrong to insist that the sexual relationship between them continued after the latter's marriage to Hermione—v. 37 makes that clear.[6] Neither *gamos* nor *posis* is used in connexion with this union. There is irony in the fact that this irregular union produces the only child for Neoptolemus, but his deficiency as a father only reinforces the disharmony of this *oikos* (49: 'the boy's father is not here to help me, and is of no use to the boy, being away at Delphi', and 75: 'your so-called father is still away at Delphi'). The news of Neoptolemus' death is received in terms of the desolation of Peleus' *domos* only (1070 ff., 1176, 1209 ff.). No mention is made of Andromache's loss; she is referred to only at 1243 as *aichmaloton*.

What then of Neoptolemus' actual marriage to Hermione? Here we are presented with a *gamos* which is clearly *agamos*; v. 33 is revealing, Hermione 'childless and hated by her husband'. The accusation is made constantly that the foreign slave is supplanting the true wife (31 ff., 122 ff., 155 ff., 370 f., 927 ff.—where Hermione protests, 'Shall we be a slave to those illegitimate beds which I once ruled before?'). Her entry at 147 ff. is important, for she appears dressed in Spartan finery in contrast to the implied poverty of the house of Peleus—'not from the house of Achilles, but from Laconia, the land of Sparta, my father gave me these as dowry with many riches'. We recall another bridal procession, that at 1–5, but here the father's house has so dominated that of the husband that the father (Menelaus) is actually present in the house (40 f., 581 f., 632 f.— where he is said to be ravaging Phthia as he had previously ravaged Troy).[7] At 619–21 Peleus reveals his persistent opposition to the marriage ('I kept telling him not to . . .'). Andromache at 205 ff. well sums up this unfortunate marriage:

> Your husband hates you not from any *pharmakon* of
> mine, but because you cannot live with him in
> harmony. . . . It is not beauty, but virtue which
> delights a bedmate. When you are annoyed at
> something, Sparta is all-important to you and
> Scyros of no account at all. You parade your
> wealth among those who lack it. Menelaus is more
> to you than Achilles. That is why your husband
> hates you.

At this point I would digress briefly to consider the *didyma lektra* motif which occurs explicitly three times and is implicit in the first part of the play. At 178–80 Hermione declares:

> For it is no good thing for one man to hold the
> reins over two women; those who do not want to live
> wrongly should look to one bedmate in love.

Later (909) Orestes will declare equally bluntly, 'you have mentioned a bad thing, for a man to have two marriage-beds'. Finally, the second stasimon explores the 'twin' theme by analogy from politics, poetry, and seamanship:

> Never shall I praise two beds for mortal men,
> nor children with two mothers,
> these are domestic strifes and grievous troubles.
> Let my husband cherish in marriage
> one bed unshared.   (464–70)

Several commentators have related the 'twin beds' and 'the children with two mothers' to an alleged decree of unknown date at Athens (D.L. 2.5.26, Ath. 556, who cite Aristotle and other earlier sources), by which Athenian men were allowed to have two wives or to have legitimate children by a second woman, the reason being either a general population shortage or the lack of adult males in particular. Some have assumed the cause to be the plague and so date this decree to the early 420s; thus this theme in

Andromache becomes a pointed topical allusion. This is not an unattractive hypothesis, but such allusions in tragedy are always doubtful at best, and the evidence for the decree, involving the personal lives of Socrates and Euripides, is not conclusive. I suspect that, while the decree may be historical, it belongs to a period after major war-losses, i.e. *c*.413 or 403.[8]

Overshadowing the entire play is the fourth relationship, the marriage of Peleus and Thetis. The prologue reveals the setting to be a shrine of Thetis, a memorial of her *nympheumata* (20). Again the image of the bride coming to her groom is invoked. But this too is a failed marriage; observe at 18 *xynōikei*, 'used to live'. From Ar. *Cl.* 1067–9 it is clear that in popular thought the goddess deserted the marriage (*apolipousa* used there is the technical term for marital desertion). Her home is not that of her husband, but with her father Nereus; Homer *Il.* 1.18 makes that clear, as well as 1225 of our play. The motif of the bride's procession has been reversed for Peleus and Thetis. At 1231 she returns from her father's *domoi* to her husband once more, 'for the sake of my marriage long ago to you'— *nympheumata*. Thus the setting of the play within the context of this marriage is both appropriate to the plot and relevant to the strong domestic theme which I am exploring.

Thetis is likewise the most appropriate deity to resolve the action—'her epiphany is one of the easiest in Euripides' (Grube, p. 212). She predicts two restorations of domestic harmony, first the marriage of Andromache to Helenus (cf. *eunaiois gamois* at 1245, which suggests a harmony unknown to Andromache and Neoptolemus or to Neoptolemus and Hermione) and the survival of both houses (Troy and Phthia) in the person of Molossus—here *katoikein* at 1244 reinforces the idea of an *oikos* restored, and second her own reunion with Peleus (1253–62). At 1256 f. we hear 'and then you will live (*synoikeseis*) with me in my father's house forever, a god with a goddess'. Critics differ on the tone of this epilogue.[9] An ironic tone is not unfamiliar (cf. the divine epiphanies at the end of *Hippolytus* and *Suppliant Women*, to say nothing of those in *Electra* or *Orestes*). On the other hand, Thetis may just be that rare creature, a truly benevolent Euripidean deity. However, there is clearly some irony present in her words 'in *my* father's house', when we consider the repeated motif of the movement of the bride from father to husband. The resolution is plainly on her terms, not his. Since this divine reunion of Peleus and Thetis appears to be Euripides' own invention,[10] we are entitled to speculate on his intentions in this last scene. I should regard Thetis' appearance as essentially positive and conciliatory, but not without certain ironic undercurrents in the domestic theme.

It must also be remembered that the marriage of Peleus and Thetis was in a real sense an *arche kakon*, since the apple of discord, cause of the 'hateful strife' of the goddesses, was cast on the occasion of their wedding.

The cause of the *eris* was left unstated at 274 ff., but its results form the substance of this tragedy (and of many others). The sensitive reader (or spectator) will recognize a grim appropriateness for the setting and relationship which hovers above the drama.

One may consider next the other union which will endure beyond the end of the play, that between Orestes and Hermione. The key passage is 957 ff., Orestes' disclosure of the events surrounding the marriage of Hermione to the son of Achilles. She had originally been betrothed to Orestes (966, 'You who were mine before'; 969 *dous*, the same verb used of Andromache at 4; 981, his use of *gamos* to describe their relationship in his eyes). What we have here is another dislocated union, presented in terms which do neither the father (Menelaus) nor the husband (Neoptolemus) much credit. In particular see 972 ff., Orestes' repeated request to Neoptolemus to release Hermione to him, arrogantly rejected out of hand by the son of Achilles.[11] Thus the marriage, opposed by Peleus (619), took place in violation of the natural union between Hermione and Orestes. At 984 ff. we hear:

> O. I shall take you from your home and give you
>   into your father's hand . . .
> H. My father will consider my *nympheumata*;
>   it is not mine to decide.
>   But as quickly as you can, send me from this house,
>   before the old man realizes that I am abandoning this home.

The motif of the bridal procession is again reversed, as (like Thetis) Hermione moves from her husband back to her father, to begin all over a new *nympheumata*, this time with her natural consort, Orestes. The marriage of Hermione and Neoptolemus has in fact been no marriage at all.

Three less obvious domestic situations may also be considered. Crucial to the war at Troy is the desertion of Menelaus by Helen (362 f., 'because of strife over a woman you destroyed the city of Troy', Andromache to Menelaus). Peleus in his famous tirade charges:

You were robbed of your marriage (*lechos*) by a man from Troy, when you left your hearth and home unguarded and unwatched, as if you had a chaste woman in your home. Not even if she wanted, could a Spartan girl be chaste; they leave their homes empty while they share the race-courses and the wrestling-grounds with the young men, their thighs naked and their clothes loose. No wonder you rear women who are not chaste. Ask Helen who left your home and went revelling off with her young man to a foreign country. And then for her sake you gathered and led to Troy a huge throng of Greeks. Rather than raise an army, you should have thrown her out, having found her worthless, let her stay there, given money not to take her back home. (592–609)

Both Menelaus and Helen have abandoned this marriage (n.b. *lipon* at 593 and *lipousa* at 603).[12] A clear parallel with Neoptolemus' abandonment of his home is created. We observe also the manner in which a Spartan girl 'deserts' her home for the playing field (597); the same verb will be used again (*exeremousan*—991) of the Spartan Hermione 'deserting' her husband's home. Notice also the inversion of the bridal dowry at 609, where a husband pays another to take and keep his faithless wife.

Less prominent is the 'marriage' between Paris and Helen, although its dreadful consequences for both Greeks and Trojans are a frequent theme of the play (e.g., 247, 'Helen, your mother, killed Achilles'). The best description is the opening of Andromache's elegiac lament:

Paris brought not a marriage (*gamos*) but a destruction (*ate*) to windy Troy, when he took Helen to his chambers as bed-mate, for whose sake, o Troy, a thousand swift war-ships from Greece took you captive by fire and by spear. (103–6)

We may call attention also to the domestic language employed to describe the aftermath of Troy, first Peleus to Menelaus (611–13): 'you destroyed many brave souls and made many women childless in their homes and robbed old men of their noble children', and next from the first stasimon:

Greece would have been spared the grievous woes which her young men endured for ten years circling about Troy in their ranks. Marriage-beds would not have been left empty, nor old men deprived of their children. (304–8)

Thus the theme of domestic dislocation is carried from the actions of Paris, Menelaus, and Helen to describe the sufferings of the Greeks and Trojans on a wider scale. Just as Peleus will curse the marriage of Hermione and Neoptolemus, 'which has destroyed these halls and my city' (1186), an earlier *gamos* has wrought a far more general havoc on both homes and cities.

The final domestic disharmony touched on in the play is that within the house of Atreus, in particular the infidelity of Clytemnestra, her murder of her husband, and the subsequent revenge of Orestes. This does lie outside the story-line of *Andromache*, but observe Orestes' first entry at 884, where before we learn his name, we learn his parentage ('I am the child of Agamemnon and Clytemnestra, my name is Orestes'). This is hardly the sort of ancestry in which one would boast. I suspect that Euripides is calling attention to one more disjointed home. Orestes' matricide is explicitly mentioned at 976 f., and in the fourth stasimon which follows this scene, the chorus comment:[13]

The son of Atreus has perished by the schemes of his wife, and she in turn exchanged murder for death at her children's hands. The prophetic command of a god turned upon her, when the son of Agamemnon came straight to Argos from the holy oracle to be the murderer of his mother. O god, o Phoebus, how shall I believe? (1027–36)

A little point, but it is worth noticing that at 1115 Orestes, scheming the death of Neoptolemus, is called 'son of Clytemnestra'.

We may extend the domestic theme past the picture of the bridal procession to the tableau of parent and child, the vertical element in the image of the *oikos*. The first note is struck by *paidopoios* at v. 4,[14] and then Euripides shows us a series of vignettes where the normal harmony is disrupted. I should cite the death of Astyanax (9 f.), the secret departure of Molossus (47 f.), Neoptolemus' abandonment of his child (49 f., 75), the patent threat to Molossus throughout the first movement of the play (the parallel with Astyanax is clear and intentional), Hermione's own childlessness, Menelaus' desertion of his daughter (854 ff.), the description of Orestes' matricide (976) which must recall the intense confrontation in *Libation Bearers*, the predicted survival of Molossus (1246 f.), and the reunion of Peleus and Thetis with Achilles (1260). The most powerful statement of this theme belongs to the first stasimon:

> If only Paris' mother had destroyed him before
> he went to live on Ida's rocks,
> when Cassandra at the prophetic laurel
> was screaming, 'Kill him,
> the destroyer of Priam's great city'.
> Whom did she not approach,
> what councillor did she not beg
> to murder the infant?   (293–300)

In this anticipation of the later *Alexandros* (415), Euripides with grim irony observes how the death of one infant would have averted the later catastrophe, felt by house and city alike.

From the domestic situations come two important results of disharmony, *eris* ('strife') and *phonos* ('murder'), the former found significantly in only three extant plays (*Andr.*, *Helen*, *Phoenissae*). In our play the judgement of Paris is the result of the hateful strife (*stygera eris*) of the goddesses (279) which results in the strife over Helen (362) and the present strife between Andromache and Hermione (122—again *stygera*, 490, 563, 960). At 467 *didyma lektra* lead to 'domestic strife', and at 490 *eris* produces *phonos* ('godless, lawless, joyless'). Perhaps the most powerful statement of the pernicious effects of domestic disharmony is the close of the fourth stasimon:

Throughout the cities of Greece would many women lament their ill-fated children; wives would leave their homes for another bed-mate. Not just on you or your friends have terrible griefs fallen.[15] Greece has endured a plague. Thunder passed through Troy, dripping on our pleasant fields a bloody *phonos*.

I have argued that in *Andromache* this theme of the *oikos* in peace and in disruption is of major importance. The ideal *oikos* is carried by certain repeated motifs, the procession of the bride from father to husband, the harmony of the marriage-bed (*lechos*), the tableau of parent and child. Against these ideals the dramatist sets a variety of dislocations; every major character in this drama is or has been involved in a *domos* disrupted. These domestic disharmonies are seen as part of a larger picture, the 'hateful strife' which marks the whole Trojan story.

We may now apply the presence of this domestic theme to the assessment of the various views of *Andromache* which I enumerated earlier. Both the simple propagandist view and Kitto's Spartan critique seem less likely in the light of a strong domestic theme. Likewise, Stevens's Trojan interpretation or Kamerbeek's concept of corruption are important themes, but not the whole story either. Garyza's emphasis on Hermione or Erbse's on Andromache are off the right track, for the domestic theme suggests that these characters are not so important for themselves as they are representatives of their *oikoi* or their *gamoi*.[16] I find the approach of Webster and Conacher reinforced by the existence of these strong domestic motifs, although Webster stresses the *persons* of Andromache, Hermione, and Peleus, and Conacher their *cities*. *Andromache* is really, I suggest, a 'Tale of Three Houses'.

The usually accepted date for *Andromache* is the mid-420s, with 425 most frequently proposed. This is based on (a) certain metrical features,[17] (b) the well-known principle of metrical resolutions in the iambic tri-meter—*Andromache* with a resolution figure of 12% should fall between the 5.8% for *Hippolytus* (428) and the 14.2% for *Suppliant Women* and 14.7% for *Hecuba*,[18] and (c) certain alleged topical allusions. Among the last are the aforementioned decree on two wives, the fall of Plataea in 427 (for Kitto, p. 236 n. 2, the probable cause of the anti-Spartan theme), the successes of Brasidas, political rivalries at Athens (Stevens, p. 154), the 'collaboration' of Aristophanes and Eupolis over *Knights* (cf. 476–8), and the identification of the hostile city of 734 with specific political events at Argos or Mantinea.[19] Collard in his introduction to *Suppliant Women* has demonstrated just how flimsy are the cases for finding such contemporary allusions in the plays of Euripides.[20]

In their recent re-evaluation of the metrical evidence, Cropp and Fick propose a slightly lower date for *Andromache*, i.e. 424–1.[21] However, the domestic theme with its key words, *oikos*, *lechos*, *domos*, *gamos*, etc., suggests to me that the play belongs closer in time to the more strongly domestic dramas such as *Medea* (431) and *Hippolytus* (428). I should make three specific points. First, the prominence of *to sophron* in *Andromache* is matched only by the appearance of that theme in *Hippolytus*, especially as it has to do with female sexuality. *To sophron* is prominent in the early plays until *Andromache*, and then not again until the very last plays. Second, the emphasis on the *lechos*-theme links this play firmly with *Medea* where female passion and sexuality is a dominant theme. In particular, Jason's complaint at *Med.* 568 f., 'you women think that bed (*lechos*) is everything', is picked up at *Andr.* 240 f., 'isn't this (*lechos*) first and foremost to women everywhere?'; cf. also 370 f. and 932–5.[22] Finally, there are several points of contact between *Andromache* and the extant portion of the lost *Stheneboea*, one of several explorations by Euripides in the 430s and 420s of the Potiphar's Wife theme—explorations which seem to have been directed into the realm of feminine psychology. The now extant thirty-one lines of the prologue of *Stheneboea*[23] mention *domos* five times (and *domata* once), *lechos* twice, and restate the familiar theme of *eros* and *to sophron* (22–6). The word *nosos* occurs twice (6, 20); the latter example ('the house is ill') is paralleled five times in *Andromache* (220, 548, 906, 949 f., 956). *Stheneboea* belongs in the early 420s after *Medea*; the resolution figure of 8.4% might suggest a date after *Hippolytus* (5.8%), but there are grounds for supposing *Hippolytus* to be something of an anomaly.[24] Schmid had in fact grouped *Andromache* thematically with *Medea*, *Stheneboea*, and *Hippolytus*, but later critics have been enticed by the metrical figures to associate it with *Hecuba* and *Suppliant Women*, with which plays *Andromache* has less in common thematically. I see Euripides in this play as a playwright in transition from a more domestically oriented to a more politically focused tragedy. Stylistically *Andromache* may look ahead, but thematically it belongs with *Medea et al.* It is a play at a crossroads in Euripides' career, and belongs, I suspect, to the first production after that of *Hippolytus* in 428, probably in 427 or 426.[25]

NOTES

1. On which see D. L. Page in *Greek Poetry and Life* (Oxford, 1936), pp. 206–30.

2. See Page (ibid.), and the discussion in P. T. Stevens, *Euripides, Andromache* (Oxford, 1971), pp. 15, 19–21 (hereafter 'Stevens').

3. The following discussions are cited by the author's name alone. Much of this survey of secondary opinion is based on the excellent summary by Stevens, pp. 5–15, and the notes in Conacher. D. W. Lucas, *The Greek Tragic Poets* (London, 1959), pp. 182–7; G. M. A. Grube, *The Drama of Euripides* (London, 1941), pp. 198–213; U. von Wilamowitz-Moellendorff, *Hermes* 60 (1925), 295; W. Schmid, *Geschichte der griechischen Literatur*, I.3 (Munich, 1940), pp. 397 ff.; D. S. Robertson, *CR* 37 (1923), 58–60; R. Goossens, *Euripide et Athènes* (Brussels, 1962), pp. 376–410; A. Garyza, *Euripide, Andromaca* (Naples, 1963), pp. i–xxxvii; H. Erbse, *Hermes* 94 (1966), 275–304; H. Golder, *TAPhA* 113 (1983), 123–33; P. N. Boulter, *Phoenix* 20 (1966), 51–8; K. H. Lee, *Antichthon* 9 (1975), 4–16; J. C. Kamerbeek, *Mnemosyne* 11 (1943), 47–67; A. P. Burnett, *Catastrophe Survived* (Oxford, 1971), pp. 130–56; W. H. Friedrich, *Zetemata* (Munich,

1953), pp. 47 ff.; H. D. F. Kitto, *Greek Tragedy* (London, 1961), pp. 230–6; D. J. Conacher, *Euripidean Drama: Myth, Theme, and Structure* (Toronto, 1967), pp. 166–80; T. B. L. Webster, *The Tragedies of Euripides* (London, 1967), pp. 118–21; P. Vellacott, *Euripides, Orestes and Other Plays* (Harmondsworth, 1972), pp. 26–43.

4. Similarly Grube, Wilamowitz, and Schmid are less than kind to the play. Most recently, G. Bond, *Euripides, Heracles*, (Oxford, 1981), p. xix pursues a similar line of criticism ('a play which may properly be termed "episodic"').

5. Against her appearance in the third movement see the arguments of Burnett, p. 154 n. 20; Stevens, pp. 10 f., 218 f.; P. D. Kovacs, *The Andromache of Euripides*, American Classical Studies 6 (Chico, 1980), pp. 43–5 (hereafter 'Kovacs'); D. J. Conacher, *CPh* (1984), 53–6.

6. Kovacs, pp. 9–20; see Conacher's rebuttal (n. 5), 54.

7. Andromache, originally from Asiatic Thebes, is completely won over to Troy, her husband's city; Hermione, on the other hand, never ceases to be a Spartan in a strange land.

8. On this decree and its relevance to *Andromache*, see Stevens, p. 151; for the historicity of the law see D. M. MacDowell, *The Law in Classical Athens* (London, 1978), pp. 90, 266 n. 193, who sees 'no reason for rejecting it'.

9. Grube, p. 212 and Burnett, pp. 153–6 insist on an essentially positive tone with no irony intended. Norwood (*ap.* Grube), Friedrich, and Vellacott, p. 43 argue strongly for an ironic tone throughout.

10. Pindar *Ol.* 2. 78–80 places Peleus with Kadmos and Achilles on the Islands of the Blessed. See Stevens, pp. 244 f. here.

11. The role of Neoptolemus, although completely absent from the action, has occasioned some comment. He has both champions and critics. Stevens, p. 6 finds 'no suggestion here of the ruthless Neoptolemus of epic tradition'. Erbse, however, regards Andromache as present during the lament over N.; her silence is a bitter condemnation of him. For Kamerbeek, p. 67 his body becomes a 'symbole de la corruption dont la guerre de Troie est la cause'. Kamerbeek, however, does not go so far as Vellacott or P. Friedlander, *Die Antike* 2 (1926), 99–102 who sees in N. the Absent Hero and unifying idea of the tragedy. For Kovacs, pp. 78 ff. Neoptolemus, rather than Apollo, is Euripides' target; he is responsible for the woes of the characters in the play.

12. Later the same verb will be used of his abandonment of his daughter (854, 918).

13. The text is corrupt here. I translate its spirit rather than its letter. See Stevens, pp. 216 f., Kovacs, pp. 38–41 for discussions.

14. E. Fantham in *Greek Tragedy and its Legacy: Essays presented to D. J. Conacher* (Calgary, 1986), pp. 267–80, arrived after this paper was completed. Her stress on the figure of Andromache as mother fits well into the domestic theme as I have outlined it. In particular, I agree with her that 'the child, not the possibility that Andromache is still sharing Neoptolemus' bed, provokes Hermione's fury'. The mother–child relationship provides a vertical element which crosses the horizontal element of the marriage itself.

15. Another *locus vexatus*: σοι should, I think, refer to Hermione, although Stevens, p. 218 *et al.* argue strongly for Andromache. I agree with Kovacs, p. 44 that the antithesis is not you (Andromache), a Trojan, *v.* Greece, but rather you (Hermione), one Greek, *v.* all Hellas.

16. See Kovacs, pp. 75 ff. and the apt comment of Conacher (n. 5), 54—'the fairly obvious fact ... that this play is not primarily about Andromache and her individual fate'.

17. On these see A. Garyza, *GIF* 5 (1952), 346–66. For the discussion of the dating as a whole see Stevens, pp. 15–19.

18. These figures are those of Webster, pp. 3–5.

19. See Stevens, pp. 15–18, 183; also Conacher, p. 170 n. 7, Kamerbeek, pp. 47–9, Kitto, p. 236 n. 2.

20. C. Collard, *Euripides. Supplices* I (Groningen, 1975), pp. 8–14, 23–31.

21. M. Cropp and G. Fick, *Resolutions and Chronology in Euripides*, Institute of Classical Studies Bulletin Supplement 43 (London, 1985), pp. 23, 70.

22. In addition to the studies of Boulter and Lee, see also Conacher, pp. 26–53.

23. Available in D. L. Page, *Select Papyri* III: *literary papyri* (London and Cambridge, 1941), pp. 126–9.

24. The figures for *Medea* (431) and *Heraclidae* (430 or 429, in all likelihood) are 6.5% and 5.9%. Cropp and Fick, p. 25 n. 22 argue that *Hippolytus* is anomalously low because of the inclusion of material from the earlier version.

25. This paper was first presented at the June 1986 meeting of the Classical Association of Canada at the University of Manitoba. I must thank my graduate student, Mr Stephen Cavan, whose reading of the play with me touched off this exploration of the domestic terms and themes.

ADDENDUM

Andromache continues to be a neglected play, as the students of Euripides continue to give first attention to the major dramas such as *Alcestis, Medea, Hippolytus*, and *Bacchae*. I would, however, call attention to five studies in English over the past five years which do bear upon this play and upon my dominant theme of domestic disharmony. First, the only major study, M. van der Valk, *Studies in Euripides: Phoenissae and Andromache* (Amsterdam, 1985), pp. 57–104, does not say much about the thematic motifs of the play or its recurrent words and images. He discusses two principal points, the unity (or rather lack of it) of the play and the possibility of contemporary references. He would see the play as having two parts only, with Andromache and Peleus as the affected characters, and denies any real dramatic unity between the two halves. What he calls the technique of 'double emotion' anticipates its more successful use in the later *Hecuba*. Certain individual points bear upon my discussion, e.g. the identification of σοι with Andromache (pp. 64–71), the optimistic epiphany of Thetis and a generally 'upbeat' ending (pp. 100–4), and the historicity of the decree on two wives and an allusion to it by Euripides (pp. 75–82). For the date he prefers 426, finding in l. 449 (wrongly cited as l. 429 on p. 74) ἀδίκως εὐτυχεῖτ' ἀν' Ἑλλάδα a reference which must antedate Sphacteria in 424.

The article by E. Fantham has been mentioned briefly in n. 14. Her stress on the maternal role of Andromache is to my mind persuasive, and as I have noted the mother–child relationship provides a vertical counterpoint to the marriage motif elsewhere.

D. Kovacs, *TAPhA* 117 (1987), 259, discusses Andromache's attitude to Neoptolemus in the light of the reading of the text at 25. He shows that the arguments of Lesky and Erbse that Andromache has nothing but hatred for her new husband are based in part on Brunck's reading of γ' for the MSS τ'. Murray's *OCT* edition followed Brunck, but more recent texts, e.g., Garyza and J. Diggle, *Euripidis Fabulae* i (Oxford, 1984), p. 278 read τ' and δ' respectively.

R. Seaford, *JHS* 107 (1987), 106–30 discusses the use of the language of marriage in tragedy. In particular he comments on the portrayal of the union of Paris and Helen (my seventh relationship) at *Agam.* 685–762 'as a marriage which brings disaster' and at *Andr.* 100–13 where Helen's marriage procession to Troy leads to a 'perverted bridal journey', i.e. the departure of Andromache to her new husband. This clearly has much in common with my emphasis on the harmony and dislocation of the marriage-bond in this play.

Finally, R. Garner, *From Homer to Tragedy: The Art of Allusion in Greek Poetry* (London and New York, 1990), pp. 132–4, deals with the allusions in the play to earlier poetry, specifically Homer and the *Oresteia*. Particularly cogent is his relation of μηχανορράφος at l. 1116 of Orestes to the only extant use of the verb at *Cho.* 221, his account of the need for deceit on Orestes' part, and his argument that the death of Neoptolemus is cast in terms which recall the death of Hector from the *Iliad*.

STRUCTURE AND DRAMATIC REALISM IN EURIPIDES' *HERACLES**

By SHIRLEY A. BARLOW

The *Heracles*, like Euripides' other middle plays, has not escaped censure for its faulty structure. From Swinburne's judgement of it as a 'grotesque abortion'[1] one comes to Norwood, who says of Gilbert Murray's view 'A great Hellenist who is the last man to hunt for blemishes in Euripides has rightly called *Heracles* "broken-backed" ', and he adds himself that the play 'at best must be called ramshackle work' or 'The action falls into 2 halves visibly separate though tied together. In each instance a champion of the poet if ingenious and resolute enough can devise some statement that will force unity of action upon his recalcitrant material, but the mere fact that he must so labour refutes him.'[2]

Kitto, who finds it the most puzzling of Euripides' plays, writes 'It is not a dramatic unity' and 'there is no connexion but juxtaposition' and complains of lack of causal unity. 'It falls into 3 distinct parts' and he adds 'But a play has no business to be a triptych.'[3]

Admittedly the picture has changed somewhat since these harsh judgements. Kevin Lee rightly acknowledges the need to dispense with concepts of Aristotelian structure as a criterion of evaluation[4] and Conacher begins from the premise that 'Any defence of the structure of the *Heracles* must rest on the assumption that there is more than one kind of integration.'[5] Yet even he, I think, reveals a traditional unease with a method of construction which is not causally set up, by using terms like '*mere* juxtaposition' and by speaking of the play as being '*saved from*' that.

This 'other kind of integration', to use Conacher's words, has received various embodiments by different scholars. There have been attempts to gloss the awkward structure by searches for over-arching thematic or linguistic unity which have somehow still obviated the need to take into account too strongly the violent wrenches of fortune which the plot reveals. Some have found a clue to continuity and development in the character or ethical attitude of the hero as for example Wilamowitz,[6] Chalk,[7] and Kamerbeek.[8]

Others have seen recurring themes or repeated patterns of language which set up a linking network across the structural breaks. Sheppard was the first to analyse the motifs of friendship, strength, and wealth.[9] Others like Chalk, Kamerbeek, and Gregory[10] have highlighted the criss-crossing of recurring ideas like that of Heracles' double fatherhood for instance, or of emblems like the bow, or of words or clusters of words like the metaphor ἐφολκίς or the image of the Gorgon.

These thematic and linguistic links undoubtedly exist in the play and perhaps in even greater measure than has always been acknowledged, and of course they themselves are creative of a structure, but are they the point from which one should start? Should one not look first at the blatant dislocation of the events in the plot—at the unconnected juxtapositions— and see whether they do not in themselves make a statement or create a logic of their own although not of an Aristotelian kind?

Arrowsmith, however, in the Introduction to his translation[11] and in his dissertation[12] unusually and unreservedly does not think he has to explain away the structure in some fashion or apologize for it. Indeed he takes it as the very root of the play. He calls it the 'most violent structural *tour de force* in Greek tragedy' and argues that the rift between two apparently autonomous actions (by which he means the first part of the play before the madness and that which comes after) jammed against each other in almost total contradiction is deliberate on the poet's part. From this he works towards a general interpretation of the play in which harsh juxtaposition is the calculated and indispensable focus of the drama.

That such juxtapositions not only exist but are underlined by the poet is undeniable. The action may be described in three causally unrelated movements.

(1) Waiting, on the part of his family, for Heracles' return from the labours.
(2) Heracles' return and murder of Lycus.
(3) Heracles' madness and murder of his children and Megara.

The return, when his death is taken for granted, provides a sudden *peripeteia* from despair to triumph and the subsequent madness, which is totally unexpected, provides a *peripeteia* from triumph to despair. There is no apparent connection between the labours and the return, or between the murder of Lycus and the onset of madness beyond the fact that they all happen to the hero and they all involve violent deeds done by him. The most severe break however is between the murder of Lycus and the murder of the children in madness.

I want to argue that these juxtaposed events are deliberately contrasted to represent three levels of violent action in an ascending order of realism, and that Euripides is manipulating our response to them through his choice of language in contrasting modes. I shall look particularly at the long first stasimon which I believe to be a crucial part of the structure and at the equally long messenger speech later in the play. I shall argue that style is an essential part of structure as being evidence of the extent to which language determines our view of actions as presented. Contrasting stylistic mechanisms may echo, indeed be a part of larger juxtapositions in the plot.

It is important to recognize that Heracles performs three sets of feats within the compass of the play (called 'trials' or 'labours'—the words πόνοι and ἀγών are used)—(*a*) the labours, (*b*) the murder of Lycus, (*c*) the murder in madness of his wife and children. Euripides, by putting the labours before the madness instead of as a penance after them, has deliberately severed any possible connection between the two actions.

The two extreme points of Heracles' experience are the labours and the murders done in madness: these represent the ultimate height and depth of his achievement at the beginning and at the end of the play. These two extreme points are marked by two reported narratives in different modes, both of exceptional length—the labours in a lyric first stasimon of 94 lines and the murder of Megara and his children in a messenger speech also of 94 lines, the third longest messenger speech in the Euripidean corpus. The chorus is longer than the others in the play which are 31, 64, 52, and 22 lines respectively and the messenger has himself more lines than many of the other important characters namely Theseus, Lycus, Iris, and Lyssa. This exceptional length in both cases must surely tell us something.

The structural importance of both these modes is evident from their placing in the play. The chorus on the labours is led up to by discussion about the labours earlier, in the prologue and in the debate between Lycus and Amphitryon about their importance, or in the discussion about the bow, and reinforced by the sudden dramatic personal appearance of Heracles after it. The absence of Heracles is not merely the absence of an ordinary man but of an almost superhuman hero of whom miracles in the past have been expected. When he does not appear the despair is therefore that much greater as is the joy when he does. The messenger speech is likewise preceded and prepared for by a very dramatic scene between Iris and Lyssa, and by an agitated lyric scene between Amphitryon and the chorus when the house is shaken as madness strikes Heracles. It is also itself the preparation for the rehabilitation scene between Amphitryon and Heracles, and Theseus and Heracles. Without it these final scenes would be utterly lacking in impact. The way these high points are therefore embedded in their context is important.

The labours in the chorus are deliberately presented in a way which undercuts their force. One might think they would be described as horrifying obstacles which the hero must overcome with difficulty. The action could be described with great violence and the monsters with grim attributes which matched their threats to the stability of law and order in the world.[13] With Euripides' ode, it is quite otherwise. There are very few adjectives expressing menace and very few strong verbs. There are no moral reflections to interrupt the description[14] (except the mention of ἀρεταί at the very beginning) and no emotive exclamations.[15] In fact Euripides' description is languid and lacking in energy. Arrowsmith refers to its 'massive strength' and Wilamowitz to its Aeschylean 'Fülle und Erhabenheit'[16] but its uncomplicated and ornamental descriptive narrative has more in common with a Bacchylides dithyramb than anything else.[17] Physical effort is deliberately not stressed—perhaps to stress the ease with which the hero accomplished his tasks. But these, the labours, in the shape of various monsters are reduced to prettily decorative scenes where the emphasis is on ornamental adjectives, not verbs of violent action. There is no horror, no pain, no moral weight—only a colourful romantic scene underlined by vagueness in the dimension of time and an order of events which is not significant. Any one labour could be substituted for any other without loss. Time does not matter. Order does not matter. All is made subordinate to the decorative. Colourful and lush detail detracts from emotive weight creating a leisurely and relaxed atmosphere familiar particularly from artistic tradition.[18] There *is* a sense of wide space indicating the breadth of the labours, the distance covered and this is to make a telling contrast later with the confined space of the palace described in the messenger speech.

Take *Labour 1* for instance. First of all he *emptied* ($\dot{\eta}\rho\dot{\eta}\mu\omega\sigma\epsilon$, an oddly neutral word) Zeus' grove of the lion and he *had his fair head covered* with the tawny creature's grim and gaping jaws and hung its skin on his back. The passive $\dot{\alpha}\mu\phi\epsilon\kappa\alpha\lambda\dot{\upsilon}\phi\theta\eta$ robs the scene of any immediacy of action and indeed the killing itself is not stressed but only the traditional pictorial scene afterwards, familiar from innumerable vase paintings.

Labour 2. Four lines are given to the shooting of Centaurs, 8 (twice as many) to the witness to the deed of the surrounding landscape where again the descriptive epithets $\kappa\alpha\lambda\lambda\iota\delta\dot{\iota}\nu\alpha s$, $\mu\alpha\kappa\rho\alpha\dot{\iota}$, $\ddot{\alpha}\kappa\alpha\rho\pi o\iota$, $\sigma\dot{\upsilon}\gamma\chi o\rho\tau o\iota$ take the weight out of the violence and stress the static scene and the textural quality of the countryside with its broad dry plains, swirling rivers, and grassy haunts.

Labour 3. In the killing of the golden hind, the action subordinated as it is by the participle $\kappa\tau\epsilon\dot{\iota}\nu\alpha s$ which is almost incidental in its positioning right at the end of a phrase overweighted by long compound adjectives, is already seen as in the past. Stress is on the colourful adjectives $\chi\rho\upsilon\sigma o\kappa\dot{\alpha}\rho\alpha\nu o\nu$, $\pi o\iota\kappa\iota\lambda\dot{o}\nu\omega\tau o\nu$, which takes the sting out of the slight menace of $\sigma\upsilon\lambda\dot{\eta}\tau\epsilon\iota\rho\alpha\nu$ $\dot{\alpha}\gamma\rho\omega\sigma\tau\hat{\alpha}\nu$. $\dot{\alpha}\gamma\dot{\alpha}\lambda\lambda\epsilon\iota$ merely presents the situation now that the deed is all over. No stress is given to the physicality of Heracles' action in doing the deed.

Labour 4 is slightly more gruesome (the horses of Diomedes) but here again the emphasis is on them not on Heracles' deed in subduing them which is expressed in the one word $\dot{\epsilon}\delta\dot{\alpha}\mu\alpha\sigma\epsilon$. After six lines the picture quickly changes to the river banks of the Hebrus past which silver-flowing waters ($\dot{\alpha}\rho\gamma\upsilon\rho o\rho\rho\dot{\upsilon}\tau\omega\nu$, a *hapax legomenon*) flow. The *hapax* draws attention to the decorative descriptive aspect.

Landscape is again stressed in *Labour 5* (the killing of the robber Cycnus) and in *Labour 6* decorative elements again prevail. In the Gardens of the Hesperides he is described as 'about to pluck the fruit from the gold metal leaves' and once again the verb of slaying is subordinated to a participle κτανών while the snake is described in detail 'fiery backed and guarding the tree with its twining coils'.

The other labours are similarly presented. No effort is to be seen in the word κατέσχεν as Heracles holds up the starry heavens for Atlas. The only violent word is in ἐξεπύρωσεν 'he burnt to ashes' the hydra of Lerna. But this is the only verb of any force in the whole ode. The rest are singularly uninteresting, being ones largely of coming and going. βαίνω in some form occurs four times (εἰσέβαινε, ἐπέβα, ἔβα, ἔβα), ἔρχομαι three, and κτείνω three. ἔπλευσε, ἐκπεραίνει, and διεπέρασεν are neutral words describing Heracles' action but hardly ones to stir the blood. On the other hand, that great care has been lavished on the statically decorative aspects as seen in the adjectives, is suggested by the fact that 10 (out of 20) of the ornamental compounds are *hapax legomena*, suggesting that the weight is designed to be here.

What does all this mean? Through Euripides' calculated use of decorative elements he is robbing the deeds of any real force, creating instead a glossy ornamental romantic atmosphere. He is not, I think, wishing to present them as pure fiction or fantasy although they have something of the miraculous about them and some of the overgloss and overglorification of mythical tradition familiar from art particularly. They have also associations of faith and belief on the part of the singers which counteract the astringent scepticism of Lycus earlier in the play.[19]

But the labours are mentioned too integrally and too often in the last half of the play for them to be dismissed as part of an imaginary world.[20] What they establish here is a sphere of action which will throw up similarities and contrasts with the actions which follow. These miraculous deeds and their beautiful setting will give place to others. The public spacious outdoor environment of the worldwide labours will change to the narrow confined domestic scene within the palace, as narrated by the messenger. There is sharp contrast here between the different settings, as well as the style. The protagonist, the weapons, and the ease of accomplishment will be the same but the objects and the environments will change. Thus the three violent actions are both inextricably bound and yet quite different in their impact. The effects are cumulatively built up throughout the play. This long elaborate ode will be stored in the audience's consciousness until the time comes for them to contrast it with the equally elaborate but much more traumatic messenger speech. Then the painless admiration they have felt here will be transferred to witnessing something nearer at hand and much more painful.

Now the messenger speech describing the murders in madness is all that that chorus is not. It is firmly fixed in a time sequence which matters: it *does* present minute detailed *evidence* of actions done with violent energy and it is not romantic, or sentimental. It expresses precision of gesture, movement, and speech within a confined space—the palace. The mode of course demands this but the use of mode in this case *coincides* deliberately with the order of realities the poet wishes to present.

Euripides had no need to use a messenger speech: he could have used another character to report the death, as Hecuba does in the *Troades* or he could have used a chorus to describe the action as he did with the murder of Lycus at 735 ff. Similarly he had no need to use a chorus to describe the labours—he could have used a messenger there instead and allowed the exigencies of the mode to conjure up a different view of the labours. But he chose not to for good reasons. It is interesting to speculate how different the labours might have appeared had a messenger described them.[21]

In the messenger speech the time sequence is everything and the order of events unchangeable, since this is an imagined factual account of a localized happening. Details are carefully amassed until the climax is reached at 977 ff. Nothing is left out, the scene is described, the physical appearance of Heracles recorded, and the subsequent observable changes that took place in him, the supposed conversations of the servants, Amphitryon, Megara, the children, and the hero himself are faithfully reported word for word as the action builds up. I have elsewhere described the stylistic traits which make up this speech. Here I simply want to stress the calculated difference in atmosphere between it and that chorus. Where there the stress was on decorative adjectives, so here it is on verbs and similes firmly drawn from the everyday world of working people. There are 132 verbs in the 94 lines, to 33 adjectives of which many are such indispensable, non-ornamental ones as δεύτερον, τρίτον, βραχύν, μέσον, μιᾶς, διπλοῦς, δεξιᾷ.

Fifteen lines each have two verbs in them (not participles): of these, six have two very forceful main verbs in them reinforcing each other in two cases by asyndeton. Other lines have one strongly weighted verb of action, e.g. συντριαινῶσαι (946), κατέστρωσεν (1000), and ἱππεύει φόνον (1001).

Of the six compound adjectives, one (καλλίμορφος) is used decoratively (the only one to be so used) to indicate the peacefulness of the scene before the violence starts, one (καλλίνικος) is a traditional epithet used ironically, one is a *hapax legomenon* used with particular force to describe an act of violence (μυδροκτύπον); two (αἱματῶπας, ἀγριωπόν) are strictly necessary to describe the horror of appearance, and one (εὐτρεπῆ) is merely traditional.

Metaphors and similes drawn from the world of work and crafts bring home the realism and reinforce the violence. Heracles chases his children round the pillars like a turning lathe (978). He digs out doorposts (999) as if he is digging a trench and he rides down his father like a horseman (1001). The tools with which Heracles intends to rip up the supposed Cyclopean walls are also mentioned (999). This language with its epic flavour, taken from crafts, could not be further from the lyric style contemplated earlier. Its hallmark is realism and physicality of a different kind from the lyric ode. The messenger speech is intended to be threatening and is meant to bring home with urgent clarity the grimness of these actions. Each mode represents a different plane of reality: one remote, romantic, decorative (adjectivally oriented), the other close, grimly unsentimental, ugly (verbally oriented).

But it is not just a question of differing stylistic tricks—the difference is also one of depth. The ode for all its formal brilliance is not profound. It is a glossy narrative devoid of moral or strong emotive weight. It has not the weighty lyrical force of some of the choral descriptions in the *Troades* for instance,[22] nor again the thought content of, say, the second stasimon of this play. The messenger speech on the other hand reaches out with implications of both a psychological and moral kind. It is all very well to point out how accurately Euripides has observed the symptoms of epilepsy in the first part of it, but it is the whole progress of the hallucination which impinges on our assessment of this dramatic action.

For this is in a sense both illusion and a hideous parody of the hero's whole life and career—close to his nature and habitual actions yet also very far removed from them. Here the ironic use of the traditional epithet καλλίνικος repeating earlier usages but in a different key, and the symbolism of the chariot drive up and down the halls of the house which echoes earlier images of chariot and race course play a very important rôle.[23] There is further irony in that Heracles thinks he is *outside* driving his chariot and fighting in *open air* contests and travelling to Mycenae, whereas in fact he is enclosed within the confines of the palace. His public and private images have become confused. It is, I think, an oversimplification to speak of the *logos* and *ergon* of the labours and the madness as Arrowsmith does,[24] for both modes involve an element of *logos* and of *ergon*. Heracles' hallucinations are fantasy though they convey events which have no fantasy in them. For he is in a way taken in by his own myth, so that there is an element of the mythical in the messenger's account also. His delusion is related to his earlier public image.

Now one might say the different modes of lyric ode and messenger speech are always contrasted stylistically. This is, up to a point, but not wholly, true. The extremes are more marked than usual here, and the relative depths are unusually unevenly weighted. It is both rare for a choral ode to be so superficial and for a messenger speech to penetrate a phenomenon in such depth.[25] Yet both are stylistic *tours de force*, and the two are deliberately kept in balance by the continuity of action referred to in the terms 'trials' and 'labours' used for both.

Chorus and messenger speech are linked by Heracles' own assertion that the murder of his children is another labour but one of a very different order. Iris links the labours and the child murders by referring to καλλίπαιδα στέφανον at 839 (στεφάνωμα μόχθων is used at 355 by the chorus) and Heracles himself puts the same perspectives on the labours and the murder of the children as I have been arguing shows in the style. He both links and distinguishes them in retrospect, making the one remote and effortless by the use of the plural and by exaggeration (μυρίων) and the other close and painful by a simple statement expressed in a telling metaphor (θριγκῶσαι):

> Why recite all those labours I endured?
> All those wars I fought, those beasts I slew,
> those lions and triple-bodied Typhons,
> Giants and four-legged Centaurs hordes!
> I killed the hydra, that hound whose heads
> grew back as soon as lopped. My *countless* labours done
> I descended down among the sullen dead.
> And now my last worst labour (πόνον) has been done:
> I slew my children and crowned my house with grief.
> This is how I stand.
>
> (1270–81)

The link between the two sequences of actions is further stressed at 1378–85 where Heracles determines with difficulty to keep the bow which performed both kinds of action, and where Theseus gives Heracles courage to endure by recalling to him his former greatness. Also at 1410–11 where Theseus specifically asks him if he remembers the labours and he replies ἅπαντ᾽ ἐλάσσω κεῖνα τῶνδ᾽ ἔτλην κακά.

Where then is the third and middle level of dramatic reality, the murder of Lycus? This is also important as it is the only violent event which is presented directly. The voice of Lycus is heard crying out as he dies at the hand of Heracles in the palace. Little space is wasted on his murder—27 lines only. The scene serves as a kind of transition between the two other sets of deeds, reinforcing the ability of Heracles to effortlessly eliminate his enemies and at the same time raising questions about the use of violence in general. The action with Lycus is linked to both what precedes and what follows by the repeated use of πόνοι, ἐκπονέω, and of the word ἀγών and the epithet καλλίνικος.

Heracles at 575 says χαιρόντων πόνοι, referring to the labours, and then goes on to ask:

> τί φήσομεν καλὸν

ὕδρᾳ μὲν ἐλθεῖν ἐς μάχην λέοντί τε
Εὐρυσθέως πομπαῖσι, τῶν δ' ἐμῶν τέκνων
οὐκ ἐκπονήσω θάνατον;[26]

What value are the labours if I don't labour to save my children's lives? A further twist is then given in the phrase τὸν λοίσθιον πόνον referring to the actual death of the children at Heracles' hands.

Lycus' murder the chorus describe at 789 as τὸν Ἡρακλέους καλλίνικον ἀγῶνα, and Heracles' words at 1229 ironically recall this, δέδορκας τόνδ' ἀγῶν' ἐμῶν τέκνων; καλλίνικος is used five times with significance in the early part of the play and again at 788 of the triumphant murder of Lycus and at 961 ironically of Heracles' deluded contest with himself.

A further hinted connection is made between the murder of Lycus and the murder of the children by Amphitryon asking Heracles at 966–7 whether the blood of those he has already killed (i.e. Lycus) has not driven him mad: οὔ τί που φόνος σ' ἐβάκχευσεν νεκρῶν | οὓς ἄρτι καίνεις; The reversal from one to the other is so quick and achieved with such ease. This is brought out by Heracles' hallucination that he is in fact murdering the children of Eurystheus. Is Euripides not asking whether there is not a very fine line between murdering one's enemies' children and murdering one's own, and even between murdering one's enemies and murdering one's friends? Heracles after all has achieved what Lycus would have liked to do and βία characterizes them both. As Chalk says, 'The essential difference between Lycus and Heracles—their motives for action—the killing of the children does not cancel; but it does reveal what actions good and bad alike have in common—violence … all βία partakes of the irrational element here embodied in the extreme form of madness.'

There are therefore implied connections between the labours, the murder of Lycus and the murder of the children.

What we have therefore are *three* juxtaposed sequences of violent action in an ascending order of horror and suffering as they impinge upon the experience of the hero and the audience. The messenger speech must be the climax of the play, both in its intrinsic depth and because it carries the cumulative effect of what has preceded it. This makes the tragedy but is led up to by the other two sequences which show, but only in retrospect, the frailty of man as he moves through different feats of action, for it is at his peak of valour that he is most likely to be struck down and experience the *same aspects of his talents negatively*. The supposed glory and heroism of the labours are converted to hideous new circumstances where the same characteristics of the hero exist but are used in a tragically inappropriate way.

The hero of the first two sequences thus becomes the villain of the third, and in learning to cope with the disgrace this brings, in a fourth closing

movement which produces no structural problems of connection, argu-
ably becomes a hero all over again, perhaps of a different sort. The
rehabilitation is undoubtedly one of the most powerful scenes in Greek
tragedy. But its full impact cannot be realized without the contrast of the
previous sequences.

The play is thus rich in contrasting levels of dramatic reality, as indeed
are many of Euripides' other plays, and this is effected through certain
juxtaposed structural high points such as I have described in the particular
styles which underline the contrast. This is a non-logical, non-Aristotelian
arrangement of sequence, but one can hardly call it 'mere juxtaposition';
rather, it is calculated juxtaposition as a dramatic method in itself. The
corresponding juxtaposition of style reveals also a method which runs
through all Euripides' work and is used repeatedly by him in large units
and in smaller ones both through different modes and sometimes even
within the same mode.[27]

NOTES

*This was given as a discussion paper to the triennial meeting of the Hellenic and Roman
Societies on 5 August 1981.

1. Quoted by A. W. Verrall in *Four Plays of Euripides* (Cambridge, 1905).

2. G. Norwood, *Essays on Euripidean Drama* (Berkeley, London, and Toronto, 1964), pp. 46,
47.

3. H. D. F. Kitto, *Greek Tragedy* (London, 1961³), p. 235.

4. K. Lee, *Vindex Humanitatis, Essays in Honour of John Huntley Bishop* (Armidale, N.S.W.),
p. 34.

5. D. J. Conacher, *Euripidean Drama* (Toronto and London, 1967), p. 83.

6. U. von Wilamowitz-Moellendorf, *Euripides, Herakles* (Berlin, 1895), p. 128.

7. H. H. O. Chalk, "Ἀρετή and βία in Euripides' *Herakles*', *JHS* 82 (1962), 7 ff.

8. J. C. Kamerbeek, 'The Unity and Meaning of Euripides' *Heracles*', *Mnemosyne* 19 (1966),
1 ff.

9. J. T. Sheppard, 'The Formal Beauty of the *Hercules Furens*', *CQ* 10 (1916), 72 ff.

10. J. Gregory, 'Euripides' *Heracles*', *YCS* 25 (1977), 259 ff.

11. W. Arrowsmith, Introduction to the *Heracles, Euripides* II (Chicago, 1956), pp. 45–6.

12. W. Arrowsmith, *The Conversion of Heracles* (Diss. Princeton, 1954).

13. Compare, for example, Seneca's presentation of the ghosts of monsters in the Underworld
and of Cerberus (*H.F.* 778–806), where verbs work with adjectives to create the impression of
energy (*territat, lambunt, horrent, sibilat*) and where Heracles is shown in motion as he puts on the
lion skin and whirls his club. Or compare the fragment of Pindar (*P. Oxy.* 2450) which describes
some of the labours of Heracles where much of the force is expressed through strong epic-type
verbs, e.g., ἀράβη[σε] διὰ [λ]ευκῶν | ὀστέ[ων] δοῦπος ἐ[ρ] ⟨ε⟩ ικομένων.

14. As frequently in Pindar, e.g., *Nem.* 1.33 ff., 4.30 ff.

15. As, for instance, in Heracles' words about his labours in Sophocles, *Trach.* 1088 ff.

16. Wilamowitz, *Herakles* III, p. 84: 'Das ganze Lied ist in der Form von aischyleischer Fülle
und Erhabenheit.' There are glyconic refrains in common between this ode and Aesch *Ag.* 367–
488 and *Supp.* 630–709 but it is hard to see any further resemblance between the highly
complicated language, thought, and content of Aeschylus' odes and the simpler descriptive
narrative of Euripides' first stasimon.

17. Bacchylides XVI (the Theseus dithyramb) is characterized by many colourful compound
adjectives; see, for example, the first few lines, κυανόπρῳρα, τηλαυγεί, πολεμαίγιδος, ἱμεράμπυκος,

χαλκοθώρακα and by colour contrasts, e.g., λευκᾶν παρηίδων, μέλαν ... ὄμμα. Lines 90 ff. involve a journey where pictorially descriptive elements prevail, e.g., 103 ff. The eleven lines of fragment XIX are similarly dominated by colourful compound adjectives.

18. See the somewhat languid and relaxed poses of Heracles on some late fifth-century vases as illustrated by Brommer, *Herakles*, particularly tafs. 29 and 30.

19. At 151 ff.

20. At 1250, 1270 ff., 1376 ff., 1410 ff.

21. There is an early messenger speech in the *I.T.*, for example, at 260 ff.

22. Especially *Troades* 1061 ff., 824 ff.

23. e.g. at 662, 777 ff., 1102.

24. Op. cit. (n. 12), p. 12.

25. Only the messenger speeches in the *Bacchae* are comparable in that they give an account of a whole phenomenon—the Dionysiac experience.

26. There is surely ambiguity here since ἐκπονέω can mean 'execute' their death as well as 'work to take it away'.

27. This is the subject of another work in progress.

DOUBLE THE VISION: A READING OF EURIPIDES' *ELECTRA*

By W. GEOFFREY ARNOTT

For double the vision my Eyes do see,
And a double vision is always with me.
(William Blake)[1]

Controversy about the evaluation of Euripides' *Electra* still rages as fiercely as empty tigers or the roaring sea. 'Euripides' play is a singular instance of poetical—or rather unpoetical—obliquity ... perhaps of all Euripides' extant plays the very vilest'; 'as a drama of character, *Electra* is supreme ... in its own genre, this is undoubtedly Euripides' masterpiece'; it contains 'a power of sympathy and analysis unrivalled in ancient drama'; its characters are 'involved in a persisting interpenetration of merit and status which accords some measure of tonal unity to this indifferent play'.[2] When a play earns judgements as contradictory and incompatible as these, one important stimulus to the verdicts is usually the critic's subjectively emotional response to a play whose views about society and society's values are provocative; more reliable (because less subjective) criteria of literary merit, such as the interplay of plot, character, structure, imagery, and ideas, are then subordinated or comparatively neglected as elements in the evaluation.[3] Euripides' *Electra* is just such a play. It attacks, both openly and implicitly, some of the traditional values still held by many Athenians in 413 B.C., the probable date of the play's production,[4] with a commitment that has engaged a great deal of scholarly attention. The techniques which Euripides deploys in his attack, however, have not been adequately studied. They provide the rationale, as well as the title, of this paper. Before the 'double vision' can be explained, however, it will be as well to outline briefly those traditional values subjected to the Euripidean vitriol.

They are the values of the Homeric poems, clearly relevant in the context of eighth-century society, but equally clearly an obsolete impediment to the effective working of democracy in Athens towards the end of the fifth century. Although their irrelevance had been paraded by a succession of thinkers—in Euripides' own time by Socrates and the sophists—there can be little doubt that these values and the system that incorporated them appealed to something deeply engrained in the Greek personality, and not confined exclusively to the more conservative elements in society. For a detailed analysis of these Homeric values and their historical development and adaptation up to the time of Euripides and beyond, the reader must turn to the seminal studies of A. W. H. Adkins;[5] the following summary of those traditional values relevant to the *Electra* is inevitably bald and oversimplified. The system was concerned with birth, status, and success rather than with morality. The prime value was ἀρετή, excellence and (for men) the summation of aggressive aristocratic 'virtues'. The prime adjective of praise, in terms of this success-oriented ἀρετή, was ἀγαθός, and the qualities that made a man ἀγαθός were those particularly needed in the unsettled conditions of the Homeric dark ages: excellence of birth (otherwise the man could not be acceptable as clan-leader); courage, physical strength, skill in organizing and making war (the qualities that promoted success against hostile neighbours); and wealth (the physical evidence of status and success). However relevant this system of values was to an eighth-century Greece divided into a large number of aristocratic chiefdoms, each trying to augment its own status and to reduce that of its neighbours, many of the system's criteria had lost their effectiveness by the time of the developed fifth-century democracy in Athens, where birth and wealth gave no advantage in the election for most offices of state, where controlled discipline was more important than fiery bravado in the hoplite line and on the trireme bench, where honest reliability rather than aggression fomented commerce. And yet, although to Euripidean Athens much in the Homeric value system was pragmatically obsolete, its emotional appeal still survived—survived, and even flourished in those few compartments of experience (the athletic festivals, for example, at Olympia and elsewhere) where the old aggressive and competitive urges were still important for success, while birth and wealth increased its glory:

> For if any man, delighting in expense
> And toil builds up high excellence (ἀρετάς) on divine foundations,
> If his destiny plants him a lovely garden of fame,
>   Already on the furthest shores of fortune
> He drops anchor, and the gods honour him.
>   (Pindar, *Isthmia* 6. 10 ff.)[6]

That this system of values, honouring high birth, the maintenance of status, and physical prowess, is provocatively challenged by Euripides in his *Electra*, has long and clearly been recognized; some of the techniques, however, which the dramatist uses to mount—and to complicate—his assault still require detailed analysis. Part of the assault is frontal and direct; part is oblique, implicit, and, in a special sense, ironically bifurcated. The open part of the assault has been eloquently discussed by previous scholars,[7] and here therefore needs only the briefest re-presentation. This attack is made on two fronts. First, Euripides emphasizes the obsolescence of the traditional code particularly in the early portion of the play by contrasting Electra's husband, a smallholder of illustrious ancestry whose present poverty has cancelled out all claims to present nobility and ἀρετή (37 f.), against Electra's brother Orestes, whose royal blood sustains his status even in exile. The husband's excellence of character, despite the degenerating pressures of poverty and banausic toil, is repeatedly emphasized; he has not consummated his marriage to Electra, because he thinks her far above his station (43 ff., 253 ff.); he is always considerate to her, trying to lighten her chores (64 ff.); he recognizes the need to be hospitable to travelling strangers (357 ff., 406 f.). This behaviour leads Orestes to comment openly on the inadequacy of the old values, in what is probably the play's most celebrated—certainly it is the most discussed—speech (367 ff.), where Orestes rejects all the traditional panoply of birth, wealth, military and physical prowess as indicators of true nobility, and concludes that character and a man's associates are better criteria of worth.

The second line of attack is so typical of the Euripidean confrontation with the myth tradition that it has become a critical commonplace.[8] The myth subject of tragedy belonged to a consciously or unconsciously distanced world of heroes and heroic actions which exemplified unquestioningly the old aristocratic code of values. In writers like Pindar and Aeschylus the heroic grandeur was part and parcel of the myth, giving a glamorous, associative aureole to actors and actions which might in themselves be sordid. By deglamorizing the myth, by presenting the story with characters who often behaved as if they were contemporary Athenians and not distanced heroes, Euripides openly challenged the values on which the myth tradition was founded and with which its rationale seemed to cohere. In the *Electra* the deglamorization shocks powerfully at first sight or first reading. The murders of Aegisthus and Clytemnestra are painted with the sordid brutality of Chicago gangland killings. But it is not the nastiness of the killings or of the murderous royal quartet involved in them that by itself makes the *Electra* a revolutionary onslaught on the myth and traditional values; Orestes and Electra may be deplorable, dehaloed hoodlums devoid of heroism or redeeming characteristics, but the revolutionism of the play lies less in the fact of deglamorization itself, and more in the use made by Euripides of two sophisticated techniques which are designed to pinpoint the dichotomy between the heroic, royal past of myth and the unglamorized, democratic present of reality. Both techniques depend on the 'double view' (hence my Blakean title) of certain characters and actions, thus creating a deliberate clash between incompatible standpoints.[9] Both use the ironic mode in a new and special way; in classical tragedy dramatic irony normally involves a clash between the characters' limited and the audience's wider understanding of a situation, but in the *Electra* Euripides complicates the mode by presenting side by side two divergent views of most of the play's characters, and in each case he leaves the audience to pick out the objectively correct view and to reject the one that is subjectively distorted. Both techniques imply the criticism of the old heroic code, or the myth tradition, or both at the same time, because in all cases the rejected view coheres with the values of that code or with the traditional presentation of character and action in the myth, while the selected view argues for their inadequacy. And finally, both techniques focus particularly on the character, words, and actions of Electra herself, thus providing an additional reason for Euripides' choice of title in this play. One of the techniques functions through imagery, the other through characterization. The latter will be discussed first.

The characters subjected to this 'double view' are the four royal participants in the dramatic action: Clytemnestra, Orestes, Electra herself, all of whom have major speaking roles in the play, and the lesser figure of Aegisthus, who never appears on stage alive. One view of these four characters is filtered through the eyes of the anti-heroine Electra. It is always a prejudiced and distorted view, interpreting the world from behind the blinkers of a naïve heroic vision which simplifies issues in terms of the obsolete values. The other view of the four characters is presented through the less biased eyes of the play's other participants: it contrasts starkly and realistically with the counterpoised Electra view. As soon as the critic realizes Euripides' aims and methods in the exploitation of this 'double view', as a result of which each reader or spectator is required to judge between Electra's assessment and that of the other characters, not only will he understand more clearly why some apparent inconsistencies of characterization occur—between Aegisthus the courteous host and Aegisthus the drunken dancer on Agamemnon's grave, between an Electra invited to a festival with an offer of clothes to wear at it and an Electra who denies ever receiving such invitations—but he will also see a clearer illumination shed over one of the play's most puzzling problems, that of Euripides' apparent parody of the recognition preliminaries in Aeschylus' *Choephoroi*.

Perhaps the clearest—because also the simplest—example of this bifocalized quartet is Orestes, Electra's lost brother.[10] Electra idealizes him in her imagination as a hero with virtues and values straight out of the *Iliad*, the bible of the aristocratic code. Before she learns that the mysterious, newly arrived stranger is Orestes, she boasts to him that Orestes is young, of nobler birth than Aegisthus, and thus capable of killing his adversary in the Homeric way—by single combat (337 f.). She tells the old servant that Orestes would never return to Argos under cloak of secrecy for fear of Aegisthus; he is 'confidently courageous' (εὐθαρσής, like his father Agamemnon in Aeschylus, *Agamemnon* 930!), 'reared in the wrestling-schools of nobility' (525 ff.). The image of Orestes as an aristocratic athlete recurs significantly after Aegisthus' murder, as we shall see. The reality is totally different from Electra's epic vision. Orestes does return to Argos secretly, reluctant to imprison himself within the city walls, and ready to run back on to foreign soil if his identity is recognized (94 ff.). He conspicuously lacks 'confident courage', in both planning and action. The scheme for the murder of Aegisthus is suggested by the old servant, that for Clytemnestra's murder by Electra. The actual murder of Aegisthus is as far removed from the haloed glory of an epic duel as possible; Euripides deliberately turns it into a revolting, unheroic butchery, described in clinical detail by a messenger who supports, not opposes, Orestes (761 ff., 767). Orestes stabs Aegisthus in the back at a sacrifice to the Nymphs, after he has been invited by the king to participate in it as his guest. Stabbing in the back offends somewhat against the heroic code of valour; murder of the host by a guest at a sacrifice is doubly an offence against the gods: against Zeus Xenios, the patron of the guest–host relationship, and against the Nymphs, in whose honour the sacrifice was being held.

Secondly, Euripides' portrait of Aegisthus: a vivid little diptych of a character seen always through others' eyes. Electra's view of him is graphically powerful. To her, Aegisthus is the embodiment of *hybris* (58; cf. 266, 331). He rides around arrogantly in Agamemnon's carriage (320). Electra alleges that

> Sozzled in drunkenness my mother's husband,
> That brilliant man, jumps, so they say, on the grave
> Of my father, pelting the stone memorial with rocks,
> And has the effrontery to say this against him and us:
> 'Where's your son Orestes? Is he here to protect
> Your grave with honour?'[11]

(326–31)

Electra jeers later over Aegisthus' corpse, calling him both a promiscuous seducer (945 f.) and a puppet controlled by a dominant wife (931 ff.). The picture that Electra paints is memorable, and in many of its details it gels with the traditional portrait of Aegisthus as an impious, weak, hen-pecked lecher that we find in other fifth-century versions of the myth, notably those of Aeschylus and Sophocles. But how accurate is Electra's picture of the king in terms of this play's objective realities? The very fact that Electra's view of him accords so well with the traditional view should in itself give us pause. Her view of Orestes similarly coincided with the traditional picture of an epic hero, and was grossly distorted. But if we accuse Electra of inaccuracy in her picture of Aegisthus, we are in effect calling her a liar.[12] Does Euripides intend this? We shall find soon enough that Euripides unambiguously presents her as a liar in other situations. Here it will be enough to demonstrate that the portrait of Aegisthus painted by other characters in the play is radically different from that

drawn by Electra. In the prologue speech Electra's husband implies that
Aegisthus was ruthless in his efforts to stamp out opposition (16, 22 ff.,
31 ff.), and the general impression that we derive from the farmer's tone
hereabouts is not one of an Aegisthus tied to his wife's apron strings.[13] The
messenger's speech later shows the king sacrificing with due piety to the
Nymphs (785 f.), welcoming the two travellers courteously (779, 786 f.),
and with typical Greek generosity inviting them to share in the sacrificial
ceremony and festivities (784 f.). This portrayal is clearly intended to
clash violently with Electra's allegations of drunken impiety against
Aegisthus in the desecration of Agamemnon's grave. But there is more to
this conflict between Electra and the others over the personality of
Aegisthus. By a disconcerting twist of irony, Electra's own later behaviour
is made to add a barbaric counterpoise to her earlier allegations. The one
outrage against the dead that we actually see happening in Euripides' play
is not committed by Aegisthus against Agamemnon, but by Electra herself
against the corpse of Aegisthus (900 ff.). It is hardly accidental that the
phrase used by Electra here to describe her action, νεκροὺς ὑβρίζειν (902,
literally 'to commit *hybris* against the dead'), echoes discordantly so much
in her earlier allegations.[14]

Thirdly, Euripides' presentation of Clytemnestra[15] complements
unproblematically the cameo of Aegisthus. There is the same kind of
differences between Electra's vivid and spiteful exaggerations and the
more complex reality. Electra claims that she was expelled from the royal
palace by Clytemnestra (61), that Clytemnestra prefers her lover to her
daughter (265; cf. 211 f.), being too preoccupied with her sexual attract-
iveness (1071 ff.) and the trappings of luxury (314 ff.). The truth is less
simple, as we learn from Clytemnestra's actions no less than from her
words. Her showy entrance in a carriage attended by Trojan slaves
(998 ff.) can be interpreted from the Electra viewpoint as evidence of a
desire for luxury, but with equal justification it can be defended as the
acceptable pomp of royalty. The accusation that Clytemnestra has little
affection for her children, however, is twice shown to be false. Electra's
husband reveals that it was Clytemnestra who rescued the adolescent
Electra from the threat of death (28 ff.), and Clytemnestra cares enough
for her daughter to visit her when Electra is reported to have had a baby.
During this visit Clytemnestra is notably worried about Electra's physical
appearance (1107 ff.)[16] and not about her own. Worry, in fact, is a
dominant factor in Clytemnestra's emotional make-up: worry about her
past actions (1105 f., 1109 f.), disquiet about Orestes and the future
(1114 f.), worry about what people are saying of her relationship with
Aegisthus (643 ff.). To all this Electra appears blind.

Euripides thus asks his audience to see each of these characters in two
ways: objectively, as contemporary, unheroic people doing everyday

things (Aegisthus in the rôle of a polite host at a sacrifice, Clytemnestra as the mother visiting her daughter in childbed), but also through the distorting lens of Electra's gaze, where the world is simplified into the traditional, heroic, and obsolete patterns of the given myth, and where Electra's friends are glorified into Homeric warriors, her enemies transformed to selfish ogres.

The unreliability of Electra's distorting spectacles[17] is further emphasized in two scenes where Electra's own egocentric character is highlighted in unsettling ways. Before she recognizes Orestes' identity, Electra makes a speech about her own condition that is a series of recriminations: she claims to be living like a farm-animal ($a\dot{v}\lambda i\zeta o\mu a\iota$, 304) in filth (305), being obliged to make her own clothes or else go naked (307 f.), fetching water herself from the river (309), and deprived of any opportunity to enjoy festivals and dancing (310). Every single one of these complaints is shown in the play to be a lie or a distorted perversion of reality. The chorus of Argive country women had already invited her to a festival at the Heraeum (167 ff.) and offered to lend her clothes and jewellery for it (190 ff.). Electra's husband had already tried to prevent her from doing menial chores like carrying water in a jar on her head (64 ff.), after she had admitted that this slavery was self-imposed (54 ff.). So too was at least one item in her squalid appearance: she had cropped her own hair (241).

The other scene which unexpectedly illuminates Electra's unreliability—this time an unreliability in judgement—is one which has fascinated scholars this century perhaps unduly.[18] It is the scene (487 ff.) where the old retainer is arrogantly criticized by Electra when he reports two signs— a lock of golden hair on Agamemnon's grave,[19] and footprints by it—and suggests that if a third sign—the clothes woven by Electra years ago for the baby Orestes—could be added to the other two, the stranger's identity as Orestes might be confirmed. It is clearly no accident that the three signs belittled by Electra are the very signs previously used by Aeschylus in the recognition scene of the *Choephoroi*, but I should hesitate to assume that parody of Aeschylus was here an important aim of Euripides in writing this scene. One major function of the scene is to provide a further ironic contrast between the fairy-tale implausibility of such tokens in the myth tradition and the deglamorized reality of everyday life (the rocky scrublands of Greece yield few footprints).[20] Another major function of the scene is to point a contrast in character between the optimism of a loyal old retainer and the pessimism of the intellectually quick, sarcastic, and superior princess Electra. But the most significant fact of all about this scene is that despite all the scorn to which the old man is subjected because of his credulity, he is right; and that despite all Electra's cocksureness and the realistic sense of her arguments, she is wrong.[21] Thus Euripides' axe of criticism is double-edged; one blade cuts through the inadequacies of myth tradition, but the opposite edge cuts through the heroine's inadequacies when she, for a change, poses as a realist. Doubtless Euripides had observed around him women like Electra, making unnecessary additions to their sufferings so that they might glory all the more in their complaints, and mingling truth and fiction in a self-absorbed obsession with their injuries. Doubtless too Euripides intended Electra to be an unconscious deceiver, believing in her own lies and misjudgements. At the same time, however, Electra's unreliability is also a part of the planned bifocal characterization of the royal quartet. Electra has a partly distorted, partly distorting view of herself—her own condition and facts relating to it— which the objective observations of other characters enable the audience to correct.

There is a subtle irony in this contrast between Electra's prejudiced distortions and the other figures' less blinkered assessments and presentations of character. A similar irony, with a similar contrast between two opposing interpretations, emerges in one of the play's climactic deeds, the murder of Aegisthus. At one level this murder is described in objective narrative as a vicious, cowardly assault. At a second level, however, the same murder is imaged, mainly but not exclusively by Electra with the chorus, as a feat of high heroism superior even to victory in the Olympic Games. Imagery thus functions as an ironic counterpoint to reality; instead of illustrating the dramatic theme by imaginative association (as do, for instance, the δίκη images in the *Oresteia*, or the sea and hunting imagery in the *Hippolytus* and *Bacchae* respectively),[22] the Olympic imagery in the *Electra* at this point runs counter to the grisly theme it embroiders.

The messenger who reports the murder of Aegisthus is on Electra's and Orestes' side, but his narrative spotlights rather than veils the gruesome horror of Aegisthus' killing. I have analysed this speech in some detail in an earlier paper;[23] here it will be sufficient merely to draw attention to the three ways in which the messenger's account underlines the sordid viciousness of Orestes' action. First, by prefacing his story of the murder with a full description of Aegisthus' courteous generosity to Orestes during the preliminary stages of a sacrifice held in the idyllic surroundings of a park, he increases the shock effect of the murder itself by the sudden contrast in tone.[24] Secondly, Euripides puts Orestes at every ethical disadvantage when he does the deed. Instead of facing Aegisthus fairly in single combat (as Electra had predicted), Orestes stabs his host in the back when off his guard during a holy sacrifice.[25] The frisson of horror that these attendant circumstances arouse is most closely paralleled in modern drama by the murder of Becket in Canterbury Cathedral as it is presented in Eliot's play. Thirdly, the horror is augmented by the clinically exact detailing of the effect of the death blow:

> While his [sc. Aegisthus'] head was bent down,
> Your brother stretched up on the tip of his toes,
> And struck him in his spine, smashing the vertebrae
> Of his back. His whole body jerked[26] up and down
> Convulsing as he died hard in his blood.

(839–44)

As a recent scholar has written, 'the realism has its effect, creating a sickening alienation from revenge'.[27] And yet, at the same time this same murder is presented on a different level as a marvellous achievement superior to one pinnacle of fifth-century aristocratic prowess, victory in the Olympic Games. This other presentation, which uses simile, imagery both visual and verbal, and motifs cunningly interwoven into the fabric of the plot at key points, merits careful analysis.[28]

First, throughout that section of the play concerned with the murder of Aegisthus, there is a tendency—I put it no stronger—to apply terms such as 'win' and 'glorious in victory' ($\nu\iota\kappa\hat{\omega}$, $\kappa\alpha\lambda\lambda\acute{\iota}\nu\iota\kappa o\varsigma$, and congeners) to the murder and the murderer, and to describe the fruits of this murder as the victor's 'garland' ($\sigma\tau\acute{\epsilon}\phi\alpha\nu o\varsigma$). When the old servant talks about killing Aegisthus and Clytemnestra, Orestes interposes 'That's the garland ($\sigma\tau\acute{\epsilon}\phi\alpha\nu o\nu$) I've come for' (614). When the messenger enters, his opening words are:

> O maidens of Mycenae, glorious in victory ($\kappa\alpha\lambda\lambda\acute{\iota}\nu\iota\kappa o\iota$),
> To all his friends I announce that Orestes is victorious ($\nu\iota\kappa\hat{\omega}\nu\tau\alpha$).

(761–2)

Victories may of course be won on fields other than those dedicated to athletic competition, and garlands commemorate military as well as Olympic success. This first group of scattered references must accordingly not be pressed too hard into any preordained mould. They are, perhaps deliberately, perhaps unconsciously, imprecise. In the key passage, however, under forty lines in length, which comprises the end of the messenger's speech, a brief choral lyric, and Electra's greeting to Orestes and Pylades as they enter with Aegisthus' corpse, the athletic images come thick and fast, and with clean precision.

We hear first, just before the end of the messenger's speech, how the servants of Aegisthus garland ($\sigma\tau\acute{\epsilon}\phi o\nu\sigma\iota$) Orestes' head immediately after the murder (854). The chorus then erupts in joyful (dare one also say, Pindaric?) dactylo-epitrites, calling on Electra to dance now because Orestes 'has won a garland of glory' ($\nu\iota\kappa\hat{\alpha}$ $\sigma\tau\epsilon\phi\alpha\nu\alpha\phi o\rho\acute{\iota}\alpha\nu$) not to be compared with those achieved 'by the streams of Alpheus' ($\pi\alpha\rho'$ $\H{A}\lambda\phi\epsilon\iota o\hat{\upsilon}$ $\acute{\rho}\epsilon\acute{\epsilon}\theta\rho o\iota\sigma\iota$). The text here (862–3) is corrupt at one point,[29] but the general sense is clear. The chorus believe that Orestes' murder of Aegisthus surpasses any victory at the Olympic Games, and they call on Electra to sing the 'song glorious in victory' (καλλίνικον ᾠδάν, 865). These words are intended to remind us that the phrase (τήνελλα καλλίνικε) ('hurrah, glorious in victory'), taken from the opening of Archilochus' poem in honour of Heracles, the legendary founder of the Olympic Games (fr. 324 West), was traditionally used to salute Olympic victors. As Orestes and Pylades enter, Electra says 'I'll garland (στέψω) my victorious (νικηφόρου) brother's head' (872), and the chorus approves with 'Then lift the glorious token on his head' (873–4). As Electra garlands her brother, she panegyrizes him in a speech loaded with games imagery and beginning with Archilochus' καλλίνικε, as requested by the chorus:

> O glorious in victory (καλλίνικε), Orestes, son
> Of a father victorious (νικηφόρου) in the battle below Troy,
> Receive this diadem for your curling hair.
> You've arrived home, not after running a useless
> Furlong contest (ἀγῶνα), but slaying the enemy
> Aegisthus, who killed your father and mine.
> And you, Pylades, companion of the shield and pupil
> Of a most reverent father, take from my hand
> Your garland (στέφανον). You have a share equal to his
> In the contest (ἀγῶνος). I wish you both good fortune for evermore.
>
> (880–9)

In this speech two details call for special notice: the careful blending of athletic and military motifs, which sum up with elegant economy Electra's prejudiced interpretation of the murder, and secondly the word 'useless' (ἀχρεῖον) in 883, which perhaps reflects a contemporary political controversy at Athens on the subject of the Olympic Games[30] more than Electra's own aristocratic attitudes.

Such a heavy accumulation of games imagery in this brief section must be deliberate. Its function is complex but primarily ironizing. First, these images form the compact centrepiece of an embroidery that covers a large part of the play. Before the recognition scene Electra imagines her brother to be an athlete trained in the wrestling-schools (528). Two further pictures, both ironically charged, are painted in the messenger's speech. It is part of the traditional myth that Orestes and Pylades should conceal their identities before the murders. In Euripides' *Electra* the messenger describes how Aegisthus asked the two strangers who they were, and

> Orestes said, 'Thessalians. We're on our way
> To the Alpheus, to sacrifice to Olympian Zeus.'
>
> (781–2)

Orestes' masquerade here as a traveller on his way to Olympia links sardonically enough with his later victorious reception from Electra and the chorus,[31] as also does a later image in the same messenger's speech. Orestes helped Aegisthus with the sacrificial bullock and stripped its hide

> more quickly than a runner
> Could complete two laps of the hippodrome.[32]
>
> (824–5)

After Electra's reception of her victorious brother, she dismisses the whole Aegisthus episode with:

> So may no criminal
> Who's run the opening stages well believe
> He's conquering (νικᾶν) Justice, till he nears
> The finishing line and reaches his goal—of death!
>
> (953–6)

There is, however, one further (and unexpected) irony in the play's epilogue, when the Dioscuri order Orestes after leaving Athens to found a new town in Arcadia, called Oresteion after him, 'on Alpheus' stream' (1273). It is the crowning irony that even this typical piece of Euripidean aetiology should be involved, albeit indirectly, in the web of games imagery. Orestes had pretended to be on his way to the sanctuary of Zeus at Olympia; his real goal, however, was to be a place 35 miles south-east of it—but watered by the same river.

Imagery thus may perform simultaneously a dual function. While enriching the texture of a play with a consistent and interlocking set of graphic patterns, it may also provide an ironic counterpoint to a dramatic theme. Here it contributes vividly to the 'double view' presentation of Aegisthus' murder. In the view particularly of Electra, but also of the chorus and of Aegisthus' retainers as described by the messenger, Orestes is a great victor and his killing of Aegisthus a heroic feat superior even to victory in the Olympic Games. At the same time and on a less subjective level the murder is brutal, sordid, and cowardly. The two views, ironically juxtaposed, are not mutually exclusive. A murder may be objectively sordid and subjectively heroic if the view of the subjectivist faction is presented as distorted. And, as Euripides is at pains in this play to emphasize, Electra's views are distorted. They glorify the myth as they glorify the aristocratic code of values in an outmoded, basically unrealistic way. They place ridiculously high regard on 'useless' things like athletic achievement in the Olympic Games. They misrepresent sordid murder as an act of epic heroism.

Euripides' message is clear and powerful, but no less important is his novel application of techniques such as the 'double view' to reinforce his message, both in the imagery and in the presentation of character. Euripides' innovations excited the interest of his contemporaries. They may not always have succeeded as well as they do in the *Electra*, but as a modern literary innovator has said, each work that a writer creates 'should be a new beginning where he tries again for something that is beyond attainment. He should always try for something that has never been done or that others have tried and failed. Then sometimes, with great luck, he will succeed.'[33]

NOTES

1. Lines 27–8 of the poem 'With Happiness stretch'd across the Hills', found in a letter to Thomas Butts dated 22 November 1802.

2. The quotations are from A. W. von Schlegel, *Lectures on Dramatic Art and Literature*, translated most conveniently in J. W. Donaldson, *The Theatre of the Greeks*[10] (London, 1887), pp. 179 f.; Gilbert Murray, *Euripides and his Age* (London, 1913), p. 154; G. M. A. Grube, *The Drama of Euripides* (London, 1941), p. 314; and John Jones, *On Aristotle and Greek Tragedy* (London, 1962), p. 244, respectively.

3. Cf. E. T. England, *CR* 40 (1926), 97 f.

4. This (the traditional) dating has been challenged (especially by G. Zuntz, *The Political Plays of Euripides* (Manchester, 1955), pp. 64 ff., and *Acta Congressus Madvigiani* I (Copenhagen, 1955), p. 159), but it has recently been convincingly defended by R. Leimbach, *Hermes* 100 (1972), 190 ff. Cf. also K. Matthiessen, *Elektra, Taurische Iphigenie und Helena* (Göttingen, 1964), pp. 66 ff.; W. Theiler, *WSt* 79 (1966), 102 ff.; and Giuseppina Basta Donzelli, *Studio sull' Elettra di Euripide* (Catania, 1978), pp. 27 ff.

5. Especially *Merit and Responsibility* (Oxford, 1960), and *Moral Values and Political Behaviour in Ancient Greece* (London, 1972). Cf. also J. D. Denniston's edition of the play (Oxford, 1939), commentary on line 253; and A. A. Long, *JHS* 90 (1970), 121 ff.

6. The translation, which aims at as literal a rendering as possible of Pindar's Greek, is my own.

7. e.g. Adkins, *Merit and Responsibility*, pp. 176 f.; Jones (n. 2), pp. 242 ff.; V. Di Benedetto, *Euripide: teatro e società* (Torino, 1971), pp. 207 f. For a dissentient voice see Philip Vellacott, *Ironic Drama* (Cambridge, 1975), pp. 49 ff.

8. Classical expositions of it will be found in U. von Wilamowitz, *Hermes* 18 (1883), 226; and S. M. Adams, *CR* 49 (1935), 120 ff. Cf. also (for example) Richmond Lattimore, *The Poetry of Greek Tragedy* (Baltimore, 1958), pp. 105, 109 f.; T. B. L. Webster, *The Tragedies of Euripides* (London, 1967), pp. 143 ff.; and Bernard Knox in *The Rarer Action: Essays in Honor of Francis Fergusson* (New Brunswick, 1971), pp. 70 ff.

9. Cf. the remarks prefaced by Emily T. Vermeule to her translation of Euripides' *Electra* (in *The Complete Greek Tragedies*, edited by David Grene and Richmond Lattimore, IV (Chicago, 1958), p. 391): 'Aegisthus we see from two angles: in Electra's prejudiced testimony, as a drunken bully and seducer; in the Messenger's speech, as an affable, pious host. Indeed this double vision is true of the whole play, as Electra's image of the truth, and the truth itself, stubbornly refuse to match. The astigmatism is deliberate.' I lit upon this quotation after completing my own paper; it gives me confidence.

10. Cf. (for example) J. T. Sheppard, *CR* 32 (1918), 138 f.; Adams (n. 8), 120 ff.; Denniston's edition, pp. xxvi f.; W. Friedrich, *Euripides und Diphilos* (Munich, 1953), p. 83; and F. Stoessl, *RhMus* 99 (1956), 52 ff.

11. This, and other translations from the *Electra* in this paper, are my own. They have no literary pretensions, aiming only at accuracy of detail.

12. Cf. England (n. 3), 101.

13. Cf. Grube (n. 2), p. 298.

14. Cf. W. Steidle, *Studien zum antiken Drama* (Munich, 1968), p. 66.

15. Cf. (for example) M. Komo, *HSCP* 71 (1966), 25 ff.; and G. Karsai, *Homonoia* 1 (1979), 15 ff.

16. The position (as well as the authenticity) of these lines has been much debated. Their diction is unimpeachably Euripidean, but there do seem to be strong grounds for removing them from their present place in the manuscript tradition to after line 1131. See Denniston's note, ad loc.

17. Cf. (for example) Wilamowitz (n. 8), 229 ff.; Sheppard (n. 10), 138 ff.; Grube (n. 2), pp. 302 f.; W. Zürcher, *Die Darstellung des Menschen im Drama des Euripides* (Basle, 1947), pp. 109 ff.; Shirley A. Barlow, *The Imagery of Euripides* (London, 1971), pp. 92 ff.; and Froma I. Zeitlin, *TAPhA* 101 (1970), 647 ff.

18. The three latest discussions are G. W. Bond, *Hermathena* 118 (1974), 1 ff. (with a useful summary of previous discourses); G. Ronnet, *REG* 88 (1975), 63 ff.; and G. Basta Donzelli (n. 4), pp. 102 ff. I take it for granted that this scene is authentic (cf. H. Lloyd-Jones, *CQ* 11 (1961), 171 ff., countering the arguments of E. Fraenkel in his edition of Aeschylus' *Agamemnon* III (Oxford, 1950), pp. 821 ff.).

19. This particular token goes back at least to Stesichorus' *Oresteia* (fr. 40 Page *PMG* = fr. 87 Page *LGS*). Cf. F. Solmsen, 'Electra and Orestes', *Med. Kon. Ned. Akad. van Wet., Afd. Letterk.* 30/2 (1967), 31.

20. Cf. L. Parmentier's Budé edition (Paris, 1925), pp. 184 ff.

21. Cf. Friedrich (n. 10), pp. 80 f.; W. Ludwig, *Sapheneia* (Diss. Tübingen, 1954), pp. 126 f.; and H. Lloyd-Jones (n. 18), 180.

22. See (for example) Fraenkel's commentary on Aeschylus, *Agamemnon* 41; C. P. Segal, *HSCP* 70 (1965), 117 ff.; and R. P. Winnington-Ingram, *Euripides and Dionysus* (Cambridge, 1948), index s.v. *Bacchae: hunt.*

23. *G & R* 20 (1973), 49 ff. = pp. 138 ff. of this volume; cf. *Mus. Phil. Lond.* 3 (1978), 2 ff.

24. An effect which film-makers have not been slow to exploit: e.g. the murder in the shower in Hitchcock's *Psycho.*

25. See above, p. 183.

26. In line 843 I read ἠλέλιζε (Schenkl) with δυσθνῆσκον (so L). See Denniston's commentary, ad loc.

27. Brian Vickers, *Towards Greek Tragedy* (London, 1973), p. 561. Cf. also the paper by Adams (n. 8).

28. Cf. here the brief but percipient remarks of Zeitlin (n. 17), 655 ff.

29. Cf. the editions of Denniston and Parmentier, ad loc.

30. It is dangerous to read into this—and other famous comments on athletes and athletics in Euripidean drama (e.g. Orestes' remark at *Electra* 387 f., and fr. 282 Nauck[2] from the *Autolycus*)—expressions of the dramatist's own personal view. After all, Euripides is not opposed to athletics in his portrait of Hippolytus, and just before he wrote the *Electra* he composed an epinician hymn to celebrate Alcibiades' victory in the chariot race at Olympia in 416 B.C. (Plutarch, *Alcibiades* 11). Alcibiades' defence of his athletic interests, before the Athenian assembly in 415 B.C., is reported by Thucydides (6.16); it implies a contemporary groundswell of criticism against athletic extravagances in current conditions. On the history of such criticism, which goes back at least to the time of Xenophanes (fr. 2 West), see especially E. Norden, *Jahrb. f. kl. Philologie*, Supp.-B. 18 (1882), 298 ff., and M. I. Finley and H. W. Pleket, *The Olympic Games* (London, 1976), pp. 113 ff.

31. In Sophocles' *Electra*, of course, the messenger's masquerade has Orestes competing in the chariot race at the Pythian Games. Which of the two plays came first? It is impossible to say with any degree of confidence, although much has been written on this question (good bibliographies in Solmsen (n. 19), 52 n. 1; and D. J. Conacher, *Euripidean Drama* (Toronto and London, 1968), p. 202 n. 9. Cf. also E. R. Schwinge, *Die Verwendung der Stichomythie in den Dramen des Euripides* (Heidelberg, 1968), pp. 300 ff.).

32. Cf. Finley and Pleket (n. 30), pp. 27 f.

33. Ernest Hemingway's speech on receiving the 1954 Nobel Prize for Literature; cf. A. Burgess, *Ernest Hemingway and his World* (London, 1978), p. 106. Professor Richard Kannicht and Mr J. D. Smart were kind enough to read and comment helpfully upon an earlier draft of this paper. To both of them my thanks are owed and most gratefully given.

ADDENDUM

Much more has been written on Euripides' *Electra* since the above paper was published. Useful general contributions in English include G. H. Gellie, *BICS* 28 (1981), 1–12; J. W. Halpern, *HSCP* 87 (1983), 101–17; E. M. Thury, *Rh. Mus.* 128 (1985), 5–22; and (challengingly dissentient) M. Lloyd, *Phoenix* 40 (1986), 1–19; cf. also A. N. Michelini, *Euripides and the Tragic Tradition* (Madison, 1987), pp. 181–228.

SUBJECT INDEX

Achilles 70–2, 104–6, 108–12, 116, 124, 182, 185
actor(s) 38–9, 41, 139, 141, 152–3, 206
aetiology 160, 214
agathos 105, 109–10, 205
agon 64, 153, 155, 157, 159–60, 163–6, 168–9, 195, 200–1, 213
aidos 22, 175
alastor 14, 34, 42
allusions, topical 183–4, 188, 191, 213
ambiguity 62–4, 88–9, 144–5, 159, 176
Antiphanes 88, 143
anti-Spartan 180–1, 185, 188
arete 96, 100, 109, 113, 156, 160, 180, 195, 205–6
Aristophanes 11, 87–8, 119, 150, 188
Aristotle 81, 85–7, 100, 104–5, 107–8, 113, 123, 183, 193–4, 202
aside-convention 84–5
Ate 14, 24, 26, 31, 34–6, 186
attention, concentration of 39 ff.

bow 64, 95 ff., 104, 106–8, 112, 193, 195, 200
burial 66 ff.

carpet scene 16–27
causation 15, 22–4, 30–1, 48
character, individuality of 60 ff.
characterization 12 ff., 58 ff., 91, 94, 149, 157, 207 ff.
charis 49–50
chorus, separation of 141–2, 152
clothes 35–6, 207, 210
context, social 2 ff.
convention(s) 6–9, 11, 13, 58, 85, 138–9, 141–2, 149–50, 158
crane 11, 148, 158
criticism, performance 1 ff.
criticism, Shakespearian 11
curse 14, 22, 24, 26–7, 69, 82–4, 87, 124

daemon 14–15, 26, 30–1, 34
death, ineluctability of 171–3
debate, formal 38, 153 ff., 168
determination, double 15, 22, 24, 26, 69, 132
deus ex machina 95, 101, 111, 119, 131, 147
disharmony, domestic 180 ff.
'double view' 206 ff.
drama, social 2, 11
dream(s) 30, 32, 36, 41, 51, 173

Eliot, George 25

Eliot, T.S. 138, 211
eris 185, 187
esthlos 109
eugenes 104, 106, 113, 175

fate 24, 51, 82
friend(ship) 18, 96–101, 110–12, 116–18, 130–3, 160, 164, 175–6, 193, 201

gamos 181–2, 185–6, 188
gennaios 104, 106, 109, 112–13, 175
god(s) 16, 19, 21, 31, 35, 39 ff., 51–2, 68–73, 79, 94, 101, 119–33, 140, 153, 162–3, 171
Great Dionysia 11
guilt 24–5, 45–6, 53, 61, 85, 174

hamartia 81
hapax legomenon 196–8
Heracles, ambivalence of 120–2, 126 ff., 132
hero(ine) 13, 29, 61, 65, 116, 118–20, 122, 126–7, 129–31, 134, 170, 193, 195, 199, 201–2, 206–8
hospitality 167 ff., 174–7, 206
hubris 20, 24, 26, 33, 35–6, 43, 81, 208–9

Ibsen 1, 13
image(ry) 26, 29 ff., 48, 64, 79, 91, 193, 199, 211–14; *see also* symbol
individuality 60 ff.
irony 59, 130, 162, 168–9, 171, 184, 187, 199, 201, 205–6, 209–11, 213–14

kakos 105, 107, 109, 111
kallinikos 120, 198–201, 212–13
kalos 105, 108, 113

lament(ation) 32, 36, 161, 171, 173–6, 180, 186
language 12, 15–17, 26, 31, 40, 64, 69–70, 83, 91, 109, 170, 172–3, 186, 191, 193–9
lawsuit 48 ff., 52 ff.; *see also* trial scene
lechos 181, 185, 188–9
love 59, 62, 79

messenger(s) 15, 30–4, 42, 64, 111, 129, 139–43, 145–6, 148, 156, 159, 194–5, 197–9, 201, 209, 211–14
metaphor 30–1, 130, 193, 200
monody 41, 145, 161
myth, knowledge of 87 ff., 142 ff., 206 ff.

name(s) 30–1, 41–2

INDEX OF PASSAGES